BUDDHIST PHILOSOPHY OF LANGUAGE IN INDIA

BUDDHIST PHILOSOPHY OF LANGUAGE IN INDIA

Jñānaśrīmitra on Exclusion

LAWRENCE J. MCCREA
AND PARIMAL G. PATIL

Columbia University Press New York

Columbia University Press
Publishers Since 1893
New York Chichester, West Sussex

Library of Congress Cataloging-in-Publication Data
McCrea, Lawrence J.
Buddhist philosophy of language in India :
Jnanasrimitra's monograph on exclusion /Lawrence J. McCrea and Parimal G. Patil.
p. cm.
Includes Jñanasrimitra's text in Sanskrit and its translation.
Includes bibliographical references and index.
ISBN 978-0-231-15094-1 (cloth : alk. paper) —
ISBN 978-0-231-15095-8 (pbk. : alk. paper) —
ISBN 978-0-231-52191-8 (ebook)
1. Jñanasrimitra. Apohaprakarana. 2. Buddhist logic.
3. Language and languages—Philosophy. 4. Yogacara (Buddhism)
I. Patil, Parimal G. II. Jñanasrimitra. Apohaprakarana. English & Sanskrit. III. Title.

BC25.M37 2010
181'043—dc22 2010004989

Columbia University Press books are printed on permanent
and durable acid-free paper.
This book is printed on paper with recycled content.
Printed in the United States of America

c 10 9 8 7 6 5 4 3 2 1
p 10 9 8 7 6 5 4 3 2 1

For Edith and Emily

CONTENTS

SANSKRIT TEXT OF THE *MONOGRAPH ON EXCLUSION (APOHAPRAKARAṆAM)* 99

PREFACE

This book was written from 2006 to 2008 while both of us were teaching at Harvard University. It is built on work that we have done both individually and together since our graduate work at the University of Chicago. At Harvard, we used to meet three times a week, for several hours at a time, to work on this and other projects. Our collaboration is such that we wrote each and every sentence of this book together, literally line by line. It is a work that neither of us would have undertaken or would have undertaken in anything like the way that we have, had we worked separately. It is in every sense a true collaboration.

Through our work on this project, we have become increasingly convinced of the need to break down the divide between exegetical and analytical work in Sanskrit studies. It has become clear to us that it is simply impossible to properly explain, translate, or even edit Sanskrit philosophical texts without a sustained analysis of their arguments and a broad and far-ranging exploration of their historical and intellectual contexts. By the same token, responsible historical and philosophical analysis necessitates systematic engagement with philological and textual details. This is particularly true for the study of Sanskrit philosophical texts, the vast majority of which have never been translated or studied, and many of which have not even been edited. Such engagement is necessary for the future of our field, despite the very strong institutional pressures against philological (and collaborative) work.

The study of Sanskrit philosophy is still in its infancy. The foundational work presupposed by almost all serious studies of Euro-American philosophical traditions has barely begun for the Sanskrit philosophical tradition, although it is comparable in its breadth, antiquity, and sophistication. As a result, even analytical and historical studies of Sanskrit philosophical work must remain very closely engaged in detailed exegetical and philological work, as virtually no Sanskrit philosophical text is yet thoroughly understood. No amount of detailed textual study and exegesis will be able to move the field forward, however, unless it also addresses larger historical and philosophical questions, despite the necessarily preliminary nature of all such efforts given the current state of the field. There may be other ways to meet these various desiderata, but the method that we have adopted here is the result of our own struggle to chart a way forward.

We are very fortunate to be part of a truly global field, and we are grateful to our colleagues in North America, Europe, Japan, and India for their interest in and support of our work. We have been challenged by our ongoing conversations with them and by their own exemplary scholarship. In particular, we would like to thank Leonard W. J. van der Kuijp, Ernst Steinkellner, Helmut Krasser, Eli Franco, Birgit Kellner, and Shoryu Katsura.

Lawrence J. McCrea and Parimal G. Patil
Cambridge, Massachusetts

BUDDHIST PHILOSOPHY OF LANGUAGE IN INDIA

INTRODUCTION

1. JÑĀNAŚRĪMITRA'S INTELLECTUAL WORLD AND ITS HISTORY

The theory of exclusion (*apoha*) has long been recognized as one of the most fundamental and distinctive components of Buddhist philosophy in India.[1] Modern scholars have tended to view the theory as primarily a theory of meaning,[2] but since its origins in the work of the sixth-century Buddhist philosopher Dignāga,[3] the theory of exclusion was used to address a much broader range of philosophical problems. Indeed, for Dignāga and his successors, it formed the basis of their account of all conceptual awareness.[4]

A distinctive feature of Dignāga's philosophy is its radical distinction between conceptual and perceptual awareness. His position is that only perceptual awareness can be genuinely free from error. Objects of awareness other than those that we directly perceive are said to exist in only a conventional sense; that is, while our awareness of them may help us attain certain practical results, they are just convenient fictions and do not correspond to anything that exists outside our own minds. For Dignāga, anything of which we are aware apart from what we directly and nonconceptually perceive can be explained only in terms of exclusion. Thus, although it includes all awareness produced through language, the scope of exclusion extends to much else besides.

In addition to restricting their discussion of exclusion to language, modern scholars have tended to focus on the theory's earliest articulations in the works of philosophers like Dignāga and his seventh-century successor Dharmakīrti.[5] Although the theory was elaborated and further developed for hundreds of years, comparatively little attention has been given to later developments.[6] The prevailing attitude seems to be that these later developments are mainly secondary and derivative and add little to the seminal treatments of Dignāga and Dharmakīrti.[7]

Despite this prevailing assumption, we show that later exclusion theorists in India did not just replicate and reorganize existing knowledge but sometimes drastically reshaped and redirected the theory. The specific theory that we will be examining here, that of the late tenth-century Buddhist philosopher Jñānaśrīmitra, was particularly radical and proved to be highly influential in the following centuries. Jñānaśrīmitra was well known to Hindu and Jain critics in the early centuries of the second millennium and seems to be have been widely regarded as the cutting-edge Buddhist philosopher.[8] His theory of exclusion was of particular importance to the great eleventh-century Nyāya philosopher Udayana, who devoted much of his own treatment of exclusion to a detailed and penetrating critique of Jñānaśrīmitra's version of the theory.[9] It is not an understatement to say that Jñānaśrīmitra's *Monograph on Exclusion* was the last and most serious attempt to provide a consistent and coherent understanding of exclusion based on and informed by the more than half a millennium of previous debate on the topic. It offers specific and up-to-date responses to the objections of non-Buddhist philosophers and provides a coherent, but critical, account of intra-Buddhist debates on the nature and function of exclusion. More than an abstract discussion of the theory, the *Monograph* offers an intellectual history of Buddhist and non-Buddhist discourse on exclusion and conceptuality.

Jñānaśrīmitra's Intellectual Contexts

The theory of exclusion is central to Jñānaśrīmitra's work, but his thought and work extend far beyond it. Jñānaśrīmitra was perhaps the most significant Buddhist intellectual of his period, and his works cover the full range of topics important to Buddhist philosophers.[10] Apart from his philosophical work, Jñānaśrīmitra also wrote on metrics and was himself a poet; several of his verses are quoted in the twelfth-century poetic anthology the *Subhāṣitaratnakośa*.[11] Even in his philosophical work, his poetic sensibilities are evident. He extensively uses complex poetic meters and often appears to choose words and phrases for aesthetic effect and not merely for their content.[12]

Jñānaśrīmitra is known as well to have been one of the "gatekeepers" at the great monastic and educational center of Vikramaśīla. Vikramaśīla, which was founded by the Pāla king Dharmapāla in the late eighth century, was the main center of Buddhist learning in India until its decline in the late twelfth or early thirteenth century. Vikramaśīla was the institutional home of many of the most important Buddhist philosophers of the tenth and eleventh centuries, for example, Jitāri, Yamāri, Durvekamiśra, Jñānaśrīmitra, Ratnākaraśānti, Ratnakīrti, Abhayākaragupta, and Atīśa.[13] At Vikramaśīla, Jñānaśrīmitra appears to have been the principal exponent of the Sākāra school of Yogācāra Buddhism,[14] which was the basis for much of the controversy between him and another leading scholar from Vikramakśīla, Ratnākaraśānti, who was the principal defender of the rival Nirākāra school.[15] One of Jñānaśrīmitra's main philosophical works, *Sākārasiddhiśāstra* (*A Treatise Proving That Awareness Contains an Image*), contains a lengthy and detailed attack on Ratnākaraśānti's position.[16] And in the introductory verse to his *Īśvarasādhanadūṣaṇa* (*Refutation of the Proof of God*), Jñānaśrīmitra's protégé, Ratnakīrti, describes his teacher as the "one who has defeated Ratnākara."[17]

Philosophical Traditions and Text Traditions

Like most of the Vikramaśīla-based Buddhist philosophers just listed, Jñānaśrīmitra worked within a textual and philosophical tradition that grew out of the work of the great seventh-century Buddhist philosopher Dharmakīrti.[18] While it thus is reasonable to label him a "follower of Dharmakīrti," this should not be taken to mean that Jñānaśrīmitra was, even in his own mind, simply seeking to clarify and defend philosophical arguments already made by Dharmakīrti himself. Although Jñānaśrīmitra's work was shaped and inspired by Dharmakīrti at every turn, he was very much an independent thinker. Unlike many post-Dharmakīrtian writers on Buddhist logic and epistemology, Jñānaśrīmitra wrote no commentaries on Dharmakīrti's work, preferring instead to produce a series of specialized monographs on particular topics.[19] In all his works, he attempts to defend positions that can be plausibly understood as consistent with Dharmakīrti's own, but much of what he says goes far beyond anything found in Dharmakīrti's work. Although the overall framework of Jñānaśrīmitra's thought is constructed from lines of argument and key phrases drawn from Dharmakīrti's texts, what he constructs from these architectural elements is his own creation.

Jñānaśrīmitra inhabited a world of Buddhist intellectuals who, while working within basically the same intellectual framework, articulated and defended a set of radically distinct and incompatible philosophical worldviews. For example, some Dharmakīrtians believed in the real existence of external objects, while others denied it. Some argued that the contents (*ākāra*) of our awareness are ultimately real, while some believed the contrary; some believed it was possible to arrive at a maximally adequate philosophical description of reality, while others believed that no such description was possible.[20] It therefore would be misleading to describe these authors as sharing a single philosophical system; it would be more accurate to describe them as belonging to a single "text tradition." Without exception, they all look back to the foundational texts of Dharmakīrti and, to a lesser extent, his predecessor Dignāga as the fundamental source of their basic concepts and arguments. They very rarely, if ever, openly contradict an explicit position taken by Dharmakīrti (although, as we shall see, according to Jñānaśrīmitra, at least sometimes Dharmakīrti did not really mean what he said).[21] What these authors really share, then, is not a philosophical position but a set of building blocks and common textual resources provided by Dharmakīrti, which constitute a common intellectual heritage, all of which, however, was subject to critical examination vis-à-vis its meaning and ultimate significance. Their work is thus directed as much toward criticizing rival Buddhist philosophers working within the Dharmakīrtian text tradition as it is toward non-Buddhists.

The concept of a text tradition can usefully be applied not only to Buddhist epistemologists but also to most historical practitioners of what today is called "Indian philosophy." We would argue that it represents a much better way of thinking about affiliated groups of philosophers than do more widely applied concepts such as philosophical "schools" or "systems." Because Indian philosophers themselves have tended to classify their own works under one or more labels—for example, Nyāya and Mīmāṃsā—modern scholars have often been too quick to assume that all philosophers or texts grouped under a certain label are committed to the same philosophical positions. This in turn has led people to assume that there is a great deal more consistency than careful observation reveals and that there is little or no real innovation to be found in later commentaries and "scholastic" works of these traditions. In fact, within each of the so-called schools of Indian philosophy there is a great deal of internal variation, debate, and polemic directed against other practitioners of that school, as well as substantive and often dramatic evolution over time. The foundational texts that form the basis of these traditions are often as much a source of contention as they are of unity. In our view, a "text tradition" model provides a better way of thinking about what those who work within these traditions do and do not have in common. It opens up a space within which the internal histories and geographies of these textual fields can be mapped out.

The text tradition growing out of Dignāga's work proved to be among the most influential in South Asian intellectual history, in that it prompted a major transformation in the self-conception and organization of Sanskrit philosophy as a whole. Dignāga's principal work, the *Compendium on Sources of Knowledge* (*Pramāṇasamuccaya*), as its title suggests, organizes philosophical discussion first and foremost in terms of epistemology. In the wake of Dignāga's work, there was a very marked "epistemological turn," not simply among Buddhist philosophers, but among all Sanskrit philosophers. In the centuries following Dignāga's work, virtually all philosophical questions were reconfigured as epistemological ones. That is, when making any claim at all, it came to be seen as incumbent on a philosopher to situate that claim within a fully developed theory of knowledge. The systematic articulation and interrogation of the underlying presuppositions of all knowledge claims thus became the central preoccupation of most Sanskrit philosophers.

With this preoccupation came a dramatic shift in the discursive practices of Sanskrit philosophy. Beginning with Dignāga, Sanskrit philosophers began to read and criticize the works of their opponents in a far more detailed and systematic way than before, criticizing not only the general positions of their rivals but also very specific textual formulations of those positions. Consequently, the critical exchange between rival philosophical traditions became far more intimate, using a shared conceptual vocabulary to formulate and pursue philosophical questions. In effect, debate over basic epistemological and ontological questions became a single, extended conversation.

Buddhist, Hindu, and Jain philosophers from the sixth century onward wrote for a general "philosophical" audience at least as much as for members of their own text traditions. It can thus be argued that Dignāga's work ushered in a shared Sanskrit philosophical culture that had not existed previously. For all their differences, most of the

Sanskrit philosophers of this period held a common understanding of what constituted the standards for rational acceptability and the proper sort of framework through which philosophical claims were to be formulated and defended. They developed an increasingly specific, shared understanding of the precise points of disagreement among their respective positions, and of the systemic consequences that would follow from resolving these disagreements in one way or another. Their disputes thus were extremely focused, with everyone understanding that these few narrowly defined points of contention were the key to their disagreements.

Sanskrit Intellectual Practices

Despite their intense philosophical disagreement, there was remarkable uniformity in intellectual and textual practices of Sanskrit philosophers. Therefore, to fully appreciate the significance of Jñānaśrīmitra's *Monograph on Exclusion* in its intellectual context, we will briefly examine some of these practices' basic features.

Throughout its history, Sanskrit philosophy has been marked by a deep scholasticism,[22] with the majority of philosophical works presenting themselves as commentaries of one sort or another on earlier works in their respective text traditions. Even those works not explicitly presented as commentaries typically formulated philosophical problems and their solutions with extensive reference to the foundational works of their respective text traditions. With this commentarial orientation came a reluctance to claim substantive philosophical originality. Even radically innovative philosophers often went to great lengths to portray themselves as unoriginal, presenting new ideas and arguments as if they were merely drawing out the implications of these foundational works. Furthermore, nearly all Sanskrit philosophical works affiliate themselves with a particular textual tradition, usually traced back to a single defining root text.[23]

In the Sanskrit philosophical world, "commentary" encompasses a broad range of genres and modes of argument. Philosophical commentaries usually do not seek merely to elucidate the meaning of the texts on which they are commenting but to elaborate, extend, and revise the texts' positions and arguments. The commentaries serve as a forum in which adherents of a particular tradition can respond to their opponents' cutting-edge arguments. In responding to arguments that were not envisioned by the authors of their root texts, they often revise and occasionally radically transform the philosophical systems that they claim merely to be explicating.[24]

Philosophical arguments often are developed through a stylized dialogue between real or constructed representatives of rival traditions. Indeed, the dialogical format is so basic to the discursive practice of Sanskrit philosophy that philosophical arguments are set forth in a dialogical format even when no real dialogue partner exists.[25] The traditional format in which Indian philosophical arguments are laid out begins with the position of an opponent, or *pūrvapakṣin*, whose views are, through a series of counterarguments and intermediate positions, ultimately supplanted by the fully established conclusion, or *siddhānta*.

Sources of Knowledge

The philosophical text traditions active in India in the first millennium CE were many and various, and there is no need to catalog them here. The text traditions most directly relevant to understanding Jñānaśrīmitra's *Monograph on Exclusion*, apart from the Dignāga/Dharmakīrtian epistemological tradition itself, are those of Mīmāṃsa (Hermeneutics) and Nyāya (Systematic Reasoning). Among the principal points of contention between the Buddhist epistemologists and their Mīmāṃsā and Nyāya rivals were the nature, number, and taxonomy of the sources of knowledge (*pramāṇa*s) and the nature of linguistic reference and its ontological implications.[26]

The principal rubric within which epistemological debate took place was that of the "sources of knowledge," that is, means of valid awareness. Rival philosophical text traditions differed over the number of distinct sources of knowledge, the precise nature of each, and the sorts of things that could be known through them. Virtually everyone at least accepted perception (*pratyakṣa*)[27] and inference (*anumāna*) as genuine sources of knowledge. Some scholars argued that verbal testimony (*śabda/śāstra/āgama*) constituted an independent source of knowledge, but others—including the Buddhist epistemologists—argued that it could be reduced to inference.[28]

PERCEPTION In general, Mīmāṃsakas and Naiyāyikas[29] believe that in order for perception to occur, there must be a sense faculty, a perceivable object, and a relation between them. In contrast, Buddhist epistemologists do not require a distinct sense faculty or object and therefore any specific relation between them. For them, the distinction between perceptual and nonperceptual knowledge is not causal but broadly phenomenal. It is not the etiology of perceptual awareness-events that is emphasized but their content, including how that content appears to us. Valid awareness-events that are free from conceptualization/conceptual content are classified as perceptual, and all other valid awareness-events are classified as inferential.[30]

INFERENCE Buddhists, Mīmāṃsakas, and Naiyāyikas agreed that inference requires an awareness of pervasion (*vyāpti*) between the inferential reason (*hetu*) and what is to be inferred (*sādhya*). In the standard example, one can infer the presence of fire on a mountain by seeing smoke rising up from it because one knows that wherever there is smoke, there is fire. Despite this general agreement, though, there is considerable disagreement over both the nature of this inference-warranting relation of pervasion and how we come to know of it in a particular case. More specifically, while the Mīmāṃsakas' and Naiyāyikas' understanding of pervasion is broadly empiricist, the Buddhists' understanding, at least after Dharmakīrti, is broadly antiempiricist. For the former, an inference-warranting relation obtains between things that are invariably observed together, whereas for the Buddhists, it obtains only between things that are invariably related, either conceptually or causally.[31]

TESTIMONY Buddhist epistemologists, Mīmāṃsakas, and Naiyāyikas all agree that certain linguistic expressions, particularly those contained in texts regarded as authoritative within their respective religious traditions, are sources of knowledge. They radically differ, however, on what exactly it means for a statement to be a source of knowledge. The Buddhist epistemologists, as already noted, reduce verbal testimony to inference. The only knowledge that one can gain directly from any statement is the expressive intent of its speaker/author, which one infers from the particular set of words used by the speaker/author. Any knowledge about states of affairs requires a further inference, for example, if a person whom I know to be trustworthy tells me that "there are fruits on the riverbank," I may legitimately infer that there are fruits on the riverbank after inferring his intent.[32] Although both Mīmāṃsakas and Naiyāyikas resist the Buddhist reduction of testimony to inference, they disagree with each other about how language works and to what words refer. The debate between them centers on whether words refer only to "universals" (*jāti*), as the Mīmāṃsakas claim, or to "particulars" (*vyakti*) as well, as the Naiyāyikas maintain. While the Mīmāṃsā position seems to have remained quite consistent over time, the Nyāya position shifted significantly with the (tenth-century) philosopher Vācaspatimiśra (and his teacher, Trilocana). The early Naiyāyikas maintained that the same word can refer, in different contexts, to a universal, a particular, or a characteristic structure (*ākṛti*).[33] Vācaspati's position, however, is that words, at least typically, refer to an individual qualified by a universal (*jātimat-vyakti*).[34] This position became the standard Nyāya position after Vācaspati and, as we shall see, was the latter position to which Jñānaśrīmitra responded.[35]

2. THE BUDDHIST EPISTEMOLOGICAL TRADITION: DIGNĀGA AND DHARMAKĪRTI

It is against the broader background of epistemological, ontological, and linguistic debate in early Sanskrit philosophy that we must view Dignāga's intellectual contributions. Dignāga's most important and radical philosophical move was to present questions of epistemology and ontology as mutually constitutive. For him, each source of knowledge has its own distinct kind of object, and there are only two sources of knowledge: perception and inference. Dignāga defined perceptual awareness as "that which is free from conceptualization (*kalpanā*)."[36] According to him, perception apprehends only bare particulars (*svalakṣaṇa*), without associating them with any label, concept, or class. That is, when we *perceive* a cow, we do not perceive it as a "cow," "brown," "four-legged," or anything of that sort.[37] Any awareness that associates an object with a label, concept, or class is conceptual and, by definition, is excluded from the domain of perception. Even though we typically think of ourselves as perceiving a "cow," our awareness of it as a cow or as possessing specific properties such as "being brown" is "pseudoperceptual" (*pratyakṣābha*), since it depends on conceptualization, the mental construction of elements that are not directly presented to us in visual awareness.[38]

These elements—concepts, labels, and class categories—are artifacts of our own mental processes and do not directly correspond to any mind-independent "objects." Dignāga therefore considered our awareness of such things as "cows" and "being brown" as being of "conventionally existent" (*samvṛtisat*) things.[39] Our awarenesses of such mentally constructed objects are sometimes accepted as correct, whereas other such awareness events are said to be a form of "error" (*bhrānti*).[40] Both are alike, however, in that they do not match up with any unconstructed object—that is, a unique particular—and thus are excluded from the domain of perception. As Dignāga says,

> Among these things, an erroneous awareness is pseudoperceptual because it operates by conceptually constructing things such as water in the case of a mirage. Awareness of conventionally existing objects is pseudoperceptual because it operates by conceptually constructing their forms by superimposing them onto other objects. Inference and the awareness that results from it are pseudoperceptual because they operate by conceptually constructing that which was previously experienced.[41]

For Dignāga, inference, unlike perception, has conceptually constructed objects but is nevertheless considered to be valid because it enables us to act successfully. For example, when we see smoke rising above a mountain, we may infer that there is fire on that mountain. The fire that we infer, however, is not an actual fire but a conceptual construction. Having previously noticed that wherever there is smoke, there is fire, we conceptually construct the fire that we infer from the smoke that we in fact see. Thus for Dignāga, there is always a gap between the conceptually constructed object that appears to us in inferential awareness and the real particular(s) that it leads us to act on. The conceptually constructed object of our inferential awareness is not any particular fire but, rather, one that is generic. Dignāga refers to such "generic" entities as universals (*sāmānyalakṣaṇa*).[42] Any awareness that is not of a particular fire must be of a constructed universal and, if valid, must be inferential.

For Dignāga, then, each of the two accredited sources of knowledge has its own distinct sort of object. Perception has only unique, unconstructed particulars (*svalakṣaṇa*) as its object, while inference has only constructed universals (*sāmānyalakṣaṇa*). The position that each source of knowledge has its own distinct sort of object, which appears to be original to Dignāga, came to be known as the thesis of the "differential application of the sources of knowledge" (*pramāṇa-vyavasthā*).

This contrasts with the more widely held thesis of the "convergence of the sources of knowledge" (*pramāṇa-samplava*). Naiyāyikas[43] and Mīmāṃsakas, among others, believe that it is possible to have valid awareness of one and the same object through multiple sources of knowledge. For example, one may hear from a reliable person that there is a fire on a mountain and conclude on the basis of verbal testimony that this is the case; if one approaches and sees smoke rising up from the mountain, one can conclude inferentially that the fire is there; and arriving on the top of the mountain, one can perceive it directly.[44] But according to Dignāga, it is impossible for the sources of knowledge to converge in this way because there is nothing that can be the object of both perception and inference. What we perceive when we see fire is a bare particular, not associated with any concepts, labels, or universals such as "fire." But what we infer from seeing smoke rising up from a mountain (or from hearing a reliable person tell us there is fire there)[45] is an altogether different kind of thing. It is a generic "fire" that is conceptually constructed on the basis of previously experienced particulars.

It is as a way of explaining the basis for the proper application of labels, concepts, and class categories that Dignāga introduces the theory of exclusion (*apoha*). As we already have seen, for him the only real objects are unique particulars. Labels, concepts, and class categories, which pick out classes of such objects, are for him always conceptually constructed. This means that members of a "class" do not share any single, real, element. The only thing that they do have in common is a shared exclusion. That is, despite being utterly distinct from one another, they are alike in being excluded from the domain of things outside this class. A generic concept such as "cow," for example, can refer to particular cows, not because it designates some real property that all cows share, but because by excluding all non-cows, it negatively defines a domain whose members can be reliably picked out by the concept "cow." Some of Dignāga's opponents saw this as viciously circular: you could know what cows are only by first knowing what non-cows are, but to do this you must already know what cows are.[46] Dignāga's successors responded to this charge in a variety of ways, as we shall see.

From Dignāga's time onward, the theory of exclusion became one of the central pillars of Buddhist epistemology. It formed the centerpiece of its argument against the reality of universals (as upheld by, e.g., the Naiyāyikas and Mīmāṃsakas) and its account of conceptual content. But this theory also created many exegetical and philosophical problems, and there was significant intra-Buddhist controversy over its nature and significance to the Buddhist account of validity.

Curiously, Dignāga does not appear to have been particularly interested in providing a general account of the conditions for validity or of the sense in which awareness events such as inference—which do not have a "real" object—can still be valid. But his successor, Dharmakīrti, building on his system, sought to construct just such an account. Dharmakīrti presented two conditions for validity, which he regarded as applicable to both (nonconceptual) perceptual awareness events and (conceptual) inferential/verbal ones. An awareness event that is "nonmisleading" (*avisamvādi*) and "reveals an object not previously known" (*ajñātārthaprakāśa*) is, by definition, valid.[47]

Dharmakīrti explained "nonmisleading" in terms of "pragmatic effectiveness" (*arthakrīyā*).[48] A state of awareness is "valid" (*pramāṇa*) only if any activity that we undertake on the basis of it could, in principle, lead us to results consistent with the expectations we form on the basis of it.[49] This does not mean that our expectations will be met in every case, but only that the objects toward which we are prompted to act will function within the parameters of these expectations. For example, suppose that upon seeing a pool of water in the distance, we walk toward it with the expectation of quenching our thirst. In such a case, owing to some obstacle, we may not succeed in reaching the pool. This lack of success does not invalidate our awareness of the pool. However, if we reach the place where we saw the pool of water and discover only sand, our initial awareness of "the pool" (which we now conclude to have been a mirage) was actually invalid. Valid states of awareness thus must *direct us toward* objects capable of meeting our expectations, that is, toward objects capable of being pragmatically effective, regardless of whether our expectations are actually met in any specific case. For Dharmakīrti, since only particulars are capable of being pragmatically effective, it follows that in order to be valid, states of awareness must direct us toward particulars.[50]

In order to satisfy the condition of being non-misleading, inferential/verbal awareness, too, must direct us toward particulars that can produce pragmatic effects that conform to our expectations. For example, when we see smoke rising over a mountain and infer the presence of fire there, the "fire" presented to us in this state of awareness is not a real, pragmatically effective, particular fire but a conceptual construct. But this conceptually constructed fire leads us to expect that if we go to that mountain, we will see a fire that we can actually use, for example, to cook. Because it is the real particular fire and not the conceptually constructed one that we can use to cook, the action that we undertake based on our awareness of the conceptually constructed fire can lead to effects that conform to the expectations that we form on the basis of it. As a result, this conceptual awareness is considered to be "non-misleading."

The second condition of validity—that a valid awareness event must reveal an object that was not previously known—was introduced in order to support Dignāga's claim that when we perceive an object, only our initial, nonconceptual awareness of it is valid. As we stated earlier, for Dignāga, all awareness events that associate perceived objects with concepts, classes, and labels are conceptual and therefore excluded from the realm of perception. Dharmakīrti accounts for this through his second condition. When we see an object, we initially have a nonconceptual awareness of it, which is typically followed by a conceptual awareness in which the object that we have perceived is associated with one or more generic labels or classes. But the conceptual awareness events that are formed on the basis of the initial nonconceptual awareness—for example, the (conceptual) awareness of a cow as "a cow"—are invalid not because they are misleading but because they are redundant.

The conceptual awareness of a cow as "a cow" attaches a label to the initially perceived object but, according to Dharmakīrti, does not present to us any additional feature of the object, which we have already perceived in its entirety. Inferential awareness, in contrast, has as its object something that we have not perceived at all, for example, the fire on the mountain that we infer but do not see. Even though inferential awareness is conceptual, in that it attaches the label "fire" to its putative object, it is nevertheless considered to be valid, since the object that it conceptually presents to us is a new object; that is, one that was not apprehended by a prior awareness. The process through which we move from conceptually constructed objects—which are not pragmatically effective—to real, pragmatically effective particulars is what Dharmakīrti calls "determination" (*adhyavasāya*). We have shown elsewhere that for Dharmakīrti, the process of "determination" occurs only in inferential/verbal awareness and not in perception.[51] It is determination that bridges the gap between the conceptually constructed objects that appear to us in inferential/verbal awareness and the real particulars that it leads us to act on.[52] In perception, the real, unconceptualized particulars themselves appear to us directly, and therefore there is no gap to be bridged.

As we will see, determination comes to play a crucial role in later Buddhist epistemology and particularly in the work of Jñānaśrīmitra. Later Buddhist epistemologists broke with Dharmakīrti by identifying in perception an analogous gap between the objects that appear to us and the objects that we act on. As a result, they further expanded the scope of determination, making it a necessary feature of all valid awareness.

Objects and Their Status

As is clear from the preceding discussion, Dignāga's and Dharmakīrti's views on the sources of knowledge rely on a distinction between "real" particular objects and "constructed" universal objects. Yet the nature and ontological status of these particulars has been the subject of great debate among contemporary interpreters of their thought. They generally acknowledge that both Dignāga and Dharmakīrti sometimes argue from a "realist" position—that there are mind-independent objects—and sometimes from an "idealist" one—that there are no mind-independent objects.[53] Contemporary interpreters do not, however, agree on their reasons for doing so. They generally agree that both Dignāga and Dharmakīrti are in fact idealists and that the "realist" positions that they adopt in various places in their works are simply instrumental; they are positions strategically adopted to help people overcome certain false views or to lead them through a series of successively superior views so as to arrive at their own idealist position.[54]

Our own understanding of Dignāga's and Dharmakīrti's reasons for arguing as they do is rather different. Although some of Dignāga's earlier philosophical works, particularly his *Investigation of the Basis of Awareness* (*Ālambanaparīkṣā*), make clear that he himself held idealist views, in his magnum opus, the *Compendium on the Sources of Knowledge* (*Pramāṇasamuccaya*), he largely avoids the question of the reality of mind-independent objects and, whenever necessary, presents parallel arguments that support both the realist and idealist positions.[55] In his *Compendium* there is no indication that he wants to support an idealist position at the expense of the realist one. Rather, he seems to be trying to create an epistemological framework that can be shared by both realist and idealist Buddhists.[56] Whenever possible, he presents arguments that are compatible with both positions and, when necessary, provides parallel arguments in support of each, without indicating any preference for one set of arguments over the other. The same strategy is evident in Dharmakīrti's major works, where the majority of his arguments are such that they could be accepted by either realist or idealist Buddhist philosophers. And on the rare occasions where he treats the two positions separately, Dharmakīrti provides parallel arguments in support of each.[57] It is worth noting that among the later authors in the Dharmakīrtian text tradition, there were both realists and idealists.[58]

The Elements of Inferential Reasoning

Because the Buddhist epistemologists maintain that perception and inference are the only two sources of knowledge and that the first of these, perception, bears upon only unconceptualized particulars, it should be clear that in general, philosophical claims can be defended only inferentially. Consequently, their approach in constructing, defending, and evaluating philosophical arguments is based on their theory of inference.

In early Indian philosophy, the theory of inference and the principles for evaluating arguments in the context of a debate were treated as separate topics, both textually and conceptually.[59] Dignāga incorporated certain elements of debate theory in his discussion of inference.[60] In his *Vādanyāya*, Dharmakīrti, building on Dignāga's work, effectively collapses the theory of debate into the theory of inference. He shows that most, if not all, of the grounds for defeat in a debate (*nigrahasthāna*) recognized by his predecessors can be reduced to defects in the inferential reason (*hetvābhāsa*) given in a particular argument. In addition, he excludes from the realm of legitimate argument those modes of sophistic or specious argumentation recognized by his predecessors as legitimate techniques for securing victory in debate.[61] The principal method for analyzing and evaluating philosophical arguments in post-Dharmakīrtian Buddhist epistemology relies on the conceptual vocabulary of inferential reasoning.

In an inference, one seeks to establish the presence of a property to be proven (*sādhya*) in a particular locus (*pakṣa*), on the basis of the presence in that locus of an inferential reason (*hetu*) invariably associated with the property to be proven. In the standard example of inference, when one sees smoke rising up from a particular mountain and infers the presence of fire there, the smoke is the inferential reason; the fire is what is to be proven; and the mountain is the locus. A necessary condition for a proper inference is a relation of pervasion (*vyāpti*) between the inferential reason and the property to be proven, such that whenever the inferential reason is present in a locus, the property to be proven also is present in that locus; for example, wherever there is smoke, there is fire. Dignāga identifies three conditions that must be satisfied by any proper inferential reason: (1) It must be present in the locus in question (e.g., the mountain); (2) it must be present in at least one similar case (*sapakṣa*)—that is, a locus other than the locus in question in which what is to be proven is also known to be present, for example, a wood-burning stove in a kitchen; and (3) it must not be present in any dissimilar case (*vipakṣa*), for example, a lake.[62] Putative inferential reasons that fail to satisfy any of these conditions are said to be pseudoinferential reasons (*hetu-ābhāsa*). These pseudoinferential reasons are generally divided into three categories: (1) those that are unestablished (*asiddha*), because either the locus in which they are to be established does not exist or the pseudoinferential reason is not present there; (2) those that are obstructed (*viruddha*) in that they are present in dissimilar cases but not in similar cases; and (3) those that are inconclusive (*anaikāntika*), because either the property to be proven is present in both similar and dissimilar cases or it is present in neither similar nor dissimilar cases.[63] Given this framework, most philosophical arguments in the later Buddhist epistemological tradition are designed to demonstrate that one's reasons satisfy these conditions and are therefore not pseudoinferential and, furthermore, that those of one's opponents fail to satisfy one or more of these conditions and hence are pseudoinferential.

3. DHARMOTTARA'S EPISTEMOLOGICAL REVOLUTION

The eighth-century Buddhist epistemologist Dharmottara proved to be one of Dharmakīrti's most influential interpreters and transformed the way in which Dharmakīrti's work was understood by most Sanskrit philosophers, both inside and outside the Buddhist epistemological tradition. Understanding his innovations is therefore essential for making sense of Jñānaśrīmitra's work. While Dharmottara presents himself as a faithful follower and interpreter of Dharmakīrti's works, his account of the two sources of knowledge, and of validity in general, is strikingly different from Dharmakīrti's.[64] Dharmottara's understanding of the two modes of valid awareness is succinctly presented in his commentary on Dharmakīrti's *Drop of Reason* (*Nyāyabindu*) 1.12, in which Dharmakīrti describes the object of perception as follows: "The object of this [i.e., perception] is a particular (*svalakṣaṇa*)." Dharmottara comments:

> The *object* of this . . . perception—that is, the thing that is cognized—is a particular. A *particular* (*sva-lakṣaṇa*) is a property (*lakṣaṇa*)—that is, a character—which is its own (*sva*)—that is, unique. For a thing has both a unique character and a general character. And of these, that which is unique is what is *grasped* (*grāhya*) by perception. For the object of valid awareness is twofold: a grasped object whose image is produced and an attainable object that one determines. For the grasped object is one thing and the determined is something else, since for perception, what is grasped is a single moment, but what is determined—through a judgment that arises by the force of perception—can only be a continuum. And only a continuum can be the attainable object of perception because a moment cannot be attained.[65]
>
> The same is true for inference: it *grasps* a nonentity because even though its own appearance is not a [real] object, there is activity through the determination of an object.[66] But since this imposed thing [i.e., the nonentity], which is grasped, is *determined to be a particular* in inference, a determined particular is the object of activity. But what is grasped is a nonentity. So here, showing the *grasped object* of this mode of valid awareness, he says that a particular is the object of perception.[67]

An episode of valid awareness, whether perceptual or inferential, is, for Dharmottara, not a single event but a process made up of two stages. In the first stage, an object is grasped; that is, its image is directly presented to awareness. In the second stage, we determine a second and distinct object that can be attained, that is, an object on which we may act.

It is clear that what Dharmottara says about inference in this passage is based on Dharmakīrti's account, as explained previously. Both Dharmakīrti and Dharmottara consider what is directly presented to inferential awareness to be not a real particular on which we can act but a generalized mental image.[68] Through determination, we treat this generalized mental image as if it were a real particular. What is most striking about this passage, however, is that Dharmottara, unlike Dharmakīrti, recognizes a parallel process at work in perception. For Dharmottara, the gap between the object that is presented to awareness and the object that we act on is equally present in both perception and inference. This is a dramatic departure from both Dignāga and Dharmakīrti, for whom the gap between the presented object and the object acted on is just what distinguishes inference from perception.

In his discussion of perception, Dharmottara raises a problem having to do with Dharmakīrti's acceptance of the widely held Buddhist theory that all existing things are momentary. According to Dharmakīrti, real, pragmatically effective objects cannot exist for more than an instant.[69] What appear to us as temporally extended objects are, in fact, continua of discrete but causally related moments. These continua are not, however, "ultimately real" (*paramārtha-sat*). Rather, they are conceptually constructed. Only the individual moments are pragmatically effective and therefore ultimately real. And herein lies the problem for Dharmottara: What directly appears to us in perception must be a real particular—that is, a single moment—but this is not the object toward which our activity is directed. For example, suppose that we see water in front of us. If we are thirsty, we will walk toward it. Assuming that it is not a mirage, we will eventually be able to take a drink and satisfy our thirst. Yet the water that we seek to obtain cannot be the single moment that initially appeared to us, since our action presupposes that the water will remain there long enough for us to reach and drink it. Thus, the object toward which we direct our activity is not a single moment but a continuum: the determined object (*adhyavaseya-viṣaya*) of perception. While the water that ultimately satisfies our thirst *is* a pragmatically effective particular, it is not *the same* pragmatically effective particular that appeared to us in our initial moment of perception. According to Dharmottara, then, in perception, just as in inference, there is a disjunction between the object that initially appears to us and the object toward which we direct our activity (and, similarly, the object that we ultimately obtain). For him, the process by which this gap is bridged is exactly the same as the process that Dharmakīrti saw at work only in inference, namely, determination.[70]

For Dharmottara, then, there is a close parallelism between the processes of perception and inference. In both cases, an object is "grasped," that is, directly presented to our awareness. But in both cases, too, this object is not something that we can either act on or even intend to act on. "Grasping" can lead to successful activity (which is the test of validity) only when, on the basis of this grasping, we construct a second object toward which we can direct our activity. In perception, this second object is a continuum, while in inference, it is a (determined) particular. According to Dharmottara, it is precisely through determination that we construct this second object: In both perception and inference, the object that appears to us is taken to be something other than what it is.

Thus, although his work builds on and attempts to harmonize Dharma-kīrti's epistemological and ontological principles, Dharmottara offers an account of validity that seems to be at odds with that of both Dignāga and Dharmakīrti. They draw a radical distinction between perception and inferential/verbal awareness, while Dharmottara sees them as essentially the same. Correspondingly, Dharmottara stresses the essential role of conceptual awareness in the perceptual process, while his predecessors dismissed it as being redundant and having a fictitious object.

Because Dharmottara's account of valid awareness takes the processes of perception and inference to be nearly identical, the question naturally arises as to how they are, nevertheless, to be differentiated. For Dharmakīrti, there is a clear difference in the kinds of mental processes that constitute perception and those that constitute inference. In inference, but not in perception, determination (*adhyavasāya*) is necessary to bridge the gap between the conceptually constructed object that we infer and the real, pragmatically effective particular that we subsequently act on. For Dharmottara, however, the difference does not pertain to mental processes (which are the same for both) but to the ontological status of the objects on which they bear.

Both perception and inference consist of two stages: One first grasps an object that is directly present to one's awareness and then determines a second object toward which one acts. In perception, what one grasps is an ultimately real, external particular, and what one determines is a continuum, which is conceptually constructed and therefore not ultimately real.[71] In inference, however, what is grasped is not a real particular but a "nonentity" (*avastu*). The determined object that one acts on is what Dharmottara calls a "determined particular" (*adhyavasitam svalakṣaṇam*). At first glance, this appears to be a simple inversion of the two objects of perception: The grasped object of one becomes the determined object of the other, and vice versa. Yet the inversion is not quite so simple as it appears from the passage just quoted. In his commentary on the *Nyāyabindu*, Dharmottara does not discuss further the nature of this "determined particular," but he does describe it in more detail in his own *Monograph on Exclusion* (*Apohaprakarara*).[72] There, in explaining the objects of verbal (and by implication, inferential) awareness, Dharmottara remarks, "That which is grasped and that which is determined are *both* exclusions-of-what-is-other (*anyavyāvṛtti*) and not real things (*vastu*)."[73] Thus, the "particular" that we determine in inferential and verbal awareness is not a *real* particular at all, but an exclusion, which is nothing other than a conceptual construct. As the tenth-century Nyāya philosopher Vācaspatimiśra says in explaining Dharmottara's position: "Even the particular that is being determined is not ultimately real. Instead, it too is conceptually constructed."[74] So, for Dharmottara, of all the objects of perception and inference, only the grasped object of perception is ultimately real. What really differentiates perception from inference is that perception begins with the appearance of a real particular in awareness, while inference has no real particular as its object, through either grasping or determination.

Dharmottara thus introduces a radical change to Dharmakīrti's system through his four-object model and the parallel role that he assigns to determination in both perception and inference, even though Dharmottara presents himself, and is presented by his commentators, as if he is merely explaining what Dharmakīrti said. Yet despite its radically innovative character, Dharmottara's new picture of valid awareness and its objects quickly became the standard account for Buddhist epistemologists, including Jñānaśrīmitra.

4. JÑĀNAŚRĪMITRA'S REWORKING OF THE THEORY OF EXCLUSION

Jñānaśrīmitra's *Monograph on Exclusion* (*Apohaprakaraṇa*) is programmatically concerned with elaborating and defending the theory of exclusion, but in fact, it incorporates Jñānaśrīmitra's views on almost all the topics just discussed. As Jñānaśrīmitra understands it, it is impossible to treat the topic of exclusion in isolation from broader questions of epistemology and ontology.

Even though Jñānaśrīmitra is often portrayed as a rival of Dharmottara, and he does criticize him on several key points,[75] his basic understanding of epistemology is closely modeled on Dharmottara's. Like Dharmottara, Jñānaśrīmitra repeatedly claims that each mode of valid awareness must have two objects, one grasped and one determined. In his *Analysis of Pervasion* (*Vyāpticarcā*), in a debate over the nature of the object of perception, Jñānaśrīmitra says:

> Now for us, both modes of valid awareness have both objects [a universal and a particular], because of the division between what is grasped and what is determined. For that which appears in an episode of awareness is what is grasped, but that [object] with respect to which this [episode of awareness] operates is what is determined. Now for perception, what is grasped is a particular and what is determined is a universal. But for inference, it is the reverse.[76]

Here, Jñānaśrīmitra basically recapitulates Dharmottara's model and differs in only one significant respect: He makes it explicit that the continuum that Dharmottara identified as the determined object of perception must be regarded as a universal, since it is not a real particular.[77]

The most significant difference between Jnānaśrīmitra and Dharmottara, however, is their attitude toward the ontological status of these objects. For Dharmottara, the grasped object of perception is a real external particular, while in inference there is neither the grasping nor the determining of such a particular. For Jnānaśrīmitra, however, there are no external, mind-independent particulars. Throughout his works, he consistently maintains that no mind-independent particulars can exist and that, as he says, "this entire triple-world is established to be nothing but consciousness (*vijñaptimātra*)."[78] Thus Jñānaśrīmitra cannot, like Dharmottara, appeal to the distinction between real and conceptually constructed objects in order to distinguish perception from inference.

For Dharmottara, the difference between the two modes of valid awareness hinges on an asymmetrical mapping of two different sets of paired concepts. In the passages discussed earlier, Dharmottara classifies the objects of awareness as those that are grasped (*grāhya*) and those that are determined, and also as those that are free from conceptual construction (*nirvikalpaka*)—and therefore real (*vastu/paramārtha*)—and those that are conceptually constructed (*kalpita/anyavyāvṛtta/āropita*)—and therefore unreal (*anartha/avastu*).[79] While all determined objects are, for him, conceptually constructed, not all grasped objects are real: The grasped object of inference is a conceptual construct, and unlike the grasped object of perception, it is not a real thing (it is a nonentity, *avastu*). Jñānaśrimitra, however, alters this conceptual map by indexing these two pairs of concepts to each other. For him, all grasped objects are free from conceptual construction, and all determined objects are the products of conceptual construction. In fact, Jñānaśrīmitra regards determination and conceptual construction as essentially the same: "The terms 'conceptualization' and 'determination' refer to the same thing. It's just that [the use of] the word 'conceptualization' is occasioned by connection with words and the like, while 'determination' is occasioned by suitability for activity, even with respect to [an object] that is not grasped [by awareness]."[80]

Thus, whatever is determined is conceptual and whatever is not determined is nonconceptual. It follows from this that the grasped (and, by definition, not determined) object of inference is, contrary to Dharmottara's claim, nonconceptual. For Jñānaśrīmitra, then, the objects of awareness fall into two neatly defined and mutually exclusive categories: those that are grasped and therefore free from conceptualization, and those that are determined and therefore conceptualized. Dharmottara's two ways of classifying objects are thus reduced to one.

This position seems to put Jñānaśrīmitra at odds with his predecessors in the Buddhist epistemological tradition. Beginning with Dignāga, this tradition relied on an ontological distinction between real particulars (*svalakṣaṇa*) and constructed universals (*sāmānya*), which were, respectively, taken to be the objects of perception and inference. Jñānaśrīmitra's reconceptualization of the objects of valid awareness effectively obliterates, however, any ontological distinction between them by relativizing the concepts of "particular" (*svalakṣaṇa*) and "universal" (*sāmānya*). For Jñānaśrīmitra, the objects that appear to us are neither particulars nor universals in and of themselves. It is only in relation to subsequent acts of determination that they can be properly classified as one or the other.[81] In his explanation of the nature of universals, for example, he says:

> From the word "cow" in the sentence "There are cows grazing on the far bank of the river," dewlap, horn, tail, and the like appear—accompanied by the form of the letters [which make up the word "cow"]—in effect, "lumped together" because of inattention to differences between things belonging to the same class. But that [conglomeration of dewlap, horn, etc.] is not itself a universal.[82]

Again, with reference to the "universal" fire, he says:

> For one and the same bare image—blazing and radiant—although it is utterly distinct from every particular when it is being made one with a particular [through conceptualization], is called a "universal." But that [image] is not itself a universal belonging to those particulars because it [the bare image] recurs elsewhere as a mental image.[83]

What we call a "universal" is for Jñānaśrīmitra simply an image that appears in awareness (just as, e.g., the image "blue" appears). Our calling it a "universal" is occasioned not by its ontological status but by the fact that we subsequently relate it to one or more putative particulars, whether real or unreal. But this subsequent relating of the image to particulars need not occur at all. When we reflect on this mental image as a mental image, for example, we are perceiving it. And relative to this act of perception, the image is not a universal but a particular (in that it is a grasped object of perception). When we reflect on a mental image, becoming aware of it *as* a mental image, we do so by assigning it to a class. For example, when we think, "The mental image 'fire' just appeared in my awareness," we are taking the unique, momentary image that appeared to us to be a member of the class "mental images of fire." This is exactly like the more familiar example of perception in which a cow appears in awareness and is subsequently conceptualized as "a cow." From this it follows that the very same image could become either a particular or a universal, depending on the kind of mental operation that follows it. If we relate the image to one or more putative particulars, it becomes a universal in relation to those particulars. But if by reflecting on the image as an image, we relate it to a class of which it is a member, it then becomes a particular in relation to that class.

Thus in claiming that "for perception, what is grasped is a particular and what is determined is a universal, but for inference, it is the reverse," Jñānaśrīmitra is making a statement that is, for him, true by definition. The image that appears in the first stage of the perceptual process is not a "grasped object of perception" because it is a particular. On the contrary, it is a "particular" because it is the grasped object of perception. In the same way, the image that appears in the first stage of the inferential process is not a "grasped object of inference" because it is a universal but is a "universal" because it is the grasped object of inference. Images are labeled as "particulars" or "universals" only in relation to a subsequent determination. Thus, for Jñānaśrīmitra, "particular" and "universal" are not really ontological categories at all. Instead, he defines them contextually. Images are categorized as either one or the other, depending on the role that they are made to play by subsequent acts of conceptualization.

Relativization of Internal and External

A similar relativization of the basic conceptual categories in the Buddhist epistemological tradition can be seen in Jñānaśrīmitra's treatment of "internal" and "external." For him, "internal" and "external" are not ontological categories but are defined relative to the activity (*pravṛtti*) of an agent.

An important element in Jñānaśrīmitra's discussion of activity is the familiar threefold division into bodily, verbal, and mental.[84] According to him, activity is not limited to physical activity involving putatively extra-mental objects but also includes verbal and mental activity that can be directed toward mental images, as well as toward putatively extra-mental objects. Even though mental images cannot be acted on physically, they can be the objects of verbal and mental activity, since we do talk and think about them. And in Jñānaśrīmitra's account, insofar as such mental objects become the objects of activity, they are "external."

That this is Jñānaśrīmitra's position is evident from his discussion of semantic value, that is, what it is that we are talking about when we use language. In his discussion, Jñānaśrīmitra makes use of the familiar distinction between what is "ultimately true" (descriptions that can withstand the most rigorous philosophical analysis) and what is "conventionally true" (convenient fictions that can help us function successfully in the world but cannot withstand the most rigorous philosophical analysis).[85] Jñānaśrīmitra argues that ultimately, given the most rigorous philosophical analysis, our statements cannot refer to anything at all. He argues further that even conventionally, when we make positive or negative statements, what we are affirming or denying the existence of is always some *external* thing. As he says,

> There is no way of *really* affirming either the mental image or the external object. Conventionally [there is affirmation] only of externals, whereas even conventionally there is no [affirmation] of the mental image.[86]
>
> For this mental image, which is indubitable and an object of reflexive awareness, cannot be what is affirmed or denied by means of words, and so forth, since this would be useless [in the case of affirmation] and impossible [in the case of denial].[87]

When one affirms the existence of a tree by saying "There is a tree here" or denies it by saying "There is no tree here," the word "tree" cannot be taken to refer to the mental image "tree." Since the mental image "tree" is present whenever one hears and understands the word "tree," it would be redundant, and therefore useless, to affirm its existence. Conversely, it would be contradictory, and therefore impossible, to deny its existence. Jñānaśrīmitra continues: "Neither can the external object, which does not appear in conceptual awareness, [really be affirmed or denied]. Since this object is not cognized, what could be affirmed or denied?"[88]

Since the external object itself does not appear in awareness (given that what appears in awareness is only a mental image), it too cannot *really* be affirmed or denied. After all, one cannot affirm or deny what one is not even aware of. Jñānaśrīmitra now concludes:

> Therefore, just as, on the basis of determination, an external tree is conditionally adopted [*vyavasthāpita*] as what is denoted by the word "tree," in the same way, it is only on the basis of determination that one talks about affirming or denying [any] external object. *Even when due to certain circumstances, one examines*

> *a mental image, having brought it to mind by means of another conceptualization, then too there is affirmation and denial of what is external to this conceptualization.*[89]

Jñānaśrīmitra's position is that even conventionally, one can affirm or deny only *external* objects, although one can affirm or deny mental images, as Jñānaśrīmitra clearly recognizes. Thus, mental images, insofar as we affirm or deny them, must be, for Jñānaśrīmitra, external. The application of the label "external," like the labels "particular" and "universal," does not depend on an object's ontological status but on the way that our awareness relates us to it. Objects are considered to be external if, and only if, they are determined, that is, not directly presented by the awareness that puts us in touch with them.

Conditionally Adopted Positions

In the passage just quoted, Jñānaśrīmitra uses the concept of a "conditionally adopted position" (*vyavasthā*), which proves to be central to his own account of what it is that words do (and do not) refer to and, as we shall see, to his understanding of traditional Buddhist claims about exclusion (*apoha*). What follows is an analysis of Jñānaśrīmitra's use of this concept, specifically in relation to his discussion of exclusion.

Jñānaśrīmitra begins his *Monograph on Exclusion* with a powerful attack on the generally accepted view of the Buddhist epistemologists, that words do not refer to real objects but express the exclusion of what is other (*anyāpoha*). Speaking in the voice of a hypothetical opponent, Jñānaśrīmitra raises two objections to the traditional understanding of exclusion. The first is phenomenological: The claim that what we understand from words, or from an inference, is merely the exclusion of others, namely, a type of negation, is directly contradicted by our experience. In both language and inference we become aware of what seem to us to be positive entities (*vidhi*), and it is argued that this would not be possible if the actual content of our awareness were simply a negation (*niṣedha*).[90] The second objection is exegetical: Dharmakīrti divides inferences into three categories, those based on identity (*svabhāva*) and those based on effect-cause relations (*kārya-kāraṇa-bhāva*), both of which establish the existence of positive entities, and those based on nonapprehension (*anupalabdhi*), which establish the absence of something (*abhāva*).[91] But if we argue that what we understand on the basis of inference, and therefore language, is nothing but a negation, that is, an absence, then the basis for this division would collapse, since all inferences would establish absences.[92] In light of these two objections, the opponent asks: "How can you say that 'exclusion is what is revealed by words and inferential reasons?'"[93]

In answering this question, Jñānaśrīmitra explains:

> It is for this reason that [in the introductory verse of the *Monograph on Exclusion*], he [i.e., I, the author] says, "This is [our] *position*." This [claim that exclusion is what is revealed by words and inferential reasons] is just a conditionally adopted position. What this means is that it is not really the case that "exclusion is primarily the object of words, etc." If you say, "So then what really is the case here?" [we say]:
>
> First of all, it is an [external] object that is primarily expressed by words. This being the case, exclusion is understood as an element of that [external object]. One [of these, the external object,] is [conditionally] adopted as an object because of determination; the other [the exclusion, is conditionally adopted as an object] because of appearance. But really, nothing at all is expressed [by words].
>
> This is the summation of the meaning of this text.[94]

Jñānaśrīmitra's response to the opponent's objections concedes that they are substantially correct: It is *not* convincing to argue that the content of our inferential and verbal awareness is simply a negation. Moreover, arguing in this manner *would* undermine the threefold division of inferential reasons, just as the opponent argues. Jñānaśrīmitra insists, however, that what the opponent is attacking is not the real Buddhist position but simply a "conditionally adopted position." Buddhists do sometimes speak as if exclusion alone were what is understood from words and inferential reasons, but this, Jñānaśrīmitra argues, is not what Buddhists take to be really the case. The real Buddhist position, as Jñānaśrīmitra understands it, is summarized in the verse just quoted: There are two sorts of things that we might conventionally take to be the semantic value of a word: the (putative) external object, and the mental image that appears to us upon hearing the word. The first of these is taken to be the semantic value on the basis of determination, in that it is an "actionable" object; that is, it is an object toward which our actions are directed, even though it does not appear in our awareness. The second is taken to be the semantic value in that it appears in our awareness, even though it is not actionable. Thus under certain circumstances, one may conventionally adopt the position that one or the other of these objects is the meaning of a word. Ultimately, however (for reasons to be discussed later), neither of these can be properly regarded as the meaning of a word, and thus the real position of the Buddhists is that "nothing at all is expressed."

Despite his ultimate view that nothing at all is expressed, Jñānaśrīmitra still provides a "conditionally adopted position" of his own in order to explain how it is that we are able, even in the absence of any real object, to engage in pragmatically successful linguistic (and also inferential and conceptual) activity.[95] Jñānaśrīmitra maintains, conventionally, that the content of our verbal (and also inferential and conceptual) awareness must be taken to be a complex object consisting of both a positive and a negative element.[96] In accordance with our everyday linguistic experience, a positive object must be taken to be what is primarily expressed by language. But an additional negative element, exclusion, must be taken to be a qualifier of that positive object. While we can act only toward positive entities, it is only through exclusion that we can pick out the appropriate objects for that activity by distinguishing them from those that are inappropriate.[97] This position has often been described as a "synthesist" view of exclusion.[98]

Yet this modified version of the theory of exclusion elicits a further objection: "Why don't you just talk in terms of the positive entity alone [when describing the semantic value of a word]? Or, alternatively, why wouldn't you be left with the unwanted consequence that one should speak of perception too as having exclusion-of-what-is-other as its object?"[99]

Here again, the distinction between perceptual and inferential/verbal awareness is seen to be problematic. We noted earlier that for Dharmakīrti, our nonconceptual awareness of a perceived object is typically followed by a conceptual awareness with a class-forming exclusion as its object (e.g., the awareness of a cow as a "cow"). And at least for Dharmottara and Jñānaśrīmitra, this second awareness is a necessary part of the perceptual process, in that it constructs one of the two objects of perception: the second, determined object. When we act on the basis of perception, the object toward which we act is understood to be a "positive entity," differentiated from other objects through conceptualization (which necessarily takes the form of an exclusion). Here, the opponent implies that Jñānaśrīmitra's theory of exclusion makes the operation of language/inference and perception essentially parallel. In each case, the object of awareness consists of a positive element that is necessarily coupled with an exclusion. The opponent accordingly argues that there is no basis for talking about the objects of perception and language/inference differently by asserting that perception deals with positive objects and language/inference with only exclusions. If it is correct to say that one "perceives" a real, positive object (*vastu*), then one could just as well say that what one refers to or infers is a real, positive object. Alternatively, if it is correct to say that because language and inference can put us in touch with objects only through the exclusion-of-what-is-other, we should say that they have exclusions as their objects, then we should also say that perception has an exclusion as its object.

Jñānaśrīmitra replies:

> In response to this, we say: By relying on a little bit of the truth, a certain conditionally adopted position is, for a specific purpose, constructed [by us], in one way, even though the actual state of affairs is different, just as in examples such as the "self" or the "arising of a thing." For "arising" can be a property only of an *existing object* qualified by a prior absence. By relying on a little bit of the truth, namely, the prior absence, we conditionally adopt the position that "[there is arising] of a nonexistent thing" in order to foreclose any worries about the doctrine that effects preexist in their causes. Or by relying on the conceptual construction of a single continuum, [we conventionally say:] "Who else will experience the [result of an] action done by this very person?" in order to frustrate the deceptive view that there is the passing away of what has been done and the onset of what has not been done.[100]

In this passage, Jñānaśrīmitra develops the theory of conditionally adopted positions. A conditionally adopted position is, as he sees it, a kind of "white lie," a statement that is not, strictly speaking, true but contains at least an element of truth and whose use is indexed to an appropriate purpose. He clarifies this by offering two examples: While it is not, strictly speaking, true that nonexistent objects can "arise," it is legitimate to make such a claim as a corrective to the erroneous Sāṃkhya position that all effects preexist in their causes.[101] "Arising" can be a property of only an existent thing. But the thing in question must be qualified by a prior absence: For example, when we say that a pot "arises," what we mean is that a pot, which did not exist previously, now exists. The prior absence of the pot is the "little bit of the truth" that we rely on in claiming that "nonexistent objects arise." And this claim, although not really true, may be legitimately offered to disabuse people of the false notion that nothing can arise that did not exist previously. In the same way, in explaining the theory of karma, one may legitimately say that a person will experience in the future the karmic results of actions that he now performs. Yet this, too, is not completely true, since there is no "person" that endures through time.[102] The statement is based on a "little bit of the truth," namely, that we, in fact, conceptually construct a mental continuum that we take to be an enduring "self." It is a "white lie" in that we use it to expose the falsity of the view that our current actions will not have karmic consequences and that what we experience in this life is not at all the result of previous actions.

Jñānaśrīmitra now applies this theory of "conditionally adopted positions" to the present case:

> Here too, [the idea that] linguistic expression takes a positive entity as its object is just the same [in that it, too, is a conditionally adopted position]. Here we conditionally adopt the position that exclusion, even though it is [really just] a necessarily attendant awareness, is the object of conceptual [including inferential/verbal] awareness, in order to set aside any suspicion that we accept [the position] pushed by [our] opponents that it is only the positive entity that is really expressed. And therefore, we don't talk in terms of just the positive entity [when describing the semantic value of a word]. But when [someone] pushes the position that "exclusion alone is the primary meaning of a word," then we put forth the positive entity as well. As stated, "First of all, it is the [external] object that is primarily expressed by words."

> But in perception, because there is no disagreement [of this sort], it is proper that one should not conditionally adopt this position.[103]

What is generally taken to be the traditional Buddhist position that "exclusion is what is revealed by words and inferential reasons" is not really the Buddhist position at all. It is just another white lie. The partial truth on which this white lie is based is the fact that as already explained, language and inference cannot effectively direct us toward the proper objects of our activities without relying on exclusion. And the purpose that makes this lie a "white" lie is that it serves as a corrective to the mistaken view that positive entities alone are expressed or inferred. Yet if someone were to mistakenly take this conditionally adopted position to be really the case, then one could adopt a new, conditionally adopted position that positive entities also are expressed and inferred, but only as qualified by exclusions. This is exactly the position that Jñānaśrīmitra sets forth in the first half of the summary verse quoted earlier. Jñānaśrīmitra understands perception to be different from language/inference, not because the latter takes exclusion as its object and the former does not, but because, for reasons to be discussed later, there is no parallel need to put forth the conditionally adopted position that exclusion alone is the object of perception. Here again, Jñānaśrīmitra's response to the opponent's argument is to concede that it is substantially correct. Perception and language/inference are alike in that they both have as their content a positive component and a negative component, that is, exclusion. The difference in the way that we talk about them is based not on a difference in their content but on a difference in the kinds of rhetorical contexts that motivate our discussions of them.

This tendency to explain distinctions among basic terms in the Buddhist epistemological tradition not in terms of real differences in their referents but in terms of the different discursive contexts in which they are used can also be seen in Jñānaśrīmitra's treatment of the terms "conceptualization" (*vikalpa*) and "determination" (*adhyavasāya*). When an objector points out that whereas Dharmakīrti uses these terms contrastively,[104] Jñānaśrīmitra does not offer any way to explain the difference between them, Jñānaśrīmitra responds: "True, 'conceptualization' and 'determination' refer to the same thing. It's just that the [use of the] word 'conceptualization' is occasioned by connection with words and the like, while 'determination' is occasioned by suitability for activity, even with respect to [an object] that is not grasped [by awareness]."[105]

According to Jñānaśrīmitra, the word "conceptualization" is generally used to designate situations in which our mental image of an object is inextricably bound up with the form of the word that is used to refer to it: For example, for a competent speaker of English, thinking of an object as a cow is typically bound up with the recollection of the word "cow." The word "determination," however, is generally applied to cases in which one treats a mental image as if it were an object that one could act on. But as Jñānaśrīmitra goes on to explain, since "thinking of" is just a kind of activity, conceptualization is really nothing but determination:

> This being the case, [just] as one concludes that an object has been apprehended through conceptualization, likewise [one concludes that it has been apprehended] bound up with the word [that refers to it]. This is because like the partial image of a thing,[106] the image of the word also appears [in this awareness]. Therefore, the conditionally adopted differentiation [*vyavasthā*][107] of conceptualization [from determination] is not based in reality [*tattvataḥ*] but is [accepted] only in conformity with the [conditional] determination that "insofar as a person conceives of himself as apprehending a thing, to that extent, he likewise conceives of himself as apprehending it together with its name."[108]

For Jñānaśrīmitra, the terminological distinction between conceptualization and determination is not based on a real difference in the mental processes to which they refer but is a contextually governed fiction that is indexed to particular purposes. Because people who have learned a language almost always associate the object that they conceptually apprehend with the word used to refer to it, they mistakenly believe that conceptually apprehending an object and associating it with its name are one and the same thing. And it is as a way of accommodating this widespread but mistaken belief that Dharmakīrti and others in the Buddhist epistemological tradition speak as if "conceptualizing" an object (i.e., apprehending it in association with a word that may be used to refer to it) and "determining" it (i.e., apprehending it as an object of activity in general: bodily, verbal, or mental) are distinct processes, even though they are one and the same.

Jñānaśrīmitra now explicitly relates this conditionally adopted position—that conceptualization can be distinguished from determination in virtue of its being bound up with language—to his earlier discussion of the distinction between perception and inference.

> And it is for the very same reason that with a view toward the practically oriented person whose mind has worn itself out due to the conceit [that conceptualizing a thing and apprehending its name are the same], the qualifier "free from conceptual construction" is included in the definition of perception [by Dignāga and Dharmakīrti] and that in the foundational text [Dharmakīrti's *Hetubindu*], there is separate mention [of conceptualization and determination with the words] "on the basis of conceptual awareness . . . by determining."[109]

This passage asserts, rather shockingly, that the claim that perception is free from conceptual construction, arguably the most fundamental and characteristic tenet of the Buddhist epistemological tradition, is itself nothing but another white lie.[110] For Jñānaśrīmitra, it is not really the case that the perceptual process is free from conceptual construction, since perception and inference each have both a nonconceptual and a conceptual object. Nonetheless, underlying this—strictly speaking, false—statement is a bit of truth, namely, that perception does in fact have a nonconceptual object that is grasped in the first moment of the perceptual process. Jñānaśrīmitra seems to believe that the reason that Dignāga and Dharmakīrti state this partial truth—that perception is free from conceptual construction—is because of the four possible objects of awareness (the grasped and determined objects of both perception and inference), it is only the grasped object of perception that can be differentiated from the other three objects without breaking down the false equation of conceptualization and language. The determined object of perception is conceptual but not necessarily linguistic. The grasped object of inference/language is, for reasons already discussed, nonconceptual but is, at least typically, bound up with language. The determined object of inference/language, however, is necessarily conceptual and typically also bound up with language. So for practically oriented people who regard conceptualization and verbalization as the same, these three objects cannot be differentiated from one another. Recognizing that it is too much to expect such people to give up this deeply ingrained equivalence, Dignāga and Dharmakīrti work around it by formulating a definition of perception that takes the first step toward clearly differentiating the objects of awareness. Accepting even this "little bit of the truth" marks a significant advance in philosophical understanding for pragmatically oriented people who already are "worn out" by the effort of accepting even this much.

Jñānaśrīmitra's theory of the "conditionally adopted position" thus provides a new and powerful tool for satisfying the dual objectives demanded by the "commentarial orientation" discussed previously: the need to be both philosophically correct and exegetically faithful to the tradition's foundational texts. This theory enables Jñānaśrīmitra to legitimate Dignāga's and Dharmakīrti's statements while at the same time taking a philosophical position that is at odds with what they appear, and have been generally taken, to mean.

5. TRANSLATION PRACTICES

For nearly a century, the Buddhist epistemological text tradition has been the object of sustained scholarly attention, and English translations of important texts in the tradition have been available since the 1930s. Yet the works of these important philosophers still remain the province of a relatively small group of specialists in classical Sanskrit and Tibetan. This is partly attributable to the linguistic and conceptual complexity of the works in question and to the widespread resistance among those educated in the Euro-American philosophical tradition to acknowledge works from outside this tradition as being properly philosophical. Nevertheless, the nature of the translations of these texts thus far produced has also contributed to the neglect of the tradition in broader Euro-American intellectual culture.

Most translations of Buddhist epistemological texts have been products of the long-standing European philological tradition. This tradition emphasizes the editing of texts through meticulous and critical study of existing manuscript materials and the production of studiously literal translations that are maximally faithful to the words on the page. Scholars in this tradition try very hard to preserve the text's lexical and syntactic features, including ellipses, ambiguity of pronouns, and the like. Furthermore, they make a conscious effort not to allow their understanding of the text's overall argument and content to shape their translation of specific words and passages. This results in translations that are highly accurate but nearly impossible for those who do not have firsthand knowledge of the primary languages to really understand. Such work is necessary for developing a rich, detailed understanding of these materials. But if these materials are to be made accessible to a broader range of educated readers, we must produce translations and studies of Sanskrit philosophical texts that can be read and understood by those with no knowledge of Sanskrit and with little or no previous exposure to the philosophical traditions to which they belong. Without such work, Sanskrit philosophers will never find a place in contemporary academic discourse and public consciousness comparable to that of Plato, Aristotle, Descartes, Kant, or Wittgenstein. In this book, we are trying to develop strategies for producing accurate yet readable translations of Sanskrit philosophical texts.

First and foremost, this means that we are willing to make judgments when more philologically minded translations studiously avoid them. Existing translations of Sanskrit philosophical texts tend to rely heavily on brackets to supply material that is necessary for understanding the text but is only implicit in the Sanskrit original. Whenever possible, we have avoided the use of brackets to supply material that is taken to be implied by the context. Instead, when it is our judgment that such material is both implied by the context and necessary for understanding the passage, we include it without brackets. For instance, when Jñānaśrīmitra uses a pronoun whose referent is clear from the context, we often supply the absent referent rather than translate the pronoun as a pronoun when clear comprehensibility or English style calls for it.

For example, in a passage that would literally be rendered

> Those things that are mutually connected by the exclusion of what does not have that form, when there is the seeing of another after the seeing of one among them, cause an awareness of that which is continuous to arise and not others. And the capacity [of these things] is precisely *this*.

We translate as follows:

> Certain things are connected with one another through the exclusion of what does not have their form. Those things, and no others, produce an awareness of a recurrent thing when, after one has seen one of those things, one sees another. And the capacity of these things is precisely this *exclusion of what does not have their form.*[111]

Rather than simply translate the pronoun as "this" in the final sentence, we supply the unstated referent.

In Sanskrit, the reference of pronouns and adjectives is often less ambiguous than in English, since in Sanskrit pronouns are marked for gender. Therefore, a pronoun of a given gender can refer only to a noun of the same gender, which restricts the range of potential referents in any given case. Thus to translate pronouns of all genders with the English "it" or to supply "it" as the unstated referent of substantivized adjectives often makes the English translation ambiguous when the Sanskrit text is not. For example, the literal translation

> Since, if, even if there is the inclusion of an additional class property, the form of the individuals is excluded only from what does not belong to that class, then how is there rejection of the awareness of the exclusion of not that, of [those individuals] that are becoming objects of language and conceptualization by just that form?

We translate as

> If you maintain that even though the class property is included as an additional element, the form of the individuals themselves is excluded from what belongs to a different class, then how can you deny the awareness of the exclusion of *those individuals* from what is not that, at the very moment they become the objects of verbal and conceptual awareness, by virtue of that very form?[112]

In this passage the adjective that we literally translated as "becoming objects" is marked with a feminine plural ending and so must refer to a feminine plural noun earlier in the passage. In this case, the only possible candidate is the word "individuals," and hence we supply the referent "those individuals," which the more literal translation supplies only in brackets.

By the same token, we sometimes supply the unstated agent of an action if it is clear from the context. For example, the literal translation "There is making of the conventional association, 'This is a cow,'" we render as "*The speaker* makes the conventional association, 'This is a cow.'"[113]

Operating on the same principle, when Jñānaśrīmitra includes a quotation that would be well known to his audience, we sometimes supply the name of the author or text quoted. For example, the literal translation "And therefore 'because, even on the basis of that conceptual awareness, by determination of it, there is activity only with respect to the real thing,'" we render as "And therefore, *Dharmakīrti says*, 'because even on the basis of that conceptual awareness, one acts only with respect to the real thing through the determination of it.'"[114]

When necessary, we also supply unspecified referents for some substantivized adjectives as well as the unstated agents of participles and agentive adjectives. For example, the literal translation

> And therefore, even if the doctrine of the difference of the contingent feature and the possessor of it is difficult to reject, then although there is a relation whose characteristic is enabling, there is capacity of the grasper of the real thing in the grasping of only what exists in the same place.

We render as

> And therefore, even if the belief that there is a difference between a contingent feature and its possessor is difficult to reject, nevertheless, given that there is a relation between them, namely, enabling, *an awareness* that grasps a thing would have the capacity to grasp *any feature* that is co-located with it.[115]

When Jñānaśrīmitra uses ellipses—that is, leaves implicit in a subsequent discussion of a topic essential qualifiers mentioned in his earlier formulation of the same topic—we include these qualifiers in our translation when they are necessary for comprehensibility. This is what Sanskrit intellectuals themselves refer to as "*anuṣaṅga*" or "*anuvṛtti*" (the "dragging" or "carrying over" of elements from an earlier passage). For example, the literal translation

> But that which Trilocana [says]: "The inherence of specific universals [i.e.,] horse-ness, cow-ness, etc., in their own loci is the occasion of the denotation and awareness 'universal,'" is discarded only by means of the rejection of inherence. Or, inherence alone is the occasion just by its own form. Thus, there is no harming of the example. And there is no mutual-power-ness of the universal and inherence by the conceptual construction of acting together, for then, there is producer-ness of even one by means of its own form."

We translate as

> But as for what Trilocana says: *The inherence of the particular universals—horse-ness, cow-ness, and the like—in their own loci is the basis for the awareness and the term "universal."* This is discarded precisely by the rejection of inherence. Alternatively, inherence itself is the basis for the awareness and the term "universal" by its very nature. And therefore, it doesn't harm our example. And it is not the case that universals and inherence jointly have that power (based on the idea that they act together). For if that were so, then just one of them would, by its very nature, produce the awareness and term "universal."[116]

The text does not itself specify what inherence is the basis for (in the third sentence) or what would be produced (in the final sentence), but it is quite clear from the context of Jñānaśrīmitra's argument that what is meant in each case is the "awareness and term 'universal'" that is mentioned in the first sentence, and therefore we include it in our translation.

Like most authors of Sanskrit philosophical texts, Jñānaśrīmitra often mentions certain relations, such as "connection between" and "difference from," without specifying one or both of the relata, either because they have been mentioned in an earlier passage or because they are clear from the context. Again, when comprehensibility or English style seem to require it, we supply the absent relata. For example, the literal translation ". . . just as the rice seed is the material cause, by the rice-ness [of it], even when the rice sprout, which is to be materially caused [by it], is that whose arising is without connection,"[117] we render as ". . . just as when a rice sprout is about to be produced, the rice seed, by virtue of being rice, is the material cause of the rice sprout, even though it arises without any connection *with the seed.*"

Or the literal translation "Because even in the treasury, there is the undesirable consequence of grasping all aspects only having put forward difference by means of enabler and that which is to be enabled," we render as "For even in the 'treasury,' Dharmakīrti points out the undesirable consequence of grasping all aspects of a thing only after he has proposed a difference between *a property-possessor and its properties* through the categories of 'enabler' and 'enabled.'"[118]

When it seems desirable, for reasons of either intelligibility or style, we sometimes render nominal expressions as verbal ones, or vice versa. For example, the literal translation "Even in both ways this is said: 'The causing of the conditional adoption of exclusion has as its highest aim the causing of the understanding of the inexpressibility of all properties,'" we translate as "But in either case it is said that *exclusion is conditionally adopted* in order to make it known that all properties are beyond the reach of language."[119]

Sometimes in order to facilitate understanding, we break up a long Sanskrit sentence into several smaller sentences in English. For example, the literal translation

> But when having shown one lump standing in front [of one], having caused the understander who rests on the conceptual awareness of the form common to all individuals dispersed in other places and times, to determine [that lump], there is the convention, "This is a cow," then, only where that [understander] ascertains that common form, he designates just that thing by the word "cow."

We render as

> But if (1) one first points out something in front of one, (2) one causes the language learner, on the basis of context, to form a

> determinate awareness of it through a conceptual awareness of a form that is common to all the relevant individuals dispersed through space and time, and then (3) one makes the conventional association "This is a cow." Then after this, that language learner will use the word "cow" only to refer to a thing in which he discerns that form.[120]

Another common feature of more philologically oriented translations is a commitment to lexical regularity, that is, a principled effort to always translate the same Sanskrit term with the same English term. Even though this is extremely useful for developing a common understanding among specialists, it sometimes results in translations that are stylistically problematic and misleading for nonspecialists. While we have made every effort to preserve lexical regularity in translating technical terms, elsewhere we allow our lexical choices to be guided by our sense of context and of English style and idiom.

Editorial Conventions

To make our translation easier to understand, we have adopted several editorial conventions to clarify Jñānaśrīmitra's discursive practices. As we noted earlier, Sanskrit philosophical works generally take the form of a constructed dialogue between a defender of the author's thesis and a series of (real or hypothetical) opponents. In our translations we indicate the "voice" of these opponents by the use of italics. We underline Jñānaśrīmitra's own summary verses, and when Jñānaśrimitra quotes and comments on portions of these verses, we underline the quoted fragments. We do not use parentheses to indicate material that we are inserting, as others often do. Rather, we use parentheses as they are used in English, to demarcate subordinate or digressive phrases or clauses.

The text included in this book is based on the printed edition in Thakur 1987. We have edited the text to incorporate our proposed emendations and, in the notes to the text, we indicate all divergences from the printed edition. We have not systematically reedited the text based on the single surviving manuscript, but we did use this manuscript when the printed reading seemed problematic or doubtful.

Numbering System

Following the page and line numbers of Thakur's 1987 edition of Jñānaśrī-mitra's *Monograph on Exclusion*, we cite (in brackets) in our translation the page and line numbers that correspond to the page and line numbers cited in our outline. In addition, we cite (in parentheses) in our translation the page and line numbers that correspond to paragraph divisions in our edition of Jñānaśrīmitra's text, even when we do not cite these numbers in our outline. We hope that these embedded page and line numbers will enable readers to work back and forth between the outline, English translation, and Sanskrit text.

JÑĀNAŚRĪMITRA'S *MONOGRAPH ON EXCLUSION*

OUTLINE

1. [201.01–201.06] Statement of the thesis: Words and inferential reasons convey only exclusions. Two explanations of the purpose in putting forth the thesis are given.
2. [201.07–202.21] Preliminary argument is made against the thesis.
   - 2.1 [201.07–201.14] The thesis is contradicted by experience.
     - 2.1.1 [201.07–201.09] Awareness that is produced by words and inferential reasons is experienced as presenting a positive entity.
     - 2.1.2 [201.09–201.14] Any philosophical thesis contradicted by experience is ruled out.
   - 2.2 [201.15–202.07] We cannot argue that exclusion is included in the awareness of the excluded thing because exclusion—as a kind of absence—cannot be included in an awareness that presents a positive entity.
   - 2.3 [202.07–202.11] If we accepted this inclusion in the case of inferential/verbal awareness, we also would have to accept it in the case of perceptual awareness.
   - 2.4 [202.12–202.22] Dharmakīrti argues that there are three types of inferential reasons, only one of which leads to an awareness of an absence. If the thesis is accepted, however, it would follow that

since exclusion is a kind of absence, all inferential reasons would lead to an awareness of an absence. Jñānaśrīmitra responds that the thesis is a conditionally adopted position.

3. [202.22–203.05] Outline (in verse) of Jñānaśrīmitra's argument in support of the thesis.
4. [203.06–208.05] The compound "object" of inferential/verbal awareness is described.

4.1 [203.06–203.11] It is true that a positive object is conveyed by words and inferential reasons, but exclusion is understood as an "element" of it.

4.2 [203.11–203.20] Six interpretations of "element" are given.

4.2.1 [203.11–203.15] "Element" as a qualifier is explained.

4.2.2 [203.15–204.19] "Element" as a subordinate element is explained.

4.2.2.1 [203.15–203.23] Jñānaśrīmitra states that exclusion must be included in verbal awareness. since it is a necessary part of what we associate with a word when learning its meaning.

4.2.2.2 [203.23–204.02] If inclusion on this basis is not accepted, Jñānaśrīmitra's opponents who argue that words refer to either universals or universal possessing particulars will be faced with the same problem.

4.2.2.3 [204.02–204.07] The opponents respond that even though we do not notice a universal as a distinct component of our verbal awareness, it is only on the basis of a real universal that we are able to pick out members of a class.

4.2.2.4 [204.08–204.19] Jñānaśrīmitra answers that the same can be said for exclusion: Even though we do not notice exclusion as a distinct component of our verbal awareness, it is only on the basis of exclusion that we are able to pick out members of a class.

4.2.3 [204.19–206.03] "Element" as property is described.

4.2.3.1 [204.19–204.20] A preliminary statement of the interpretation is given.

4.2.3.2 [204.21–204.24] Vācaspatimiśra's criticism and Jñānaśrīmitra's reply are stated.

4.2.3.3 [204.24–205.09] Exclusion is defined as a conditionally adopted position.

4.2.3.3.1 [204.24–204.25] Criticism: Why do you say that exclusion is an element of inferential/verbal awareness but not that it is also an element of perceptual awareness?

4.2.3.3.2 [204.26–205.09] Jñānaśrīmitra responds.

4.2.3.4 [205.09–206.03] The distinction between those inferential reasons that establish positive entities and those that establish negations is justified.

4.2.3.4.1 [205.09–205.12] The first justification is given.

4.2.3.4.2 [205.12–206.03] The second justification is given.

4.2.4 [206.04–207.07] "Element" is described as an element of an assertion.

4.2.4.1 [206.04–206.14] If exclusion were not included as an element of any positive assertion, there would be nothing to properly limit the scope of the assertion.

4.2.4.2 [206.15–206.24] Rejection of sequentialism: We cannot become aware of the positive entity first and then become aware of the exclusion of what is other.

4.2.4.3 [206.25–207.07] The view that the exclusion of what is other is a real property of mind-independent particulars is rejected.

4.2.5 [207.08–207.19] "Element" is defined as a desirable property: Although inferential/verbal awareness contains both a positive component and an exclusion, exclusion is the more desirable, that is, the more important, element.

4.2.6 [207.19–208.05] "Element" is defined as a desirable element of language, given that exclusion is expressed. The inclusion of exclusion in inferential/verbal awareness is necessary if this awareness is to have the desirable property of being free of the aforementioned defects.

5. [208.05–225.11] Internal and external objects are differentiated.

5.1 [208.05–220.01] The object of inferential/verbal awareness is not a particular.

5.1.1 [208.05–208.09] Opponent: But if you accept that a positive object is what is directly expressed, you contradict your thesis that "nothing at all is expressible."

5.1.2 [208.09–208.18] "Objects" are of two kinds, external and internal. The external object is conditionally adopted as the semantic value of a word only on the basis of determination and not because a real particular appears in inferential/verbal awareness. This is established by the fact that the object of inferential/verbal awareness appears different from that of perceptual awareness.

5.1.3 [208.19] Opponent: One and the same real particular could be the object of both perceptual and inferential/verbal awareness, although it would appear differently in each.

5.1.4 [208.20–210.27] Jñānaśrīmitra extends his argument that awarenesses with different appearances cannot have the same object.

5.1.5 [211.01–220.01] If the semantic value of a word really were a real, external particular, we would be aware of it in its entirety and would have no need to affirm or deny anything about it through the use of additional words.

5.1.5.1 [211.01–213.09] Affirming or denying property possessors is impossible.

5.1.5.2 [213.10–220.01] Affirming or denying properties is impossible.

5.2 [220.02–225.11] The object of inferential/verbal awareness is not a universal.

6. [225.12–228.03] The object from the perspective of determination is described.

6.1 [225.12–225.15] Objection: How can you say that the external object is "expressed by words" when in your account, it does not appear at all in inferential/verbal awareness?

6.2 [225.16–225.19] The external object is taken to be the object of conceptual awareness in that it is determined by it, even though it does not appear.

6.3 [225.19–225.26] Objection: How can you say that it is "through determination" that externals are the object of conceptual awareness when determination and conceptualization are really just the same thing?

6.4 [226.01–227.15] It is true that the words "conceptualization" and "determination" refer to the same thing; It is just that we use them on different occasions.

6.4.1 [226.01–226.02] Our use of the word "conceptualization" is occasioned by connection with words and the like. Our use of the word "determination" is occasioned by fitness for activity even with respect to something that has not been grasped.

6.4.2 [226.02–226.25] How determination works is explained.

6.4.2.1 [226.02–226.09] Determination is an inherent capacity of conceptual awarenesses to direct our activity to only certain particulars and not others.

6.4.2.2 [226.09–226.18] This capacity is not based on any similarity between the image in conceptual awareness and the real particulars that it determines.

6.4.2.3 [226.18–226.25] Determination provides a workable basis for everyday activity and for inferential and linguistic behavior.

6.4.3 [226.25–227.15] Why does it seem to us that conceptualization and determination are different?

6.4.3.1 [226.26–227.01] Determination governs all three forms of activity, physical, verbal, and mental.

6.4.3.2 [227.01–227.10] The image in conceptual awareness can include abstracted features of both things and the words associated with them. We associate the word "conceptualization" specifically with awareness containing a verbal component, but the process of determination is equally operative in all such awareness, regardless of whether they contain such an element.

6.4.3.3 [227.10–227.15] "Determination" is a "property" of conceptual awareness, but for us, property/property-bearer relations are ultimately fictitious and so they are really the same thing.

6.5 [227.16–228.03] Determined objects are defined.

6.5.1 [227.16–227.21] Our activity is always directed toward determined objects.

6.5.2 [227.22–228.03] We call the images that do appear in our conceptual awareness "unreal" because they are not the same as the objects that we act on.

7. [228.04–230.08] The object from the perspective of appearance is described.

7.1 [228.04–228.19] The mental image is taken to be an object of awareness because it is what appears, but it is not determined by it.

7.2 [228.19–229.02] Such images are said to be "unreal" in that they do not correspond to the external objects that we act on, but they nonetheless really do exist as mental images.

7.3 [229.03–229.13] What we affirm or deny through language, even conventionally, is always the external object and never the mental image.

7.3.1 [229.03–229.08] It is useless to affirm the existence of the mental image that directly appears to us, and it is impossible to deny it.

7.3.2 [229.08–229.13] Even when we act on mental images by thinking about them, those images themselves are in fact external relative to the conceptual awareness that determines them.

7.4 [229.14–230.08] Dharmottara's account of exclusion is rejected.

8. [230.08–232.04] The conditionality of both perspectives is explained.

8.1 [230.16–231.16] There really are no "objects" at all.

8.1.1 [230.16–231.02] In order to really be an object of awareness, something must both appear in that awareness and be determined by it, but nothing satisfies both criteria.

8.1.2 [231.03–231.16] In perception, too, just as in inferential/verbal awareness, there can be no real object, since nothing can both appear in perceptual awareness and be determined by it.

8.2 [231.16–232.04] An alternative explanation is that exclusion really is an object of inferential/verbal awareness, but still nothing is expressed because exclusion is itself an absence.

9. [232.05–232.19] Summary and conclusion

9.1 [232.05–232.11] What is the object of inferential/verbal awareness? It depends on the perspective from which the question is asked: from the perspective of determination, it is the external object; from that of appearance, it is the mental image; but from the perspective of ultimate reality there is no object at all.

9.2 [232.12–232.19] Concluding verses: The key to establishing exclusion is the nonappearance of the external object in awareness. If this can be established, everything else follows easily.

TRANSLATION

[201.01] Exclusion is what is revealed by words and inferential reasons.[1] This position is established in order to demonstrate that all properties[2] are inexpressible.

"Position," that is, a conditionally adopted position.[3] Everything up to the word "established" explains that exclusion is the topic to be discussed in this text. The rest explains the purpose of demonstrating this. Alternatively, it means "It is for this purpose that Buddhist teachers have conditionally adopted the position that exclusion is revealed by words and the like." But in either case, it is said that exclusion is conditionally adopted in order to make it known that all properties are beyond the reach of language.

[201.07] *But it is contrary to experience to say,* "Exclusion is what is revealed by words and inferential reasons." *That is, the awareness that "there is fire on that part of the mountain," whether from words or from an inferential reason, is seen to depict only the form*[4] *of a positive entity and not to present to us the mere exclusion "there is no non-fire there."* [201.09] *And when something is contradicted by experience, one needn't think about other ways of proving it, since every means of valid awareness*[5] *derives its power from experience alone.*[6] *This is because it arises from experience and culminates in it. For no other means of valid awareness can arise without the help of perception. Nor is someone who pursues a means of valid awareness satisfied merely by the arising of valid awareness that is nonexperiential as long as there is no experience of the pragmatic efficacy*[7] *of the things that were presented in it. Therefore, if it does not depend on experience, this other means of valid awareness, being either incapable or useless, is by itself nothing. When something has been proven or disproven by experience, no other means of valid awareness finds an opening. So how can you say that exclusion is the object of words and the like?*[8]

[201.15] *If you say this:* Even if one does not have the conceptual awareness,[9] "I am aware of an exclusion," nevertheless, the depiction of the excluded thing is itself the depiction of the exclusion. This is because there cannot be an awareness of a qualified thing that does not include an awareness of its qualifier(s).[10] For our opponents, conceptual awareness is an awareness of a universal because a shared image appears[11] in it, even in the absence of the conceptual awareness "I am aware of a universal."[12] In just the same way, the awareness of the exclusion implied by the awareness of the excluded thing makes it possible for us to be aware of and to talk about exclusion.

(201.19) *We reply: When there is the appearance of a shared image, one can take the position that there is the awareness of a universal by virtue of its having a positive form. But what does that have to do with taking the position that there is awareness of an exclusion in a mental state in which a negative image does not appear? Therefore, if even in the absence of a conceptual awareness of the form "I am aware of an exclusion," there were an appearance that constructs the form of an absence, then who would object to the position that there is awareness of an exclusion?*[13] *If one didn't take this view, there could be talk of the awareness of a thing even when it doesn't appear, and thus why not say that there is the awareness of a horse, even in a mental state that has the image of a cow?* [202] *If you say,* "The awareness of an exclusion is included as a qualifier," *then we reply: If the conceptual awareness had a form such as "excluded from non-cow," then let exclusion be introduced as a qualifier. But the awareness is "cow." And therefore, because the qualifier, exclusion, even if it exists, is not depicted in that awareness, how can we adopt the position that there is awareness of that exclusion? So from your position, it follows that one does not take the positive entity to be the object, even though it appears in awareness, but one does take the exclusion to be the object, even though it does not appear in awareness. What kind of thinking is this? And it is for just this reason that Dharmakīrti says, "How can it be that something that is not ascertained"*[14] *by ascertaining awarenesses "is the object of those states of awareness?"*[15] *Something that does not appear in a conceptual awareness surely cannot be ascertained by it.*

[202.07] "When a positive form appears, its exclusion from other things also is contained within it, and so there is awareness of that exclusion." *If this is your position, we reply that even in that case, exclusion is just something related to the positive entity, but it is the positive entity that directly appears. And so there is no escaping from the problem mentioned previously. And furthermore, if this were the case, it would unavoidably follow that exclusion would be the object of perception as well,*[16] *especially of perception that, owing to conceptualization, depicts a single excluded thing, that is, which sees it as excluded from all other things. Therefore, because it apprehends a positive image, conceptual awareness, like perception, has the positive entity as its object and does not have exclusion as its object.*

[202.12] *But as for the analyses of the word "exclusion" as "that which is excluded from other things" or "that in which other things are excluded"—which declare the external object (which is excluded from what belongs to a different class) or the mental image, respectively, to be "exclusion of what is other"—they are of absolutely no use. This is because one is just using the term "exclusion" to mean a positive entity, and making up another name does not alter the nature of a thing.*[17] *Therefore, in accordance with our experience, let us just say that it is the positive entity, that is, the external object, which is understood from words and the like. Moreover, there are these authoritative texts:*[18] *"Among the three types of inferential reasons, two establish positive entities and one is a basis for establishing a negation."*[19] *"Nonapprehension is a type of inferential reason that establishes the negation of a thing, not entailing any positive element. But the other two types of inferential reason, because they make a positive claim, establish an implicative negation."*[20] *And if there is just the awareness of pure absence, even from other types of inferential reasons, as if a negative particle had been used, then they are no different from nonapprehension. And from this would follow the instability of the entire framework built on the division of inferential reasons. So how can you say, "Exclusion is what is revealed by words and inferential reasons"?* It is because of this that I said, "Position." The claim "Exclusion is what is revealed by words and inferential reasons" is just a conditionally adopted position. What this means is that it is not really the case that exclusion is literally the object of words and the like.

[202.22] If you say, "*So then what really is the case here?*" we say,

First of all, it is an external object that is primarily expressed by words. This being the case, exclusion is understood as an element[21] of that. One object is adopted as expressed on the basis of determination, another, on the basis of appearance. But really nothing at all is expressed by words.

This is a summary of the meaning of this text.

[203.06] Indeed, no authoritative text can triumph over experience. Thus, first of all, no one can deny that a conceptual awareness can only arise insofar as it presents to us a positive entity: this is what the first line of the verse means. (We are not concerned here with cases in which the negative particle is used, because there is no disagreement about them.)[22] Now, "*by words*" is a partial indicator:[23] It should also be understood to include "made known by inferential reasons" and "made into an object by conceptual awarenesses."

(203.09) *If this is so, forget about exclusion's being expressed. Even as a conditionally adopted position, it has now been abandoned. For even that position is asserted on the basis of two things: on the basis of a connection between the conditionally adopted position and what is really the case and on the basis of some purpose. In this case, even if a purpose has been stated, namely, making it known that all properties are inexpressible, there still is no connection.*

[203.11] With this objection in mind, the author replies, "This being the case, exclusion. . . ." Given that the positive entity is primarily what is made known, exclusion must be understood as a subordinate element because it is a qualifier of it. "As an element of that" shows the connection of exclusion with the external object. "Is understood" shows the connection of it in our awareness. And so exclusion is both connected with the external object and present in our awareness. So, leaving aside the positive entity, exclusion is, for the purpose just stated, said to be the primary meaning of a word. This is so, even though it is the positive entity that one is primarily aware of.

[203.15] Or on another interpretation, "it is understood" only "as an element of that" and not as the primary thing. Thus, those who maintain that exclusion is directly presented are refuted. And even if it is said that words such as "exclusion of others" and the like are not depicted in our awareness, nevertheless it cannot be said that there is no awareness at all of exclusion as a qualifier, since words such as "cow" and the like are introduced to us only as referring to things excluded from non-cows. For there is an authoritative text that begins: "A word is introduced, when one has excluded that from which the thing is different."[24] It is just like this. When from the word "*indīvara*" (which has been introduced as referring to a blue lotus), there is an awareness of a blue lotus, the appearance of blue in our awareness is undeniable. In the same way, when from the word "cow" (which has been introduced as referring to what has been excluded from non-cows), there is an awareness of a cow, the appearance of exclusion in our awareness is undeniable.

[203.23] But as for those who imagine that there is circular reasoning (which deceives simple-minded people) in taking the conventional association[25] of the word "cow" to be with what is excluded from non-cows,[26] how do they, who argue that the conventional association of words is with universals or with what possesses a universal,[27] see themselves as being free from the same problem? That is to say, by "universal" they cannot mean any universal at all, because it would follow that the word "cow" would be conventionally associated even with a horse. Instead, what they mean is a universal such as "cow-ness." This being the case, [204] if reference is determined in this way—"There is the conventional association of the word 'cow' either with the universal 'cow-ness' or with what possesses it"—then there is the very same problem, since one cannot know what the universal "cow-ness" is without knowing what a cow is, and one cannot know what is expressed by the word "cow" without knowing the universal "cow-ness."

[204.02] *Now there would be a problem if the conventional association were made with words of this sort: "The word 'cow' refers to the universal cow-ness or to what possesses it." But if (1) one points out something in front of one; (2) one causes the language learner, on the basis of context, to form a determinate awareness of it through a conceptual awareness of a form common to all the relevant individuals dispersed through space and time; and then (3) one makes the conventional association "This is a cow," after this, that language learner will refer only to a thing in which he discerns that form with the word "cow." So why is there the problem of mutual dependence? And insofar as this is the case, the statement that "a conventional association is made with respect to the universal 'cow-ness' or with respect to what possesses it" is a commentators' gloss on the empirically established fact. But this is not the way that those who impart those conventions teach them.*

[204.08] If you say this, then in the same way, if the form of the conventional association were stated with words of this sort—"The word 'cow' refers to what is excluded from non-cows"—then this would be a problem. But how could there be a problem if (1) the language learner has, with respect to the individuals intended by the speaker, a reflective awareness[28] (*pratyavamarśa)* containing a single image, and (2) on the basis of context, he is caused to form a determinate awareness of them, and then (3) the speaker makes the conventional association "This is a cow"?[29] For this language learner understands that all the individuals falling within the scope of his own conceptual awareness (which are themselves excluded from all individuals that do not belong to that class, without relying on words such as "excluded from non-cows") are expressed by the word "cow." Therefore, by the word "cow," he refers to only those individuals in which he apprehends the exclusion of what does not belong to that class. Accordingly, the statement that "The word 'cow' refers to what is excluded from non-cows" is just a gloss on the empirically established fact and is not the form of the convention itself. This is because it is only when this application of the word "cow" has been accepted that everything else can be denoted by the word "non-cow." But whether the shared image that is excluded from what does not belong to that class is the appearance of a universal in conceptual awareness or is the real nature of the individual will be determined later.[30] But it is established that there is no circularity. And just as when one hears the word "*puṇḍarīka*," one becomes aware of a white lotus flower, so too when one hears the word "cow," one becomes aware of something that is excluded from non-cows. Therefore it is established that even those who believe in real class-properties[31] (*jāti*) must accept that a positive verbal content[32] (*vidhi*) is necessarily linked with awareness of exclusion as a qualifier of it. And this is not just some vague connection; rather, it is in fact the immediate awareness of both the positive verbal content and the exclusion as primary and subordinate. This is the difference between them.

[204.19] Or on a third interpretation,[33] the word "*element*" expresses a property because there is awareness of the positive entity having the exclusion of others as a property. [204.21] Now in denying the similarity (produced by the exclusion of what is other) of a third form existing in both the externally projected mental image and the external object, Vācaspati says, "*Furthermore, you do not accept that exclusion is a property [dharma] of a particular [svalakṣaṇa].*"[34] This is completely wrong. If you say that what is meant here is a "real" exclusion,[35] this still is of no use, since we take the property/property-possessor relation to be purely conceptual.[36]

[204.24] *Why don't you just talk in terms of the positive entity alone? Or why wouldn't you be left with the unwanted consequence that one should speak of perception as also having exclusion-of-what-is-other as its object?* [204.26] In response to this, we say: Here, by relying on a little bit of the truth, we construct in one way a certain conditionally adopted position for a specific purpose, even though the actual state of affairs is different. This is similar to cases such as the "self" and the "arising of a thing." For "arising" can only be a property of an *existing object* qualified by a prior absence.[37] [205] By relying on a little bit of the truth, namely, the prior absence, we conditionally adopt the position that "there is arising of a nonexistent thing," in order to foreclose any worries about the doctrine that effects preexist in their cause.[38] Or by relying on the conceptual construction of a single mental continuum, we conventionally say, "Who else will experience the result of an action done by this very person?" in order to frustrate the deceptive view that there is the passing away of what has been done and the onset of what has not been done.[39] Here, too, the claim that linguistic expression takes a positive entity as its object is exactly the same. Here we conditionally adopt the position that exclusion—even though it is really just a necessarily attendant awareness—is the object of conceptual awareness, in order to set aside any suspicion that we accept the position pushed by our opponents that it is only the positive entity that is really expressed. And therefore we don't talk in terms of just the positive entity. But if someone pushes the position that "exclusion alone is the primary meaning of a word," then we put forth the positive entity as well. As it is stated, "First of all, it is an external object that is primarily expressed by words." In perception, though, because there is no disagreement of this sort, it is proper that one should not conditionally adopt this position.

[205.09] But it has already been said[40] that there is no advantage in saying that a positive entity is a qualifier of the exclusion of what is other. For there are authoritative texts such as "It demarcates that. It excludes what is other than that."[41] But as for the thing negated, there it is specifically the function of negation that is foregrounded by the word "nonapprehension."

[205.12] Alternatively, just as in the case of nonimplicative negation, the nonincorporation of the role of the positive entity is simply the capacity to produce conceptual awareness of absence, owing to the experience of a specific property (*rūpa*), in the same way even for conceptual awareness of positive entities, the incorporation of negation is just the capacity to produce activity suitable to a given practice (*tantra*), and the capacity to produce reflective awareness such as "I am aware of fire."[42] And in the case of implicative negation, there is, of course, the awareness of a definite form (*niyata-svarūpa*).[43] In both cases, there is the incorporation of a negation.

(205.16) And Dharmakīrti, the author of the authoritative texts, accepts both implicative and nonimplicative negation. In some cases, when appropriate to the context, his statements are made with reference to nonimplicative negation, such as "in the form of that, there is nothing,"[44] but sometimes they rely on implicative negation as in "because it establishes something excluded from what does not have that form."[45] There is no definite rule. Therefore, what Dharmottara, the author of the *Commentary*,[46] says in his own *Proof of Exclusion* and what Trilocana,[47] who is confused by his descent into the meaning of that text says, namely, that "the teacher, Dharmakīrti, is properly understood to be partial to nonimplicative negation,"[48] is refuted.

(205.21) And it is not the case that talking about qualification is impossible in the absence of a distinction between a qualifier and what is qualified by it. This is because talk of qualification based on a speaker's intention remains, as in cases like "Rāhu's head" or "the universal, cowness."[49] Moreover, you yourself talk about a qualifier/qualified relation[50] between the absence of a pot and the place where it is not or between the absence of goblinhood and the pillar that is not a goblin. So why should this be forbidden to us? If you say, "*Because you maintain that absences lack any real nature*," we respond, "But at this point we are not investigating the nature of absence, but rather we are investigating our awareness of it." And this awareness cannot be denied. In the case of implicative negation as well, the negation of what is other than a thing is just the affirmation of that thing. Thus there is no obstacle to our being aware of an absence or to its being a qualifier. Since in this very sentence—"The negation of what is other than a thing is just the affirmation of that thing"[51]—we see that affirmation and negation are coreferential. [206] And for this reason, the objection that there is a contradiction is also not a problem.[52] For there is a contradiction between a positive entity and the absence of itself, not between it and the absence of something else, since these necessarily exist together. Therefore, it was rightly said, "This being the case, exclusion is understood as an element of that."

[206.04] Or on another interpretation,[53] this negation of another thing is indeed an "element" of the positive assertion of the external object.[54] Therefore, this is said to be "understood."[55] As the authoritative text says, "One acts by avoiding what is other than that"[56]—it is for this reason that language is used. "Otherwise, language use would be pointless"[57]—this shows that exclusion is the whole point of language use and that it does not fail to cover any cases.[58] Even in the sentence "This road goes to Śrughna,"[59] this principle is easily satisfied. It is just "this," relative to roads other than the intended one; it is just "to Śrughna" relative to undesired places other than Śrughna; it just "goes" because it doesn't end like a forest path; and it is just a "road" in virtue of excluding caravans, messengers, and the like.[60] If you say, *The meaning of the word "road" is understood from pointing one's finger*, we reply that first of all, there is exclusion of other things, and this is what we want. In any case, in everyday life, one does see the use even of words whose meaning is already understood, as in the examples "he advances *toward*" or "both those *two* Brahmins." For just as by excluding the caravan, people, and the like, one asks, "Which *road* goes to Śrughna?" In the same way, the answer is also "This *road*." For in each and every case, there is affirmation or negation only of what is marked by doubt regarding what is to be communicated.[61] And if, when hearing the words, the exclusion of what is other were not noticed, then how could one act by avoiding what is other? Thus, when told to tie up the cow, we would also tie up horses and the like.[62]

[206.15] But as for the view *When there is the awareness of a cow, the exclusion of what is other is ascertained subsequently, by implication, with the thought that "what is not that is other than that."* This doesn't hold up. This is because one does not see this sequence of awarenesses even in a first-timer. For even when one has just learned a verbal convention, when told, "Bring the cow," one does not *subsequently* deduce the exclusion of what is other than that. And if the awareness that arises from the word "cow" were mixed up with what is other than a cow, then it would not be possible to ascertain what a cow is. Or if the awareness were like that, then how even subsequently could the deduction arise? For the "cow" would be grasped along with other forms. How is that "cow" capable of attaining a state in which it is not mixed up with them? Therefore, the awareness of what is excluded from non-cows is called "the awareness of a cow." And for this reason, the time when we are aware of the word's own object is the time when we are aware of the exclusion of other objects. Just as when the word "moon" is used, the time of our awareness of the moon is the same as that of its brightness. And what sort of awareness of the moon can there be if there is no awareness of its brightness? Likewise, what sort of awareness of a cow can there be if our awareness of it is mixed up with other forms? The two are just the same. Nor is it possible to be aware of a thing as neither mixed nor unmixed. This is because even subsequently it could not possibly have that capacity.[63] Therefore, it is not desirable to rely on the capacity of the positive entity to make one aware of the negation.

[206.25] In regard to what Vācaspati says in addition to this: "*Individuals characterized by a class property*[64] *are the objects of both words and conceptual awarenesses. And the form of those individuals characterized by that class property is excluded from what does not belong to that class. Thus because the awareness of that excluded form arises from the object itself, when one is told, 'Tie up the cow,'* [207] *one does not tie up horses, and so forth.*"[65] This, too, is rejected by very same argument, since (1) if you maintain that even though the class property is included as an additional element, the form of the individuals themselves is excluded from what belongs to a different class, then how can one deny that there is awareness of the exclusion of those individuals from what is not that, at the very moment they become the objects of verbal and conceptual awareness by virtue of that very form? Or (2) if the form of the individuals is not excluded from what does not belong to that class or is not cognized in that way, then this awareness of exclusion is just the gift of a class property. So how can exclusion be understood from the object as well? This has effectively been explained already. If it is excluded from what is other only by virtue of the class property, then since that class property existed previously but was not previously suitable for ascertaining that exclusion, how then could it subsequently be suitable? For it is only when connecting something with its name that one requires the memory of the linguistic convention as an aid. But the conceptual construction of something as other than what does not belong to that class depends merely on seeing it, just as in the case of a prelinguistic infant. Therefore, this argument is not significant.

[207.08] Or on another interpretation,[66] the term "element" means a desirable property in that it is "repeated," that is, "repeatedly sought out."[67] Therefore, what is being indicated in the summary verse is preeminence. Therefore, "in these," that is, words,[68] it is that desirable element, the exclusion, that is the main thing. In the case of words that denote real things, it is precisely the exclusion, by virtue of its being a desirable element, that is said to be "understood," and not the positive entity, because even though it also appears in awareness, it is not the main thing. As the authoritative text says, "Because it requires that one see the use of the word in some cases"—that is, those that belong to the same class—"and it requires not seeing the use of the word elsewhere"—that is, in what does not belong to that class—"therefore, exclusion is connected with the word."[69] Moreover, even though both the positive entity and the negation appear, because of the absence of a knowable object that conforms to that appearance, and because the picking out of the real object is owing to the exclusion of what is other, exclusion alone is the main thing (as it is said in the authoritative text: "So there can be a connection between the word and a real property if the word marks a distinction,[70] since that distinction is really there in the real thing");[71] but in words that express an absence, the exclusion alone is the main thing precisely because there is no real thing (as it is said in the authoritative text: "Words for absences cannot be supposed to denote a positive form because absences do not have a positive form; they are established as producing an awareness of a distinction").[72]

[207.19] Or on another interpretation,[73] words have that desirable element, the absence of defects, only given that exclusion (or given implicative negation, the excluded image) is expressed, and therefore, it is just exclusion that is said to be expressed. Just as Dharmakīrti says, "Because exclusion does not have an essence, there is no point in talking about whether it persists or not; but the idea of a universal flounders. For this reason, too, there is no problem with this."[74] [208] Thus, given the conditionally adopted position that exclusion is what is expressed, those factors occasioning the use of terms, which are spoken of in the authoritative text and which speak against the view that exclusion is what primarily appears on the basis of a word, are to be understood as applying to words that express a positive entity. In the section on words that express absences,[75] it is said, "This distinction itself is primary."[76] He explains that for words that express a positive entity, distinction is not primary in that it is a subordinate element. For this, in particular, must be understood: for words that express absences, exclusion is itself the referent of the word. But for words that express positive entities, the referent is excluded from what is other and the other is excluded from the referent. These two differ in name alone.

[208.05] *If the conditionally adopted position that exclusion is what is expressed rests on such a foundation but really it is the positive entity that is primarily expressed, well, hell, then the convention that all properties are inexpressible is sunk. And you have already indicated that this entire enterprise is for the sake of that convention. And as for what was already said—namely, that the conditionally adopted position that exclusion is primarily what is expressed is for the sake of rejecting the false imputation that the real thing is expressed*[77]*—here, too, it is a great wonder: You yourself accept that the positive entity is expressed, but you tell your opponent something else.*

[208.09] Anticipating this objection, I said, "The first is adopted as an object. . ."[78] This is what it means: Objects are of two sorts, external and internal, because there is no other possibility. Now of these, the first, the external, is conditionally adopted as what is expressed only on the basis of determination, and not through the appearance of a particular.[79] If you say, "*How is this so?*" We say, "Purely on the basis of experience." For the way in which particulars are experienced when they appear in perceptual awareness—fixed with respect to place, time, and condition, and having a clearly manifest form—is not the way they are experienced when we have a conceptual awareness of them. For when we have a conceptual awareness of them, the object of our experience appears having a certain form (1) which is not familiar from perceptual awareness, (2) which is really excluded from what belongs to a different class, (3) which seems as if it were mixed up with each and every individual form, and (4) which seems as if it were unclear. As it is said in the authoritative text, Dharmakīrti's *Pramāṇaviniścaya*, ". . . because through language, an object does not appear in the awareness of someone whose eye is inactive as it would in visual awareness."[80]

[208.19] If you say, *Because of a difference in method of awareness, there is a difference in the appearance of one and the same thing. For the basis of one awareness is the sense faculty and that of the other is language, and the like.* [208.20] In response to this, Dharmakīrti has said, "There would have to be a different basis for each awareness of a single real thing. But how could the form of one and the same thing appear as having different images?"[81] For a single thing, there cannot be two mutually exclusive forms, clear and unclear, such that it could appear with one form in a sensory awareness and with another form in a conceptual awareness. If this were so, it would follow that the object itself would have to be different. [209] For a difference between things is nothing but a difference in their forms, and a difference in their forms is nothing but a difference in their appearance. Otherwise, the entire world would be just one thing.

(209.02) But if you say, *Even though in the case of one and the same tree, there is a difference between the clear appearance for someone who is standing nearby and the unclear appearance for someone who is standing far away, there is nevertheless no difference in the tree because there is no difference in its pragmatic effect. Only when it is accompanied by a difference in pragmatic effect does a difference of appearance differentiate things.*[82] *And here, there is no difference in pragmatic effect, so how is the object (e.g., cow) of the awareness episode produced by a sense faculty any different from that of the awareness episode produced by language?* We don't say a difference in appearance is invariably associated with a different thing but that it is invariably associated with not having the same object. That is, whenever an appearance is different from an appearance in a perceptual awareness of a certain thing, it does not have the same object as that perceptual awareness, just as the appearance of cloth is different from that which grasps a pot or the appearance of yellow is different from that which grasps a conch shell.[83] And likewise, in the case of a cow, the appearance during conceptual awareness is different from the appearance in perceptual awareness. Thus, there is the apprehension of something that precludes a pervading factor.[84] For having the same object is pervaded by a lack of difference in appearance, just like what is seen by the right and the left eye. There would be nonpervasion either if there were another perception with a different appearance or if the thing itself had two forms. And neither of these is the case; therefore there is definitely pervasion. In the case of awareness based on a difference in location, which is the subject of this inference,[85] a difference of appearance that precludes this nondifference of appearance is established. Therefore, when a difference in appearance is accompanied by a difference in pragmatic effect, there are different things, such as a pot and cloth. But one who acts without the benefit of a difference in pragmatic effect invariably rejects the existence of a single object. So, in this case, one appearance is definitely erroneous, like the appearance of yellow in a conch shell.[86]

(209.15) If you say, *Even in that case, the very same conch shell is the object,* we reply, Oh yeah, this is a great thing to say: "The awareness has the conch shell as its object, even though it doesn't touch its whiteness." If you say, *I am aware of the mere conch shell,*[87] we reply, No, because the "mere conch shell" doesn't appear as something distinct from that yellow conch shell. If you say, *The mere conch shell appears in the conceptual awareness that follows,* we reply, That is fine. But we have established that the nonconceptual appearance of yellow does not have the conch shell as its object. *In the same way, in the case of a tree, from a distance, even an awareness containing a nondescript image and not containing the specific features of the leaves, and so on (which enable us to determine that it is, e.g., a fig tree) would not have a tree as its object.* This is a question-begging response.[88] Now since there isn't a difference in pragmatic effect, the thing is not different. Thus because this error is attributed to one of these appearances, if the perceptual appearance is not erroneous, then the other appearance must be an error. This is what we say. Thus the same principle applies to both the appearance of yellow and the conceptual appearance of a cow.

(209.24) If you say, *The superimposition of one thing onto another is due to some similarity, and it is not the case that a completely individualized image has ever been apprehended to be like a conceptual appearance, even in another life, so what is superimposed on what, and what is the basis for this error?* This is just another problem for you: Namely, conceptualization does not have as its object the cow that was perceptually apprehended, nor does it have any other object; but you can't call something an error if it doesn't even have an object.[89] But for us, conceptual awareness does not have a perceptually apprehended thing as its object, and just this much establishes what we set out to prove. But if you say, *The very same thing appears differently, and therefore conceptual awareness does have that thing as its object;* we would say, Since that thing exists in the form presented by perception, therefore (since there is no real thing apart from that) [210] what is it that is appearing differently? For that thing[90] does not appear at all. Enough with all this talk. Therefore, it is right to say that particulars do not appear in conceptual awareness.

(210.03) Therefore, what Vācaspati says—"*It is not the case that there is no difference between linguistic and perceptual awareness, even though both have the real thing as their object, since it makes sense to say that they differ in remoteness and nonremoteness because of a difference in their causes*"[91]—is of no use, because it has not been established that the "remote" awareness has the real thing as its object. The purpose of differentiating causes based on remoteness is accomplished simply by not grasping the same object as the senses.

(210.06) *But you yourself argued for the unwanted consequence of the nondifference between linguistic and perceptual awarenesses if they had the real thing as their object. So just by rejecting this unwanted consequence, we have established that they do have a real thing as their object and (since there is no other real thing) that they have the same object.* This is not so, since the unwanted consequence that we raised was based on our establishment of the pervasion of "dissimilarity of appearance" by "not having the same object." And this effort was made precisely to refute our pervasion.[92] *If it is possible that the dissimilarity of appearance is produced by a dissimilarity in the cause of awareness, then how can there be pervasion by "not having the same object"?* In what context does this apply? Is it if a difference in cause can be shown to be pervaded by having the same object in general? But this is not the case, since the function of "difference in cause" is accomplished just by the nonapprehension of the real thing. If it is not, then it is just a fantasy that a difference of appearance is imagined to arise from a difference in cause, even when two awarenesses have the same object. Why then don't we imagine that the awarenesses of the scent of myrrh and a sweet taste have the same object, since there too there is a difference of cause?[93] *Both the nonconceptual and conceptual awarenesses of fire depict fire as such, and therefore one feels confident that they have the same object. But in each of those two awarenesses there is a failure to depict either the scent of myrrh or sweetness.*

(210.16) Oh, how stubborn you are! This is the result of an absolute difference in causes. But the belief in their having a single object will result, finally, from the depiction of a real thing. When there is uncertainty about the difference in causes, there is a depiction of an intermediate property such as "fire-ness." But in the final analysis, there is the depiction of an utterly unique property. Thus from this alone, it does not follow that they do not have the same object. And the intermediate property of sweetness does, in fact, carry over to the scent of myrrh. If you say, *That is a different kind of sweetness.* In just the same way, the fire-ness is different from what is depicted in conceptual awareness. The appearances of two intermediate properties do not have the same object, even if a single form is depicted in them, as in the case of mother-of-pearl and silver: For the appearance of mother-of-pearl does not have silver as its object, and the appearance of silver does not have mother-of-pearl as its object, even though the depiction of whiteness is common to them both. Therefore, even if the real thing did appear in the conceptual awareness of fire, because the intermediate property "donkey-ness" does not appear, it would not have a donkey as its object. And in just the same way, even though the intermediate property "fire-ness" does appear, because the exact image of the particular does not appear, there isn't the appearance of another substance. This is the rule, because the substance, fire, is only the particular. Therefore, let it be the case that a difference in cause produces a difference in the appearance of awareness. But the appearances do not both have the real thing as their object; this is established. And therefore it is demonstrated that the particular is not the object of language and so forth.

[211.01] And furthermore, if this were so, there would be no statements of affirmation or negation, since they would be useless. For they would have to be either of a property possessor or of its properties, as, for example, "There is a tree" or "There is not a tree," or "The tree is blue" or "The tree is not blue." The first of these is not the case, for the tree that is referred to by the word "tree" must either exist or not. If it must exist, it is useless to say "It exists" and it is wrong to say "It does not exist" because it is contradictory. But if the word tree describes an absence, then the converse is the case. And when we hear the word "tree," we do require either affirmation or negation. Therefore, from the word "tree" comes not the external tree but the appearance of a tree, which is common to cases where the tree exists and where it does not. This is the rule.

(211.07) But in the Nyāya system there is this complaint that the author of the *Tātparyaṭīkā* makes after he has declared, in his very own words, that it is the individual qualified by the universal that is expressed: "*But it is not impossible for a universal, as the meaning of a word, to be common to cases of existence and nonexistence. For that universal, even though by its nature it is eternal, being common to cases of existence and nonexistence in that it resides in various individuals scattered through space and time, is therefore suitable for connection with the expressions 'exists' and 'does not exist.' For the 'existence' of a universal is its connection with currently existing individuals and its 'nonexistence' is its connection with past and future individuals. Thus, because its negative concomitance is in doubt, 'commonality to cases of existence and nonexistence' is either Inconclusive or Otherwise Established.*"[94] Just this much does no harm to the argument being discussed, since you yourself accept that particulars are not expressed, in that you place the burden on the universal. And furthermore, even the universal, which is denoted by a word prior to the use of expressions such as "exists," is denoted as connected with present individuals, as connected with past and future individuals, as connected with both, or as not connected at all: these are the alternatives. And no one who is well versed in the old objections will let you take refuge in any one of these alternatives. For on the first alternative, it would have to exist. On the second, it would have to not exist. Even on the third alternative: If what you want is to apply the terms "existence" and "nonexistence" to the universal based on its connection with existing or nonexisting particulars, then, just as it makes one aware of the universal, the word would also have to make one aware of all those instances on the basis of which the universal is said to be in contact with present individuals or of all those instances on the basis of which it is said to be in contact with past and future individuals. (If this were not the case, it would not be made known as being connected with both sorts of individuals.) And this being the case, there would be the very same problem, that one would not use words such as "exists."

(211.21) Or this may be your idea: *The universal's being connected with individuals of both sorts is certainly conveyed by the word, but there is no awareness of the individuals of both sorts that are connected with it. A single relatum does not entail the awareness of the other relatum, as in the case of the awareness of things like "being a son."* Given this position, if there is no awareness of the *relata*, there can be no awareness of the relation either, since "there is no awareness of a connection, which depends on two things, from the awareness of the form of just one of these things. There is an awareness of a connection only when there is the apprehension of the form of both."[95] [212] Therefore it is like this: Someone, who is really the son of some person, is understood merely as a person when there is no awareness of his father or of the relation between them and is therefore a freestanding thing, like a pot. In the same way, even though it is cut through with the universal, if it is cognized as freestanding, a real thing is not cognized as having the form of that universal. In this way, the fourth alternative is rejected. Even on this alternative, because the *relata* are not indicated, it is established that one would not use words such as "exists." For if a thing is ascertained as freestanding, then the use of words such as "exists" would have to be occasioned by the existence and the nonexistence of just that thing and not anything else. Even if we are aware of a relation, the use of words such as "exists" for one *relatum* is not governed by the existence or nonexistence of the other *relatum*. And it is not the case that due to the existence or nonexistence of Caitra, Maitra—even though he is known to be his son—can be connected with words such as "exists" or "does not exist." How much more so is this the case for a universal, which does not make us aware of a connection? If you say, *The connection there is of a different sort*. Let it be of any sort, but a thing that has not risen to the level of awareness is as good as nonexistent. So it is not appropriate to use words such as "exists" in connection with the thing that is cognized—which is like an iron bar—because of the existence or nonexistence of some other thing, because there would be overextension.[96] And the nature of this universal has been explained as perpetually subsistent, and thus the uselessness of the word "exists" and the contradiction in the expression "does not exist" apply to this alternative as well.

(212.11) Therefore, the inferential reason used in response to the argument that what appears in conceptual awareness is an external object, that is, "commonality to cases of existence and nonexistence," is neither Inconclusive nor Otherwise Established.[97] For the conditional adoption of objects is restricted; that is, it is pervaded by "being restricted." And no other basis for this makes sense apart from the establishment of the existence or nonexistence of the object, because there would be overextension. Therefore, the quality of possessing an object (which would not exist in the absence of that, because of the absence of a pervading factor), being restricted to cases where there is the establishment of existence or nonexistence, is pervaded by that. So how could it subsist in something contrary to that?[98] If an awareness has an appearance common to cases of the existence and nonexistence of a thing, then it cannot be on the basis of that thing that the awareness has an object, just as it cannot be on the basis of a horse that an awareness of a cow has an object. And the conceptual awareness of a tree has an appearance common to the existence and nonexistence of the external object, thus there is the apprehension of something contradictory to the pervading factor.[99] For this commonality, which consists in not establishing existence or nonexistence, is contradicted by the establishment of existence or nonexistence, which is a pervading factor of having that external thing as its object. Thus, even if the individual were expressed as qualified by a universal, there would be the very same problem. If it establishes the awareness of an individual, then whether or not one is aware of the universal as an additional element, there is no escape from this problem.

(212.19) Regarding what is said by the followers of Kumārila: *Precisely because a thing has parts, the problem of commonality doesn't arise. For tree-ness is understood from a word without its existence or nonexistence being ascertained. It is its connection with one or the other of these two that is understood from another word.* Here, too, if what is meant by "tree-ness" is the universal, then it is finished off by the very same refutation. Now if what is meant is tree-ness, without regard for its difference or nondifference from the individual, then it must be restricted to existence or nonexistence and must be expressed by the word in just that way. Thus, what is the use of words such as "exists" even on this view?

(212.24) *It could be like this: Even though it is restricted to existence and nonexistence, only the tree-ness part is expressed by the word and not the existence or nonexistence part.* If you say this, we reply, Well then, is the difference between these two parts conceptual or real? This is the way it is. If it is conceptual, [213] then how can this verbal awareness, which apprehends the cow as if it were not a real thing, have a real thing as its object? If it is real, then it would be impossible for the words "existing tree" to be used coreferentially,[100] like the words "pot cloth." As for someone learned in the Nyāya system[101] who says, "The two properties are restricted to a single thing," this will be refuted later.[102] Likewise, the view of difference/nondifference is refuted elsewhere.[103]

(213.03) And as for this: *The manner in which words make one aware of objects is not the same as in the case of perception, such that there would be no need for words such as "exists," as in the case of what is seen by perception. This is because the modes of valid awareness have different capacities.*[104] This, too, is refuted by the refutation of different appearances when there is a single object. Therefore, if a word were to make known the object of perception, then the appearance would be just the same. And if it were not the same, then it could not present the object of perception. Thus even for him, the notion that the modes of valid awareness have different capacities is produced merely by the determination that one has experienced the form of a real thing.[105] It is not produced by a difference in appearance, even when the object is the same. This is because if there were a difference in appearance, then the existence of a single object would be precluded by valid awareness. Therefore it is established that if the particular is denoted, a property possessor cannot be affirmed or negated. Thus, let's be done with the use of the words "exists" and "does not exist."

[213.10] The affirmation or negation of properties also is not possible. Since the property possessor is made known in its entirety by the word "tree," as in the case of perception, what opportunity is there for affirming or negating a property such as "blue" either by another word or by some other mode of valid awareness? If you say, *Even in the case of perception, one sees the need for other modes of valid awareness.* We reply, This may be so, since even perception is not decisive in the case of an object whose form we are not accustomed to. But when a conceptual awareness, which is itself decisive, grasps a thing, what need would there be for anything else? But there is a need for other words and inferential reasons. Therefore, it does not grasp the form of a real thing. Instead, it is just awareness based on the arising of a conceptualization that mimics the appearance of a single property. This has been proven.

(213.15) *No, it has not been proven, since properties such as universals are distinct from one another and from their property possessors. So even when a tree has been cognized through one of its properties, that is, its universal, it has not been cognized as having other properties. Thus, why shouldn't there be awareness of another property such as "being blue," "moving," or "being taller than," which is dependent on another expression?* This is wrong. For if it is because of their difference that one does not become aware of properties through either words or inferential reasons, even when one is aware of the property possessor, then one should also not be aware of them through perception. So if you say, *When the property possessor is related with the sense organ, through contact or inherence, the properties participating in relations such as inherence also become objects of awareness.* We reply, This same set of causal factors would apply to the inferential reason as well. It is not deficient even in the smallest degree. Even if there is neither contact nor inherence between the word and the thing expressed by it, a connection is still desired, namely, an expresser-expressed relation, since if that did not exist, there would be the unwanted consequence that there would no awareness of the thing expressed. Or if it were understood, what need would there be for relations such as contact? And for those who depend on a "natural connection," it would be the same when there is the awareness of a thing on the basis of an inferential reason.[106] And as long as there is awareness on the basis of a word, there is no worry about there being an obstacle that precludes our basis for using that word. This is because for you there is the determination (1) of the individual (2) qualified by the universal, at one time, on the basis of a word. There could never be awareness of an individual qualified by a universal on the basis of the awareness of each one of these in sequence. And we do not notice a sequence in our ascertainment. Therefore, let the universal be understood as something extra, but the individual property possessor, being understood, cannot become fixed in our minds without making us aware of qualities, actions, and the like that inhere in it. Otherwise, even in perception, our awareness of other contingent features[107] would have no basis.

(214.01) *This being the case, let there just be the awareness of an individual by means of words. Why do we need to accept that it is accompanied by conditioning factors?* If you say this, we respond, So now, are things abandoning their own nature out of fear that your position will become irrelevant? You may or may not have this additional problem. But whatever produces awareness of a certain object cannot stop without producing awareness of those things that are connected with it, as in the case of a sense faculty. If you say, *It is only from a sense faculty that something is seen in this way. Thus, there is no problem with anything else.* If so, then, from the fact that a grass fire is seen to be capable of producing smoke (which is invariably connected with a transformation of its fuel), it would not follow that a wood fire would be the same. But if you say, *In both cases, there is pervasion by a universal,* we respond, There is no difference in this case. Therefore, if in the case of a wood fire there is no transformation, then it is not smoke but some dust being blown around by the wind. Or there is no fire there, but rather the collected light rays from a pile of shining rubies, rising up. But if that is smoke and this is fire, then there must be a transformation in the wood. In the same way, if that is the awareness of a property possessor and language is what produces it, then certainly there is the problem that there should be the awareness of the properties located in it. And if there is no awareness of the properties located in it, then this is not the awareness of a property possessor, and a word does not make one aware of a property possessor. Whatever produces an awareness of something invariably produces the awareness of its properties, just like a sense faculty. And you accept that words and inferential reasons produce awareness of things that you take to be beyond the range of sense perception. This is an inferential reason of the identity type that leads to an unwanted consequence.[108] Moreover, this is not the case because one does need other words or inferential reasons.[109] What does not produce an awareness of the properties that inhere in a thing does not produce an awareness of the form of that thing, just as the word "cow" does not produce an awareness of the form of a horse, or a horse of a donkey. And the word "cow" and the inferential reason, smoke, do not make one aware of other properties that inhere in what you take to be their own objects. Thus there is the nonapprehension of a pervading factor in the contrapositive inference.[110] Even in a dream, one cannot think of seeing something without its class properties, qualities, actions, and so on. And for this reason, seeing a thing is pervaded by an awareness of those other properties that arise along with its sheer existence. Thus, in neither of these inferences is the inferential reason inconclusive.[111] For there can be disagreement about class properties and the like only if they are different from their property possessor. But even on the view that there is no difference, the word "inherent" indicates the nonseparate emergence of those things appearing in conceptual awareness as if they were separate. Therefore, it is better that there be no difference between the property and property possessor. In any case, if you accept that there is the awareness of a thing, the objection that one would have to be aware of its properties is unavoidable. So why then do you accept this difference that goes against our experience? Class properties and the like are simply the nature of the thing.[112]

(214.22) But what is said in the *Bhūṣaṇa*—"*It is not the case that what is connected with the nature of a thing is the nature of the thing. If that were so, it wouldn't be connected at all, since a thing cannot be connected with itself*"—is not so.[113] In the expression "connected with the nature of a thing itself," it is the nature of some thing that is meant; and there is no difference between those two. For if there were a difference, it would be outside the realm of ordinary usage to say it is its "nature." Thus the question "How is that very thing connected with itself?" is rejected. Otherwise, how could one use the possessive expression "the nature *of it*"?[114] If you say, *What is meant by "nature" is just the universal, and so on, and therefore there is no problem.* We respond, There is a problem when we consider the nature of the thing itself, having distinguished it from the universal and so on, for the nature of the thing itself cannot be stated. And it is this nature that is meant in the expression "what is connected with the nature of a thing." This is because what is meant by the phrase "what is connected" is the universal, and so on. [215] Therefore, when even though one thing is not different from another, it is seen to be different through conceptual awareness, then that thing is "connected" with it; this way of way of talking is unavoidable.

(215.03) And what Vācaspati says—"*And it's not the case that when a thing is grasped as qualified by one contingent feature, that is, existence, there is the undesirable consequence that it would be grasped as qualified by its other contingent features. For the nature of a particular thing is qualified by its contingent features, but neither its contingent features nor its being qualified by them is its nature*"[115]—flounders as well, for the grasping of a thing's other contingent features is not based on their nondifference. For even in the "treasury,"[116] Dharmakīrti points out the undesirable consequence of grasping all aspects of a thing only after he has proposed a difference between a property possessor and its properties through the categories "enabler" and "enabled."[117] *But you have said that there is a nondifference between a capacity possessor and its capacities.* That is not even touched on in this discussion.

(215.08) But as for the criticism raised in the *Bhūṣaṇa* on this point, namely, the undesirable consequence that when one grasps a thing such as the sun, one would grasp the entire collection of things "enabled" by it:[118] This is the result of not getting our point. That is to say: The idea is this. Since you believe that the property possessor and its properties are different, you, the best of the Naiyāyikas—to support the denial of inherence that you yourself will state later[119]—must accept that when the property possessor is connected with the sense organ, there is awareness of its properties, universals, and the like, owing to the nondifference of their capacities to "enable" that thing, insofar as it is assisted by them. For if there were no "enabling," there would be no connection between any one thing and a different thing. Thus, by forcing on the opponent the nondifference in the capacities of the property possessor, he says, "If they . . . are different from the thing, then in what sense do they belong to it? If they are not enabled by it, then there would be an infinite regress of capacities."[120]

(215.16) But I have refuted the basis for this discussion—that "capacity," whether it is an innate universal, a contingent feature, or a totality of assisting causal factors, is in fact distinct from the thing—in my *Study of Moment-by-Moment Destruction* (*Kṣaṇabhaṇgādhyāya*), in which I conclude that "capacity" is just the nature of the thing when it acts to produce an effect.[121] And the view that enabling, which consists of the attainment of a common effect, is possible even for what is not produced is demolished in the very same work. Really, there is no difference at all between an effect and an enabled thing. In ordinary usage, however, when there is the arising of something new, it is called "being an effect," owing to exclusion. But for something that is the object of the misconception that it existed previously, it is called "being enabled" because we experience a difference. But really it is contradictory to say that a thing existed previously but is now different.[122] So here, when we consider this by introducing a putatively stable universal, the talk of being enabled must depend either on being an effect or on the individual and the universal really being one and the same thing. Thus there is no problem. This being the case, since one must accept a close relation in the form of enabling whether or not one likes it, the deviation from experience in the case of things enabled by the sun and the like, which undesirably attaches to our argument, is the same for both of us.

(216.01) But as for what Vācaspati says, *The connection of an individual with its universal, being natural, does not require enabling.*[123] With respect to this, we say that there is no "natural" connection different from those that are well known. But when there is in fact a connection, such as contact, one just conditionally adopts the position that it is either a "conditional connection" or a "natural connection" because it behaves differently depending on the deviation or nondeviation of the *relata.* The investigation of this may be seen in the *Study of Pervasion* (*Vyāpticarcā*).[124] And just as the connection of an individual with a universal is "natural" because of their nondeviation, in the same way the connection of the universal with the individual also is "natural" precisely because of nondeviation, in accordance with the principle that "there cannot be a universal without particulars, just as there cannot be a horn on a rabbit."[125] So because there is no other form of contact between the two and because inherence[126] is a pure fiction, if even a relation between enabler and enabled, such as that between the seed and the earth, did not exist between them, for those addicted to the idea that there is a difference between the individual and the universal, the rule of nondeviation itself would be untenable because it is overextensive.[127] For only when there is enabling is the nature of a thing or some special feature of it invariably connected with another thing. Only in this way is a thing nondeviant and not in any other case. Thus, there is no overextension.

(216.12) But in the absence of that enabling, there are two ways of rejecting that overextension, by relying on either the doctrine of "nature" or the power of inherence. It cannot be the first alternative because of the unwanted consequence that everything, being seen to have a capacity only with respect to a some particular or the other, would go astray. Enabling is seen to be the cause of nondeviation of things like smoke, a pot, and clouds with respect to things like a fire, a potter, and water. The only difference is with respect to place, time, and the like.[128] Therefore, for one who says that "*even though there is a difference between a property possessor and its property, there is nondeviation precisely because of their 'nature'; there is no enabling*," capacity must be conceptually constructed through exclusion. And the second view is impossible because inherence itself does not exist. For inherence is accepted as the basis for the awareness that "this is in that." But this thought cannot be accepted in the case of visual awarenesses which are mixed up with a lot of errors owing to the acceptance of common conventions. This is because of the unwanted consequence that everything would establish everything, since conceptual awarenesses arise depending only on one's own desire.[129] And other people certainly do not have this awareness with respect to anything that we disagree about, because there is no reason for it. For the appearance of two things, neither of which is mixed up with the form of the other, is the cause of the conceptual awareness "this is in that," which constructs a division between a subject and its location. This is because the appearance of two things does not exist for someone who sees only a pot. For even when there is water in a pot, someone who just sees the pot will not have the experience of two things, even though he has all the other requisite causal factors. But for the person so situated, this experience of two things will exist only subsequently, when he apprehends the second thing. And this appearance of two things does not exist in any locus of inherence at all.[130] So the object of the conceptual awareness "this is in that" is just that of the conceptual awareness of a connection. When there is not the apprehension of two owing to the separation from each of what does not have its own form, no one who is not crazy would think "this is in that," just as when there is nonapprehension of either a pot or a fruit.[131] And there is no experience of the universal and the individual that possesses it with a difference in the appearance of their own forms.[132] Thus there is the nonapprehension of a cause.[133] This inferential reason is not inconclusive because the cause-effect relation between the two intended things is established, as in the case of fire and smoke. So these people,[134] constructing another object through a word that they themselves have made up, are chasing after an imitation of a horse. As Dharmakīrti himself will say, [217] "Expressions such as 'the cloth is here in the threads' are things that you have made up yourself."[135]

(217.01) *But we say that through nonconceptual awareness, one grasps the real thing with both individual and universal natures. So how is it that both forms do not appear? This "nonapprehension of the cause" is thus not established.* This is even worse. For when a thing is apprehended through perception, another person's statements about it do not bear any weight. If you say, "*But the appearance is just like that*," this is the result: "when these five fingers appear clearly in perceptual awareness, one who sees here a sixth thing common to them sees a horn on his own head."[136] For we leathery-eyed people, no matter how wide we open our eyes, even if we look a hundred times, don't see another thing. Even if it appears that way to you, by the grace of some unseen divinity, that doesn't establish this sort of awareness for another person.

(217.09) Therefore, it is seen that Trilocana, too, when he says, "*Perception itself shows viewers a visible thing that is single but common to various individuals*," is seeing as if with some other eye. And as for what he says—"*The universal, even though it is seen, because it doesn't exist in a location separate from the individual, is not seen to be separate from the individual, as another individual would be*"—there too, when he says that the universal is seen, but not separately, he must say that it is an object that is perceived as nondifferent. And since even for you, it is the entire thing that is grasped by perception, it is not proper to offer a proof or disproof of that.[137] And therefore, there is no opportunity for justifying your position in this way: "*But the continuity of awareness will differentiate the universal from the individual*."[138] Nor is it right to say that "*it is just like the way in which tactile awareness differentiates touch from smell and the like*." For perception does not also grasp the nondifference between smell and touch.[139] Accordingly, even if one explains this by saying, "'*Not seen to be separate' means 'not ascertained to be separate,*'" does "*the universal, even though it is seen* . . ." mean "as separate" or "as nonseparate"? If it means "as nonseparate," then let it be ascertained as either separate or nonseparate: Why bother with thinking about this, since nonseparation is established by perception?[140] If it means "seen as separate," this again is impossible because we already have said that there is no difference in appearance. If you say "*the difference in appearance is established by reasoning*," this is just embarrassing. This is because we have already investigated this in the *Section on Uncaused Absence*: "Something that does not appear is established through the appearance of something else. But it is not the place of reasoning to say, 'This appears but that does not.'"[141] Furthermore, if you accept that even when there is the appearance of a single image, another appearance can be established by reasoning, then you cannot say that the statement "fire is not hot" is contradicted by perception, since the appearance of the absence of heat also is possible in that case, just like the appearance of the universal in the individual.

(218.05) If you say, *They are not the same because there is no inferential reason establishing the appearance of the absence of heat in the case of fire*. Nevertheless, there could be doubt. So how does perception contradict the absence of heat? And why is there is no inferential reason, since the inferential reason "being known" exists there?[142] If you say, *An inferential reason has to be nondeviant*, then we say that deviation, too, has to come from perception, either directly or indirectly. And given your position, as I have already explained, a contrary appearance cannot be ruled out. And if the absence of heat is not proved by "being known" because of a defect in the inferential reason due to its being inconclusive, then it is seen that there is no defect in the conclusion that "fire is not hot" because there is no way of refuting the absence of heat in fire. Even perception cannot prove it.[143]

So, heat is just heat; it is not "heat and the absence of heat." Therefore the awareness of a specific appearance must necessarily be accepted as precluding a different appearance, whether or not one likes it, because otherwise the indiscriminate mixing up of activity would follow. And thus he says, "For even one who sees fire. . . ."[144] Therefore, when those who have fallen into these floodwaters shout, "*If the linguistic convention is made with respect to individuals possessing universals, then wherever one sees the universal, one has the awareness that that thing is expressed by that word,*" this is like a cloth with no threads, since even in a dream, one does not see anything different from particulars. For this very reason, we reject the validity that you take to belong to the conceptual awareness that links the contingent feature and its possessor once they have been grasped through their individual natures. This is because before that, one does not see two things at all. Therefore, the "nonapprehension of the cause" is not unestablished.[145] But the awareness "here" is not established, so why this useless talk of inherence and this useless notion that "there is a natural connection of individuals with a universal"? And therefore if even now, the belief that there is a difference between a contingent feature and its possessor is difficult to reject, nevertheless, given that there is a relation between them, namely, enabling, an awareness that grasps a thing would have the capacity to grasp any feature co-located with it. Thus, the argument against deviation in the case of an imperceptible enabled thing is the same.[146]

(218.22) Therefore, if there is an awareness of the nature of a thing by even one of its properties, there is the awareness of it in its entirety. So, what room is there for affirmation or denial by means of another word? So even now, what use is the word "tree" by itself?[147] And therefore, why adopt the position that the individual is co-located with the universal and that there is a qualifier/qualified relation between them? But if "no thing at all is expressed, [219] owing to the denotation of which one could understand the whole just by the nature of that thing, then the word, having a single expressive basis, could have multiple results."[148] For if the thing were expressed, we would be aware of it in its entirety, and there would be no sense in affirming or denying it. But if there is just an awareness whose principal feature is an image constituted by a single exclusion (due to the influence of the beginningless karmic traces left by the repeated occurrence of false conceptual awarenesses), which arises from the awakening of a karmic trace for some reason, then what room is there for the already stated problems that would arise if there were the capacity to grasp a real thing? That is, when someone says "tree," a "universal"—whose real object is the exclusion of non-trees—is established, owing to an appearance whose form is common to things such as oaks and elms. And that form requires the use of other words, since in it distinguishing features such as existence and nonexistence are neither asserted nor denied. Thus, a word such as "tree" is used coreferentially with words such as "existing," "blue," and "moving," as if they were linking one property possessor with another property possessor. And then when in accordance with one's thought, one needs to emphasize one part, one mentions it separately: "The existence of the tree." Thus both sorts of qualifier/qualified relation are established.[149]

(219.10) And this being the case, it is like this: Because of contact with water or fire, either growth or diminution is seen in a tree, and because of the imposition of unity on it, one thinks, "That very tree has become like this." And even though no properties arise that are fit for connection with it, the tree is conceptually determined as if it were fit for connection with them.[150] In the same way, in conceptual awareness, too, even though other properties do not appear, the image of the tree is conceptually determined to be fit for them. Thus, when expressions such as "blue" and "not fruit-bearing" are used, it appears as if the "tree" grew or diminished, yet it is determined to be "that very same one."[151] But even when those words are uttered, the external tree cannot grow or diminish in the way that it does when it is connected with water, and so forth. And this would not be possible if words had external things as their objects, since their nature would not accord with their appearance, and their appearance would not accord with their nature.[152] Likewise, it would not be possible to use other expressions even when we needed a separate qualifier, as in "Caitra's cow" or "Maitra has a cow but not a horse."[153] This is because the appearance of growth or diminution produced by those expressions does not exist externally.

(219.19) Therefore, this is just the play of the mind. And given this confusion concerning the "real thing" that is progressively excluded from others,[154] people who have achieved their desired pragmatic effect do not make any effort to notice this distinction and are not able to do so.[155] Thus, worldly activity does not break down. And even though there is a discrepancy, people do not conclude that "this is false." But this is not the case at other times, since philosophers are able to think that "it is not due to external things that words have objects." Why talk about anybody else? Therefore, it is established that particulars are not the objects of words and the like.

> This primary awareness picks out a single property possessor, which is the locus of various properties (which take the form of exclusions) but which has an invariant appearance even when one of these properties is affirmed or denied and thereby causes one to go astray. But people when going astray in this way, as long as they attain satisfaction through some bit of reality, do not think there is any error.

[220] This is a summary verse.

[220.02] Nor are universals are not the objects of words and the like. That is, from the word "cow" in the sentence "There are cows grazing on the far bank of the river," dewlap, horn, tail, and the like appear, accompanied by the form of the speech sounds that make up the word "cow," in effect "lumped together"[156] because of inattention to differences between things belonging to the same class. But this conglomeration of dewlap, horn, and so on is not itself a universal. For "Cow-ness is said to be devoid of color, shape, or form of the letters."[157] And, as in the case of "space," nothing else appears.[158] Otherwise, there would be the undesirable consequence that there would be no difference between the conceptual awareness of cow-ness and horse-ness.[159] For one and the same bare image, blazing and radiant, although it is utterly distinct from every particular, when it is being made one with a particular,[160] it is called a "universal." But that image itself is not a universal belonging to those particulars because it recurs elsewhere as a mental image. For as it is said in the authoritative text: "If the universal is not distinct from awareness, how could it carry over to another thing?"[161] Nor does any other thing appear in conceptual awarenesses such as "This is that," "This is like that," or "This is a cow," which arise immediately after the initial sense impression[162] and are thought to be produced by the sense faculty and the object. But insofar as one joins this "lumped-together-form"—which appears to oneself, but which does not exist in the world—with the thing that appears in front of one, to that extent there is, in fact, an error because that external object does not exist, like a clump of hair that appears to someone with cataracts.[163]

(220.15) *If you say,* This is so because there is a blocking awareness.[164] *But in the case of the clump of hair there is a discrepancy, because of the absence of things such as resisting the pressure of a hand that is pressed on it with effort. In this case, if there is some defeating factor, just say what it is.*[165] The experience of the individual is the blocking awareness. What is the use of anything else? But people lack the capacity to distinguish; this has already been said.[166] Alternatively, why is the absence of resistance to the pressure of a hand not a blocking awareness in this case, too? For those very horns and the like, set in their proper places, without having a clear form, and not fixed with respect to place or condition, having endless instantiations due to differences of space, time, and the like, appear even now as if they were mixed up together, and since those horns and so on are invariably resistant to pressure and so on, how are they different from hair and the like, so that there would be no blocking awareness in this case?

(220.21) Therefore, because of latent karmic traces, let it be the case that the awareness itself appears as if it has that nature or let it be the case that the form of it appears but is entirely nonexistent or that the individuals themselves appear in a manner other than they really are (due to the suppression of differences between things belonging to the same class), [221] or let us say that there is an overlooking of memory because it overlays experience.[167] But in any case, talk of a universal regarding what is external is just an error. And it makes good sense that there is this error, since it arises from experiencing the thing that exists in front of one as "this."[168]

(221.02) *But the causes of error—cataracts, rapid motion, and so on, which result in a disruption of the sense faculty—have already been enumerated,*[169] *and none of these is present in this case. So how can there be this error that has no cause? If you think that those are just the causes of nonconceptual error but that this is a "mental error," then this too is based on seeing the similarity of the thing superimposed to the object on which it is superimposed. Thus, because of the absence of such nondifferentiation, how can there be even a mental error? And all errors must be based on similarity; they could not arise without seeing something similar, even if that was in another birth. And nothing that has a conglomerated image has been seen, even in another birth. Thus, how can there be the superimposition of it?*[170] Oh, how powerful this is! That is, if it is not possible to reject the objectless-ness in the stated manner, you could talk about this as an error or not.[171] But by just this much we have established what we set out to establish. Why worry about this?

(221.11) In any case, it is not right to say that it is without a cause, because even you must accept a difference in the set of causal factors[172] that gives rise to this awareness. Otherwise, how could the sense faculty and the object, which are seen to invariably produce nonconceptual awareness, produce conceptual awareness? Therefore, this set of causal factors, when its capacity is heightened by a cooperating factor, namely, the memory of the sight of prior lumps,[173] produces the conceptual awareness. Which is to say, it produces an awareness without an object. This is because the conceptualization of a thing through one of its parts requires that it not have an object. Therefore this is better: just like the conceptualization of a thing as not belonging to a certain class, the conceptual awareness of something as belonging to a certain class also is entirely different from the experience of the thing, because it has an indistinct appearance.[174] This alone is right, and so one cannot establish a universal on the basis of perception.

(221.17) Nor can one do so on the basis of inference, since no one can grasp the cause/effect relation between them[175] in virtue of their being the objects of perception, as one can in the case of fire and smoke.[176] It would be possible, however, if the arising of the awareness were owing to a universal, just as sometimes, apart from the visible causes, another required cause can be established, as in the case of the sense faculties[177] if in the presence of all of the other causes, one were to sometimes notice the absence of the desired effect, that is, awareness. But in the present case, this is not possible. For if one were to point to the absence of the awareness "cow" in another lump or in the intervening space, the absence of the awareness "cow" could be accounted for simply by the absence of a cow lump. So, how could it indicate the need for another thing, such that you could hope to say, "That very thing is 'cow-ness'"?

(221.22) *But it is only because of the universal cow-ness that something is "a cow lump." Otherwise, even a horse lump could be a cow lump.* If this were so, then one might just as well say that it is only due to the cow lump that there is the universal cow-ness, otherwise even horse-ness would be cow-ness. Also, neither the presence nor the absence of the imperceptible universal can be ascertained anywhere, as can the lump. This doesn't amount to anything. *But if this were so, then, since there is not the awareness "cow" with respect to a horse, due to the absence of the mottled-cow lump, there should not be the awareness "cow," even with respect to spotted-cow lump. This is because the particular does not recur in any case.*[178] It is true that the particular does not recur. But just as when the cognizer remembers seeing other lumps that belong to the same class, a mottled cow has the capacity to produce a reflective awareness containing an image of those lumps, [222] so too does the spotted cow. Therefore, not just one cow lump but in fact all the lumps enter into such a conceptual awareness. Thus, there is no awareness "cow" with respect to a horse.

(222.03) *But a capacity is just a power. Thus, it is just what we call a universal. For is this power different or nondifferent from the individuals? If it is nondifferent, then just like the particular, it doesn't recur, and thus neither would have that power. If it is different and common to others, then it is just a universal; the disagreement is only about the name.* To this we respond: In each and every thing there is a capacity that is not different from that thing. But what sort of problem does it create if, in the same way as one thing has a capable nature, another one does too? For just as, for you, one universal causes the arising of a common thought and word, and another one does so too just by its nature, owing to the absence of any other universal, in the same way, for us, even the individual independently, and merely by its very nature, is the cause of a common thought and word, although it is different from other individuals.[179] But the nature of that individual is tied to its causal chain.

(222.10) But as for what Trilocana says, *The inherence of the particular universals—horse-ness, cow-ness, and the like—in their own loci is the basis for the awareness and the term "universal."* This is discarded precisely by the rejection of inherence.[180] Alternatively, inherence itself is the basis for the awareness and the term "universal" by its very nature, and thus, it doesn't harm our example.[181] And universals and inherence do not jointly have that power (based on the idea that they act together). For if they did, then just one of them would, by its very nature, produce the awareness and term "universal." Thus the awareness and term "universal" are given their last rites. For the complete set of cooperating causes is an imposed capacity belonging to things like seeds, which are by their very nature, producers. Thus, the fact that universals produce things by their nature would have to be admitted.[182] So this reliance on inherence is just a trick. And it is not the case that without the functioning of that universal, an awareness having the form of that universal could simply arise from some other cause. Otherwise, why couldn't the particulars themselves be successful in producing an awareness having a recurring image?[183] Thus the very idea of a universal is pulverized down to its root. Likewise, if there is no cause, there is the very same problem. Thus those who accept universals without themselves imposing any additional universals[184] are forced to accept, with a foot to their throats, that a universal acts to produce a recurrent awareness by its very nature, out of fear of an infinite regress. So how can they reject this, by way of inherence? *Inherence may or may not exist as an additional cooperating cause, but the universal, independent of any other universal, possessing power by its nature, produces a recurrent awareness, but, since the nature of things cannot be questioned, an individual does not do so.* You cannot say this without some royal edict.

(222.23) "*How could this recurrence of awareness, which requires that there be a recurrent thing, exist in individuals, which are absolutely distinct and fall within the scope of differentiated awarenesses?*"[185] This line of reasoning of his is also rejected by the same argument. This is because it deviates, since there is a recurrent awareness in the case of the universals themselves, which take on the status of individuals insofar as they are differentiated from one another.

(222.25) Now if you say, *Because universals are not seen, where is there the recurrent awareness on the basis of which there would be deviation?* we say, no. This is because in this manner we have explained that you contradict a position that you yourself have accepted. [223] That is, the recurrence of awareness has been introduced in order to prove that there is a recurrent thing. And that recurrence of awareness occurs together with the absence of a recurrent thing.[186] If you say this is the proof of a recurrent thing, then who can tolerate this contradiction except out of idiocy? Moreover, even if universals were conceptually constructed, there would be deviation regarding those conceptually constructed universals themselves.[187] What is the use of this position in this case?

(223.05) Now if you say, *This principle is restricted to objects that are seen*, we say, no. This is because even in this case an invariable connection cannot be established because there is no ruling out of counterexamples.[188] And because one sees deviation in the case of the universal, there is a seed of doubt in other cases, too. And if one avoids deviation in the case of the universal by relying on a difference between it and a visible thing, then you cannot say, "*When there is recurrence of awareness and terminology with respect to different things, it is occasioned by a recurrent thing, as with the recurrence of awareness and terminology of "thread" in the case of the flowers in a garland. And in the same way, there is recurrence of the awareness and the term "cow" with respect to different cows.*"[189] This is because the reliability of the pervasion of the "recurrence of awareness and terminology" by "being occasioned by a recurrent thing" is restricted to cases in which this continuity is occasioned by something visible. And this is quite right. Indeed, even in the case of the thread, there is no recurrence of the awareness "thread" with respect to those flowers that are not within our sight. For except in the case of inference, a conceptual awareness that has a real thing as its object is proven to be the effect of seeing that real thing.[190] Thus, the pervasion of the recurrence of awareness by a recurrent thing, which ceases to apply because of the nonapprehension of a cause on the basis of this counterexample, is reliable only when it is occasioned by something visible, as long as it has a real thing as its object. But if there is a disagreement about whether it has a real thing as its object, there is no such rule.

(223.15) But as for his stated way of ruling out counterexamples: "*The recurrence of awareness and terminology, which occurs only in some cases, avoiding others, must be occasioned by something. But there is no other occasion.*"[191] This is not right, because we have established that even without a recurrent thing, the recurrence of awareness and terminology must be accepted on the basis of the specific character of the thing. Therefore, just as in virtue of some connection (*pratyāsatti*), there is the recurrence of awareness and terminology—"This is a universal, that is a universal"—only in the case of universals, for example, cow-ness and horse-ness, ruling out particulars, in the same way, let it be the case for particulars as well. Thus, one should recognize that both these things are inconclusive: (1) the recurrence of awareness and terminology when a recurrent thing is to be proven; and (2) the nonapprehension of a pervading factor, which would rule out counterexamples to the pervasion of the recurrence of awareness and terminology by a recurrent thing. And this "connection" is nothing but the exclusion of what is other. For just as cow-ness is excluded from nonuniversals, in the same way horse-ness, substance-ness, and the like are excluded from nonuniversals. In the same way, just as one individual cow is excluded from non-cows, so is another excluded from non-cows. If you go on and on about the idea of difference and nondifference in the case of this individual as well, the answer is the same as in the case of capacity.[192] And therefore, certain things are connected with one another through the exclusion of what does not have their form. Those things, and no others, produce an awareness of a recurrent thing when after one has seen one of those things, one sees another. And the capacity of these things is precisely this exclusion of what does not have their form. It does not have the nature of a universal. If this were not the case, "that nature itself would be the cause even in a single case; thus the cooperating factors would be useless."[193] You can learn about this from the discussion of cooperating factors in my "Breaking into Moments."[194] And it has just been explained that this connection ensues from a causal sequence.[195] And certainly it must be accepted that a particular connection is produced by a cause, since only some individuals are fit for establishing a universal, and not others. Otherwise, the statement of the *Nyāyabhūṣaṇa*— "*An effect possesses a particular universal owing to the restriction of its causal complex*"[196]—would be indefensible. And that being the case, "given that they are similarly distinct,[197] the basis of verbal awareness is just the connection by which the 'universal' comes to mind in the case of one individual but not another."[198] What is the use of a universal here?

(224.09) But as for the other stupid objection[199] that he raises in connection with this verse: *For it is not the case that anyone would say: "Let the basis for expressions such as "possessing a stick" or "possessing a thread," when applied to persons or crystals in a necklace, be just that connection by which the stick and the thread come to mind with respect to one individual but not another—what is the use of the stick or the thread?"*[200] Under what circumstances does this seem right? Only if a certain capacity with respect to certain things, which has been established by valid awareness, were to be denied. The connection (whose basis is the awareness of proximity and the like), which causes the stick and the thread to come to mind in connection with the person and the crystal, is established by valid awareness such as perception. And for a cognizer who remembers the verbal convention, the experience of the person and the crystal that are connected with them is established as the basis for the awareness of the "stick possessor" and the "thread possessor." But the awareness "cow" is not seen in this way to track with the presence or absence of cow-ness. Rather, this is just groping around with your hand in the dark with the thought that "there must be some such basis for the awareness 'cow.'"[201] If there is nothing standing in the way of the establishment of this in some other way that must be accepted, then why bother postulating anything whether it is ontologically promiscuous or not? Otherwise, having postulated that thing, there would be nothing to prevent you from postulating a hundred useless things. But if this case were like the nearness of the stick and so on to the person and so on, which is seen to track with the existence or nonexistence of the awareness of proximity and the like, and the awareness of "stick possessor," which is seen to track with the existence or nonexistence of the nearness of the stick and so on to the person and so on, then, the collection of causal factors would operate only when something has a specific universal. This is not so on a single observation. But if on a single observation, one had the experience that "this very universal is now operating," then there would be a fault on the part of someone who rejected this.[202] Insofar as this is a mere convention—since it has already been explained that the universal is beyond the range of our experience—how then would the objection that this universal is useless also include within its scope even such things as the stick? In the same way, a counterargument can be analogously devised for other objections of this sort.

(225.02) If you say, *There is this inference: Whatever awareness there is of a qualified thing is invariably connected with the apprehension of its qualifiers, like the awareness "stick possessor." And the awareness "This is a cow" is an awareness of a qualified thing. This is, by implication, an effect type of inferential reason.*[203] *For in the example it is established that the awareness of the qualified thing is an effect of the experience of its qualifiers.* There is a question about this: Is it to be established that the awareness of the qualified thing is invariably connected with the apprehension of qualifiers distinct from it, or merely that it is invariably connected with the experience of any sort of qualifier? In the first case, the blocking by perception of the locus of the inference leaves no room for considering the inferential reason, because the perception that grasps the thing lacks the appearance of both the qualified and the qualifier.[204] And the inferential reason—the universal "being an awareness of a qualified thing"—is inconclusive, since this is seen even without the apprehension of a distinct qualifier, for example, "the pot possesses a nature" and "the universal cow-ness."[205] But in the second case, you are establishing what has already been established, since we accept that just as in "the pot possesses a nature" there can be a qualifier/qualified relation based on a conceptually constructed difference, for example, "The lump possesses the universal cow-ness." This is because the expression "This is a cow" arises from the experience of what is excluded from non-cows. So, therefore, in verbal awareness and the like there is no appearance of an external thing, either a particular or a universal. And it has been shown that universals are not established by valid awareness. And other contingent features[206] should be thought of in just the same way.

[225.12] *If so, then how does this text make sense:* "First of all, it is an external object that is primarily expressed by words"*?*[207] *For it makes no sense to say that something is made known by an awareness but does not appear in that awareness.* [225.16] In response, I say "because of determination."[208] There are two ways of talking about objects, on the basis of appearance and on the basis of determination. So here, even though it does not appear, the particular that is excluded from what is other is said to be an object simply on the basis of determination. And therefore, Dharmakīrti says, "Because even on the basis of that conceptual awareness, one acts only with respect to the real thing through the determination of it."[209]

[225.19] *Now what is this "determination" apart from conceptualization, since there is no difference in meaning between "conceptualized" and "determined"? Why are they mentioned separately*: "on the basis of conceptual awareness" *and* "through the determination"? *Also,* "The particular that is excluded from what is other does not appear in conceptual awareness. It is made known on the basis of determination." *What kind of reasoning is this, on the basis of which even this particular is conditionally adopted as an object of conceptual awareness on the basis of determination? Furthermore,* "The external object is not the object of conceptual awareness" *and yet* "There is the grasping of it after having joined it together with a word." *Thus, conceptualization, too, is hard to explain. Moreover, there is no grasping of itself.*[210] *Thus conceptual awareness doesn't even exist.*[211] *So what is it whose object we are considering? And if, on the basis of a word, there is activity with respect to a particular that has not been grasped, there would be activity everywhere without distinction. This is because there is no distinction, since everything is ungrasped, and therefore one could not even reliably obtain what is desired. Thus, inference would flounder as well.*

[226.01] To this we reply: It is true that "conceptualization" and "determination" are one and the same thing. It is just that the word "conceptualization" is occasioned by connection with words and the like, while "determination" is occasioned by suitability for activity even with respect to an object that is not grasped. [226.02] And although everything is ungrasped, activity has a specific object because the conceptual awareness has a specific form. For things that have specific capacities and whose natures have been established by valid awareness are not liable to questions about the mixing up of their capacities, as in, for example, the arising of a nonexistent thing. For even though everything is not present, there is the arising *only* of a sprout from a seed.[212] This is because the seed is ascertained by valid awareness to have capacity only with respect to that. Here, too, in the same way, for a person who seeks the pragmatic effects of fire and has a memory of a conceptual awareness containing the image of fire, it is known through valid awareness that this conceptual awareness has capacity only with respect to activity that has fire as its object. How would this capacity fall prey to overextension? And when we consider the connection between them, both the real fire and what is depicted by our conceptual awareness have a blazing and radiant image. Thus, on the basis of just this, the conceptual awareness of fire has the capacity to cause one to act only with respect to that real fire, and not water and the like. [226.09] And we do not say that there is activity because there is superimposition based on similarity, such that there would be an opportunity to criticize us for imposing the external object on the image or the image on the external object.[213] *What then?* The awareness, which arises only because of the maturation of its own karmic traces, even without seeing the external object, produces activity with respect to the external object. Hence, it is just a form of error. As the authoritative text says, "It is not the same in the case of awareness, because there is the arising of conceptual thought which is of just that sort."[214]

(226.16) Therefore, activity is not due to superimposition, as in the case of silver and the like, but due to a specific capacity invariably connected with the arising of an image of just that sort. Just as when a rice sprout is about to be produced, the rice seed, by virtue of being rice, is the material cause (*upādāna*) of the rice sprout, even though it arises without any connection with the seed. This is because the persistence of things like "rice-ness" has been rejected by rejecting endurance. [226.18] And the undesirable consequence that a philosopher who ascertains that he is not seeing a real object would not act does not follow. For even if he does not see it, he acts by virtue of the associated pragmatic efficacy, and the pragmatic effect is attained given the restriction that the thing exists. And just as a restriction is produced by a connection with the thing on the basis of observation, there is a restriction, even if indirect, on the basis of a particular conceptual awareness. And inference, therefore, is not without foundation. But on the basis of language, there is sometimes activity with the thought that there might be some satisfactory result, and in that case, there is no restriction, even with respect to the attainment of pragmatic effect.[215]

(226.23) Therefore, the meaning of "determined" is "made an object of activity, even when it does not appear." Even though it does not appear in the conceptual awareness, nothing prevents the external object from being determined. And this is precisely what is meant by "making what is seen and what is conceptualized into a single thing," "the apprehension of nondifference," and so forth.[216] [226.25] And on this basis, it is shown that the objection that "it is not cognized, but there is the appearance of nondifference from it" doesn't arise, since we have already established the basis for the meaning of this.[217] [226.26] And just as the determination "there is fire here" produces bodily activity, in the same way it produces verbal activity as well: "Fire has been apprehended by me." [227.01] It also produces mental activity, that is, a reflective awareness having the same form. This being the case, just as one concludes that an object has been apprehended through conceptualization, likewise one concludes that it has been apprehended bound up with the word that refers to it. This is because like the partial image of a thing,[218] the image of the word also appears. Therefore, the conditionally adopted differentiation of conceptualization from determination is not based in reality but is only accepted in conformity with the conditional determination that "insofar as a person conceives of himself as apprehending a thing, to that extent he likewise conceives of himself as apprehending it together with its name."[219] And therefore, I say,

> There is no connection with words anywhere, either externally or in one's awareness, but a little bit of the image of the thing appears mixed up with the image of the speech sounds. And it is because the determination of the awareness itself invests both of these aspects[220] in the external object and in the verbal expression that conceptual awareness is established.

[227.10] And it is for just this reason that, with a view toward the practically oriented person whose mind has worn itself out because of this conceit,[221] the qualifier "free from conceptual construction" is included in the definition of perception[222] and that the authoritative text mentions separately "on the basis of conceptual awareness . . . through the determination."[223] Furthermore, in that passage, the word "determination" is not used to denote the conceptualization, which is the *property possessor* but, rather, a property belonging to it, namely, determination. So this is what it means: "There is activity on the basis of conceptual awareness by reason of that property, namely, suitability for activity even when the thing is not seen." And if the object is conditionally adopted as "known" conventionally, on the basis of determination, then our way of talking about objects is attained as well. Thus it is right to say that there is objecthood merely by means of determination. [227.16] For this reason, it was said: "The first is adopted as an object because of determination."[224] As the author of the *Bhāṣya*[225] says, "How can that be an object? Because there is activity with respect to it."[226]

(227.20) But the lion's roar that he makes when faced with the question, "How is there activity with respect to something unseen?"—namely, "In every case there is activity only with respect to what is unseen!"[227]—is something that we will not elaborate on, for fear of making our book too long. [227.22] Thus, in this passage too—"Even though its own appearance is a nonobject, there is activity through the determination of an object"[228]—given that the appearance of the awareness itself is not an object, there is determination, just as before. But "object" refers to the external thing, which is capable of pragmatic effect, and it is in contradistinction to this that the mental image is a "nonobject." Thus it is seen that the mental image is a "thing" but is "unreal." This is made clear by Dharmakīrti's words in the *Pramāṇavārttika* itself, in the "Proof That Awareness Contains an Image."[229] [228] By saying that inference acts through the determination of an object, he means that inference is the determination of an object. But the way the author of the *Ṭīkā*, Dharmottara, explains this in his own *Proof of Exclusion* is to be rejected altogether. But we won't explore this for fear of getting caught up in an extended discussion.

[228.04] *If so, then the external is expressed through determination. But how is the mental image expressed? As the authoritative text says, beginning with (1) "The meaning of a word rests on a conceptual awareness that arises from beginningless karmic traces";*[230] *(2) "The word is connected with conceptual images that rest on the exclusion of what is other";*[231] *and (3) "On the basis of a word, an image of the thing appears in awareness as if it were distinct."*[232] *For you cannot say that there is determination with respect to the mental image as well, since that has been conditionally adopted in connection with the object of activity. And for someone who seeks pragmatic effect, the object of activity is just the external object.* In response to this, I say, "The other" object is "expressed," "on the basis of appearance."[233] "Other" means other than the external object, that is, the mental image. Since in awareness generated by language and the like, it is just the image that appears, that image is called an object, just as color is the object of vision. But this is not due to determination; this is the idea. And as it is said, "This is said to be the meaning of a word in accordance with awareness."[234]

[228.19] But it is "unreal"[235] because it does not exist externally in accordance with its appearance and because the discussion began with reference to what is externally directed. And this is just what is meant by "because it does not really exist in the way that it is determined and it is not determined in the way that it really exists."[236] This is because its meaning depends on the statement "Since determination is a synonym for conceptualization, it appears in accordance with conceptual awareness."[237] And the meaning of "the appearance of an unreal object" is just its not existing externally in accordance with one's awareness. And error, as well, is only relative to what is external. Thus, it all [229] makes good sense. But because the object of reflexive awareness is an object insofar as it has the form of an awareness, it is not right to say that it does not exist,[238] just as in the case of the image of hair and so forth.[239] Therefore, even if the mental image is expressed: [229.03]

> There is no way of *really* affirming either the mental image or the external object. Conventionally, only externals are affirmed, whereas the mental image is not affirmed.

For this mental image, which is indubitable and an object of reflexive awareness, cannot be what is affirmed or denied by means of words and the like, since this would be either useless or impossible.[240] Neither can the external object, which does not appear in conceptual awareness, be what is affirmed or denied. Since this object is not cognized, what can be affirmed or denied? Therefore, just as on the basis of determination, an external tree is conditionally adopted as what is denoted by the word "tree," it is only on the basis of determination that one can talk about affirming or denying any external object. [229.08] Even when, owing to certain circumstances, one examines a mental image, having brought it to mind by means of another conceptualization, then, too, one affirms or denies only what is external to this conceptualization. For "analyzing the image, one falls into the object,"[241] as the authoritative text says. Therefore, there is really neither affirmation nor denial of either, but conventionally, it is unavoidable that there is affirmation or denial only of the external. This is because otherwise there would be the unwanted consequence of having to abandon all ordinary activity.

[229.14] Therefore what the author of the *Ṭīkā*[242] says—"*Affirmation and denial have as their object the external existence of the superimposed*"—does not conform to the understanding of ordinary people, lacks any scriptural support, doesn't stand to reason, and is rejected out of hand. For there cannot be a conditionally adopted position that does not depend on either conventional or ultimate truth. Now among these, this is not conventional truth, since that consists in the understanding of ordinary people, and the understanding of ordinary people, which is the universally accepted basis for action and inaction, is that it is the external object alone that is the meaning of a word that is either affirmed or denied. Ordinary people do not touch on things such as "the externality of the superimposed." Nor is this ultimately true, since there is no affirmation or denial of what is not expressed. And scripture states that "nothing at all is really expressed." Nor does reason lead in any other direction. And you yourself proclaim that "there is no affirmation or denial of what is not determined, and on the basis of language, there is no determination of anything other than a particular."[243] What, then, becomes of "the affirmation or denial of the externality of the superimposed"? All conditionally adopted positions arrived at on the basis of appearance or determination fail to touch on ultimate truth. And in this case, the "superimposed" or "the externality of the superimposed" is the object of neither appearance nor determination. On the one hand, the superimposed does not touch on appearance, as you yourself [230] say: "The object of conceptual awareness is the superimposition, which occurs at the same time as the experience of delineation, which does not at all have the form of appearance and which is not a real thing."[244] And for that very reason, its externality also does not appear, since that is a property of that superimposition. But there is no determination of either of these two things precisely because this is restricted to external particulars. So enough of propping this up. Even this "superimposed" is just a way of saying "conceptually constructed," and the object of conceptual construction is either an appearance or something determined. So what reason is there for this third category called "superimposed"? Therefore, it is proper that our analysis should rest on only external objects and mental images, from the perspective of either conventional or ultimate truth. If what this means is that there is an appropriate pragmatic effect, then why resort to such a convoluted and difficult way of saying this?[245] So enough with troubling ourselves excessively in this way. It has been established that the external object is expressed by a word on the basis of determination but that the mental image is expressed on the basis of appearance.

[230.08] *But if you explain things in this way, you have accepted that the entire collection of both sorts of objects is expressible. So how is it that this has been introduced in order to establish the inexpressibility of all attributes?*[246] In response to this, I say, "This is conditionally adopted." The idea that things can be expressed either merely by determination or merely by appearance is just a conditionally adopted position made with another purpose in mind. So someone who accepts external objects merely as a conditionally adopted position on what is ultimately real says, "Only the particular that is excluded from others is the object" in order to rule out the mass of contingent features.[247] Similarly, in order to rule out all external objects, one says that "the image that is excluded from what is other—which is what conceptual awareness consists of—is the object." But neither of these is said for the purpose of finally settling on the position that there is objecthood in either the external object or the image itself; thus, there is no contradiction.

[230.16] *But how is it that even when you say there is objecthood in one or the other, what is intended is not to settle on this but, rather, the intention is only to reject the other?* In response, I say, "But really, nothing at all is expressed by words."[248] As far as the practically oriented person is concerned, it is the appearance that is excluded from what is other, together with determination, that leads us to the belief that a really knowable object is the object of awareness, just as in the case of perception. For a mere appearance, either which is devoid of determination or whose functional role has been interfered with by a contrary determination, is not capable of establishing, for the person desirous of activity, that something is an object—like the touch of grass to one who is moving through it,[249] in the first case, or like the superimposition of water onto the rays of the sun, in the second case.[250] Nor is mere determination detached from an appearance capable, again, like the superimposition of water. Therefore, given that the establishment of something as an object is pervaded by suitability for activity, it is vitiated by the absence of a pervading factor if either appearance or determination is absent. Since it is necessarily connected with the presence of both, it is merely conventional to accept it when just one is singled out. Whatever does not appear in a certain episode of awareness, or is not determined by it, is not the object of that awareness, just as a horse is not the object of the awareness "cow." And a particular does not appear in verbal awareness, and a mental image is not determined by it. Thus, a pervading factor is missing. Since an invariable connection has been established,[251] this is not inconclusive. And even if, in the case of completely habitual behavior, things are seen to be objects of activity merely by appearance, [231] nevertheless, that very habituation could not exist without determination. Thus, determination itself has this power. Therefore, this qualification is required: "Whatever is not determined by it *when there is no habituation* is not the object of an episode of awareness."[252]

[231.03] *But even in perception, there is no determination of the grasped moment but, rather, of the continuum, and there is no appearance of the continuum.*[253] *So how can even perception have an object, since the pair*[254] *is absent in the moment and in the continuum? And this investigation is itself about inference. And there is no other instrument of valid awareness that could have an object by virtue of there being both.*[255] *Thus, this is impossible.*[256] *Therefore, given that being an object is due to either one or the other, it is established that everything, whether external or internal, can be expressed.*[257] To this, I say: What I have stated is a conditionally adopted position about the way things really are. There is objecthood only in virtue of the existence of both appearance and determination. It is just that the convention[258] is said to be "the way things really are," relative to a lower-order convention, with a view toward the practically oriented person. This is because, for the practically oriented person, things are not destroyed at each moment, since pragmatic activity breaks down when one gets down to the division between moments. Even with perception, there is really no possibility of both. Thus, there is no problem.

(231.10) Now if you say, "*For an ordinary person, there is surely a failure to grasp even the difference between what is seen and what is conceptualized, such that for him the determined fire is the very same one that appeared.*" We say "no." This is because it is due to the recollection of other appearances that people fall into the error that there is the appearance of that determined fire. And since in perception it is possible to show an appearance of the thing, which is definitely different from the conceptual appearance, and likewise that this conceptual appearance is different from the perceptual appearance, therefore—because it is only in perception that one can settle on the appearance of a thing—for anything other than perception, it is better to deny that there is the appearance of a thing. Therefore, it was rightly said, "This is conditionally adopted. But really, nothing at all is expressed by words."[259]

[231.16] Or on another interpretation: Even if no other thing is expressed, by saying "This being the case, exclusion is understood as an element of that," we really do accept that exclusion is expressed. *Why, then, are all properties beyond the reach of language?" As was said:* "But really, nothing at all is expressed by words." This is the idea: First, on the view that there is implicative negation,[260] just like the form of the real thing, exclusion, too, is expressed only as a result of determination, not on the basis of appearance, just as in perception. But on the view that there is nonimplicative negation, although the mere exclusion of what is other is no different even in other cases, nevertheless this exclusion is not a thing.[261] So, the stated problem does not apply. Or through my summation—"But really nothing at all is expressed by words"—I show the real basis of the conclusion stated in the authoritative text: "Therefore it is established that all words and conceptual awarenesses have differentiation as their object."[262] Because it has already been shown that conventionally, something can be expressed through mere appearance or determination, I said, "really." [232] This is what it means: When the authoritative text sums up by saying "differentiation alone is expressed,"[263] what it means is that nothing is really expressed. Just as the expression "an absence exists" means "a certain thing does not exist," in the same way "exclusion is expressed" means "there is the exclusion of anything being expressed." And we have already explained that this is made clear by the authoritative text itself when it makes a division of inferential reasons into three types, and so on.[264]

[232.05] So when one is asked, "How is exclusion expressed by a word?" We answer, "As an element of that," the meaning of which is as described. If the question is, "Why are the mental image, or the particular, or the contingent features not expressed?" these questions are dispensed with in order by saying, "This is because of the absence of determination, the absence of appearance, and the absence of both." But if the question is "What is it that is expressed by words?" then, having set out these options (1) on the basis of appearance, (2) on the basis of determination, or (3) really, the answers are, in order, (1) "the image that is excluded from what is other, that resides in conceptual awareness";

or (2) "the particular that is excluded from what is other"; or (3) "nothing." This has already been said. Therefore, establishing the position that words and inferential reasons have exclusions as their objects is for the sake of making it known that all properties are inexpressible; this is the summation of the meaning of the first verse.

[232.12] Accomplished people can go on and on about exclusion,
but the secret is the fact that the form of a real thing does not appear.
If that is not firmly established, everything is effortlessly cut to pieces.
But if it is firmly established, it all stands firm by that alone.

The justification for this line of reasoning
has been revealed by us, without extensive discussion.
But the extensive discussion of this in the treasury[265] should be considered
by those who would brush aside the statements of
our opponents as if they were a bit of fluff.

SANSKRIT TEXT OF THE

MONOGRAPH ON EXCLUSION (APOHAPRAKARAṆAM)

[201.01] apohaḥ śabdaliṅgābhyāṃ prakāśyata iti sthitiḥ |
sādhyate sarvadharmāṇām avācyatvaprasiddhaye ||

sthitir vyavasthā | sādhyate[1] ityantena apoho 'tra abhidheya uktaḥ | śeṣeṇa tatprasādhanaphalam | athavā yad ācāryair apohaḥ śabdādinā prakaśyata iti vyavasthā kriyate tad etadartham ity arthaḥ | ubhayathāpi sarvadharmānabhilāpyatva pratipādanaparam apohavyavasthāpanam ity uktaṃ bhavati |

[201.07] nanv apohaḥ śabdaliṅgābhyāṃ prakāśyata ity anubhavabādhitam etat | tathā hīha mahīdharoddeśe vahnir astīti śabdāl liṅgād vā pratītir vidhirūpam evollikhantī lakṣyate | nānagnir na bhavatīti nivṛttimātram āmukhayantī | [201.09] yac cānubhavabādhitaṃ na tatra sādhanāntaracintā, sarvapramāṇapauruṣasya tatraiva viśrāmāt [8b] tat-prasūtes tatphalatvāc ca | na hi pratyakṣopakāranirapekṣaḥ pramāṇāntarodayaḥ | nāpi pramāṇāntaro dayamātreṇa kṛtārthaḥ pramānānusārī yāvan na tadupanītasādhanārthakriyānubhavaḥ | tasmāt tadanapekṣāyām asāmarthyavaiyarthyagrastaṃ pramāṇāntaraṃ svayam eva na kiñcid iti na tena sādhite bādhite vāvakāśam āsādayati | tat katham apohaḥ śabdādigocara ucyate?

[201.15] atha yady api nivṛttim ahaṃ pratyemīti na vikalpaḥ, tathāpi nivṛttapadārthollekha eva nivṛttyullekhaḥ | na hy anantarbhāvita-viśeṣaṇapratītir viśiṣṭapratītiḥ | tato yathā sāmānyam ahaṃ pratyemīti vikalpābhāve 'pi sādhāraṇākāraparisphuraṇād vikalpabuddhiḥ sāmānyabuddhiḥ pareṣām, tathā nivṛttapratyayākṣiptā nivṛttibuddhir apohapratītivyavahāram ātanotīti cet?

(201.19) nanu sādhāraṇākāraparisphuraṇe vidhirūpatayā yadi sāmānyabodhavyavasthā, tat kim āyātam asphuradabhāvākāre cetasi nivṛttipratītiv-yavasthāyāḥ ? tato nivṛttim ahaṃ pratyemīty evamākārābhāve 'pi nivṛttyākāraṇasphuraṇaṃ yadi syāt, ko nāma nivṛttipratītisthitim apalapet? anyathā vātatpratibhāse[2] tatpratītiv-yavahṛtir iti gavākāre 'pi cetasi turagabodha ity astu | atha viśeṣaṇatayā antarbhūtā nivṛttipratītir ity uktam, tathāpi yady agavāpoḍha itīdṛśākāro vikalpas tadā viśeṣaṇatayā tad anupraveśo bhavatu, kiṃtu gaur iti pratītiḥ[3]| tadā ca sato 'pi nivṛttilakṣaṇaviśeṣaṇasya tatrānutkalanāt kathaṃ tatpratītivyavasthā? tad etad āyātam, sphurato 'pi vidher na viṣayasthitir apohasya punar asphurato 'pīti ka eṣa nyāyaḥ? tathā ca niścayair yan na niścīyate rūpaṃ tat teṣāṃ viṣayaḥ katham? na ca vikalpe 'sphuratas[4] tena niścayanaṃ nāma |

[202.07] yad vidhirūpaṃ sphuritam antarmātrāyāṃ tasya parāpoho 'py astīti tatpratītir ucyate | tatrāpi sambandhamātram apohasya | vidhis tu sākṣān nirbhāsīti na pūrvadoṣān muktiḥ | api caivam adhyakṣasyāpy apohaviṣayatvam anivāryam, viśeṣato vikalpād ekavyāvṛttollekhino 'khilānyavyāvṛttam īkṣamāṇasya | tasmād vidhyākārāvagrahād adhyakṣavad[5] vikalpasyāpi vidhiviṣayatvam eva nānyāpohaviṣayatvam |

[202.12] yat punar anyasmād apohyate, apohyate 'nyad asmin[6] veti vijātivyāvṛttaṃ bāhyam eva buddhyākāro 'nyāpoha iti gīyate | tena na kaścid upayogaḥ, apohanāmnā vidher eva vivakṣitatvāt, na ca nāmāntarakaraṇe vastunaḥ svarūpaparāvṛttiḥ | tasmād anubhavānusārād vidhirūpam eva bāhyaṃ śabdādigamyam astu | śāstraṃ ca, atra dvau vastusādhanāv ekaḥ pratiṣedhahetuḥ |[7] anaṅgīkṛtavastvaṃśo niṣedhaḥ sādhyate 'nayā | vastuny api tu pūrvābhyāṃ paryudāso vidhānataḥ||[8] yadi ca nañprayogavat[9] [9a] abhāvamātrasyaiva hetvantarād api pratītiḥ, tadā nānupalambhād bheda iti liṅgavibhāgapūrvakāśeṣavyavasthādauḥsthyam āyātam iti katham apohaḥ śabdaliṅgābhyāṃ prakāśyata ity ucyata āha, sthitir iti | vyavasthāmātram etat | mukhyatayāpohaḥ śabdāder viṣaya iti nedaṃ vastutattvam ity arthaḥ |

[202.22] kiṃ punar atra vastutattvam iti cet?

śabdais tāvan mukhyamākhyāyate 'rthas, tatrāpohas tadguṇa-
tvena gamyaḥ |
arthaś caiko 'dhyāsato bhāsato[10] 'nyaḥ, sthāpyo vācyas tattvato
naiva kaścit ||

iti prakaraṇārthasaṃgrahaḥ |

[203.06] na khalu śāstram anubhavaṃ paribhūya bhavituṃ kṣamam iti vidhirūpam āmukhayann eva vikalpa upajāyata iti tāvan na śakyam apahnotum iti prathamapādārthaḥ | nañyoge vivādābhāvāt na tatra cintā | śabdair iti copalakṣaṇam | liṅgaiḥ pratipādyate vikalpair viṣayīkriyata ity api draṣṭavyam |

(203.09) evaṃ saty āstām apohasya vācyatā, tadvyavasthāmātram api viluptam | sā sthitir api hi dvidhā vidhīyate, sannikarṣāt prayojakāc ca | tatra yady api sarvadharmānabhilāpyatvapratipādanaṃ prayojakam uktam, na tu sannikarṣaḥ kaścid

[203.11] ity āśaṅkyāha- tatrāpoha iti | vidhau hi mukhyatayā pratipādyamāne tadviśeṣaṇatayopasarjanatvena gamyata evāpohaḥ | tatra tadguṇatvenety arthasannikarṣaḥ | gamya[11] iti pratītisannikarṣaḥ | tataś cārthasaṃbaddhaḥ pratīyamānaś cāpoho mukhyapratītikam api vidhiṃ tiraskṛtya prādhānyena sa evābhidheya ity ucyate, uktaprayojanāt

[203.15] athavā tadguṇatvenaiva gamyo na mukhyatveneti[12] sākṣādapohavādino nirastāḥ | yady api cānyāpohādiśabdānullekha uktas tathāpi nāpratītir eva viśeṣaṇabhūtasyāpohasya, agavādyapoḍha eva gavādiśabdasya niveśitatvāt | śāstraṃ hi, niveśanaṃ ca yo yasmād bhidyate vinivartya tam[13] ityādi | yathā hi nīlotpale niveśitād indīvaraśabdāt tatpratītau nīlimasphuraṇam anivāryam, tathā gośabdād apy agavāpoḍhe niveśitād gopratītāv ago'pohasphuraṇam anivāryam |

[203.23] ye punar ago'pohe gośabdasaṅketavidhāv anyonyāśrayaṇaṃ grāmyadhandhīkaraṇam udbhāvayanti, te 'pi sāmānye sāmānyavati vā saṅketavādinaḥ katham ato doṣān mucyamānam ātmānaṃ paśyanti?

tathā hi sāmānyaṃ nāma na sāmānyamātram abhipretaṃ, turage 'pi gośabdasaṅketaprasaṅgāt, kiṃtu gotvasāmānyam abhipretaṃ | tāvatā ca gotvasāmānye tadvati vā gośabdasaṅketa ity arthaniṣṭhāyāṃ sa eva doṣaḥ, gavāparijñāne gotvasāmānyāparijñānāt, gotvasāmānyāparijñāne gośabdavācyāparijñānāt |

[204.02] atha gotve tadvati vā gośabda itīdṛśākṣareṇa yadi saṅketas tadā doṣaḥ | yadā tu [9b] puraḥsthitaṃ piṇḍam ekam upadarśya deśakālāntaraviprakīrṇāśeṣavyaktisādhāraṇarūpavikalpasthāyinaṃ prakaraṇādeḥ pratipattāram avadhāryāyaṃ gaur iti saṅketaḥ tadā yatraivāsau tat sādhāraṇaṃ rūpaṃ nirūpayati tam eva gośabdena vyavaharatīti kathaṃ mithaḥprārthanādoṣaḥ? tāvatā ca gotve tadvati vā saṅketa iti vyākhyātṝṇāṃ siddhāntānuvāda eṣaḥ, na tu saṅketakartṝṇām upadeśakramas tādṛg iti cet.

[204.08] evaṃ tarhi yady agavāpoḍhe gośabda itīdṛśākṣaraṃ[14] saṅketākārakīrtanaṃ tadāyaṃ doṣaḥ | yadā tu vivakṣitavyaktiṣv ekākārapratyavamarśavartini prakaraṇād avadhārite pratipattari saṅketakaraṇam ayaṃ gaur iti, tadā kva doṣāvakāśaḥ? sa hi svavikalpatalpaśāyinīḥ sakalavyaktīr agovyāvṛttādyakṣaram anapekṣya svayaṃ tadvijātīyāśeṣavyaktivyāvṛttā gośabdavācyāḥ pratipadyamāno yatraiva vijātīyavyāvṛttiṃ pratipadyate tā eva gośabdena vyavaharatīti, tāvatā agovyāvṛtte gośabda iti siddhāntānuvāda eva na saṅketākāraḥ, abhimate gośabdavṛttāv agośabdena śeṣasyābhidhātuṃ śakyatvāt | sa tu vijātīyavyāvṛttaḥ sādhāraṇākāro vikalpe sāmānyasya pratibhāso vyakter vā svātmaiveti paścān niśceṣyate | itaretarāśrayas tu nāstīti siddham | siddhaṃ ca puṇḍarīkaśabdaśrutau śvetaśatapatrapratipattivad gośabdaśrutāv apy agavāpoḍhapratītau jātivādināpy avaśyābhyupagantavyam apohaviśeṣaṇaśe-muṣīnāntarīyakatvaṃ vidher iti | na ca saṃbandhagandhamātraṃ sākṣād eva dvayoḥ pratītir mukhyopasarjanabhāveneti bhedaḥ |

[204.19] dharmavācī vā guṇaśabdaḥ, anyāpohadharmaṇo vidhirūpasya pratīteḥ | [204.21] yat tṛtīyākārasyāropitabāhyayor anyanivṛttikṛtaṃ sādṛśyaṃ dūṣayan vācaspatir āha- na ca svalakṣaṇadharmo vyāvṛttir bhavadbhir abhyupeyata iti,[15] tad duṣṭam eva | atha bhāvikīti vivakṣitaṃ tatreti cet ? tathāpi nopayogaḥ, kalpanārūḍhasyaiva dharmidharmabhāvasyeṣṭatvāt |

[204.24] kevalaṃ kiṃ na vidhinaiva vyapadeśaḥ pratyakṣasyāpi vā parāpohaviṣayatvavyavahāraprasaṅga ity avaśiṣyate | [204.26] atra brūmaḥ| iha kācid vyavasthā tattvaleśam āśritya prayojanaviśeṣād anyathā sthitāv apy anyathā kriyate, yathātmatadupāda iti | utpādo hi prāgabhāvaviśiṣṭasya vastunaḥ sata eva dharmaḥ | atha ca prāgabhāvalakṣaṇatattvaleśam āśrityāsata iti vyavasthāpyate satkāryavādaśaṅkāsaṅkocāya | yathā vā 'nenaiva kṛtaṃ karma ko 'nyaḥ pratyanubhaviṣyatīty ekasantānaprajñaptim āśritya kṛtanāśākṛtābhyāgamavañcanāvimohāya, tathādyāpi vidhiviṣayābhidhānam |[16] [10a] vastuto vastuna eva parāropitavācyatāsvīkāraśaṅkānirākaraṇāya nāntarīyakapratītir apy apoha[17] eva vikalpaviṣaya iti vyavasthāpyate | ato na vidhinaiva vyavahāraḥ | yadā tv apoha eva mukhyārthaḥ śabdasyety āropaḥ, tadā vidhir api puraskriyate | yathoktam, śabdais tāvan mukhyam ākhyāyate 'rtha iti | pratyakṣe tu vivādābhāvān naivaṃ vyavastheti yuktam |

[205.09] anyāpohaviśeṣaṇaṃ tu vidhiḥ |[18] tatrātiśayo netyuktam eva | śāstraṃ hi, tat paricchinatti tato 'nyad vyavacchinattītyādi |[19] niṣedhyāpekṣayā tu tatrānupalabdhiśabdena niṣedhavyāpāraḥ puraskriyata eva |

[205.12] yathā vā [vidhivṛ]tter agrahaṇaṃ nāma prasajyapakṣe niyatarūpānubhavād abhāvavikalpotpādanaśaktir eva, tathā vidhivikalpānām api tantre 'nurūpānuṣṭhānadānaśaktir eva niṣedhagrahaṇam agnir mayā pratīta ity anuvyavasāyaprasavaśaktiś ca | paryudāsapakṣe ca niyatasvarūpasaṃve[da]nam eva | ubhayatra[20] niṣedhagrahaṇam |

(205.16) ubhayaṃ caitad abhimataṃ śāstrakārasya | kvacit tasya prastāvānurūpaṃ prasajyapratiṣedhādhikāreṇa, rūpe tasya na kiñcanetyādīni[21] vacanāni, kvacit tv atadrūpaparāvṛttavastumātraprasādhanād ityādīni[22] paryudāsāśrayāṇi | na tv ekaniyamaḥ | tato yaṭ ṭīkākāraḥ svāpohasiddhau tadarthāvatārataralas trilocanaś cāvocatām ācāryaḥ prasajyapratiṣedhavallabha unnīyata iti tan nirākṛtam |

(205.21) na ca bhedābhāvāt viśeṣaṇavyavahārahāniḥ, rāhoḥ śiraḥ gotvaṃ sāmānyam ity ādivad vivakṣākṛtasya anapāyāt | kiṃ ca vyavahriyata eva bhavatāpi ghaṭābhāvapradeśayoḥ piśācatvābhāvastambhayor vā viśeṣyaviśeṣaṇabhāvaḥ | tat katham asmākaṃ niṣedho[23] niḥsvabhāvābhāvavāditvād iti cet? nedānīṃ svarūpanirūpaṇam abhāvasya, kiṃtu pratītinirūpaṇam | sā cāśakyāpahnotum[24] | paryudāsapakṣe 'pi tadvidhir evānyaniṣedha iti na pratītikṣatiḥ | nāpi viśeṣaṇabhāvasya | anenaiva vākyena vidhiniṣedhayoḥ sāmānādhikaraṇyapradarśanāt | ata eva virodhacodyam apy avadyaṃ na, svābhāvena hi vidher virodho, nānyābhāvena, sahaiva sthānāt | tasmād yuktam uktam, tatrāpohas tadguṇatvena gamya iti |

[206.04] athavā tasyārthākhyānasya guṇo 'yam eva yad anyaniṣedhanaṃ nāma, tenāsau gamya[25] iti vyavahartavyam | yac chāstram, tadanyaparihāreṇa pravarteteti śabdaniyogaḥ, vyartho 'nyathā prayogaḥ syād iti | etena tātparyārthatvam apohasya darśitam avyāpitvaparihāraś ca | eṣa panthāḥ śrughnam upatiṣṭhata ity atrāpi prakṛtapathāntarāpekṣayaiṣa eva | śrughnapratyanīkāniṣṭasthānāpekṣayā śrughnam eva | araṇyamārgavad vicchedābhāvād upatiṣṭhata eva | sārthadūtādivyavacchedena panthā eveti sulabho niyamaḥ | tarjanīnirdeśād gatārthaḥ panthā eveti cet ? paravyavacchedas tāvad astīṣṭaś ca | prayogas tu gatārthasyāpi loke dṛśyata eva | abhyāgacchati, [10b] brāhmaṇau dvāv ity ādivat | yathā hi sārthapuruṣādivyavacchedena kaḥ panthāḥ śrughnam upatiṣṭhata iti praśnaḥ, tathottaram apy eṣa panthā iti | sarvatraiva hi pratipādyaśaṅkāṅkitasyaiva vidhipratiṣedhāv iti | yadi ca śabdaśrutikāle kalito na parāpohaḥ katham anyaparihāreṇa pravṛttiḥ ? tato gāṃ badhāneti codito 'śvādīn api badhnīyāt |

[206.15] yat tu goḥ pratītau na tadātmā parātmeti sāmarthyād anyāpohaḥ paścān niścīyata iti matam—tad asaṅgatam, prāthamikasyāpi pratītikramādarśanāt | na hi tatkālavyutpannasaṅketo 'pi gām ānayety uktaḥ parato nivṛttāv arthāpattim anusarati | na ca gośabdād anyāvakīrṇapratipattau goniścayo yuktaḥ | tathā pratipattau vā paścād api katham arthāpatter udayaḥ? pararūpaparikaro hi gaur gṛhītaḥ | kathaṃ sa tadanākīrṇatāsamarthane samarthaḥ? tasmād goḥ pratītir ity ago'poḍhapratipattir ucyate | ataḥ svārthapratītikāla evārthāntarāpohasya pratītikālaḥ, candraprayoge candrapratītikālavad avadātatāyāḥ | yathā ca śuklimāpratītau kīdṛśīndupratītiḥ, pararūpasaṅkīrṇapratītāv api kīdṛśī gopratītir iti samānam | nāpi na saṅkīrṇaṃ nāsaṅkīrṇam avagantuṃ śakyaṃ vastu, paścād api sāmarthyasyāśakyatvāc ca | tasmān na niṣedhabodhāyārthasāmarthyālambanaṃ śreyaḥ |

[206.25] yad apy uvāca vācaspatiḥ,—jātimatyo vyaktayo vikalpānāṃ śabdānāṃ ca gocaraḥ, tāsāṃ [ca] tadvatīnāṃ rūpam atajjātīyavyāvṛttam ity arthatas tadavagater gāṃ badhāneti codito nāśvādīn badhnātīti, tad apy anenaiva nirastam | yato jāter adhikāyāḥ prakṣepe 'pi vyaktīnāṃ rūpam atajjātīyavyāvṛttam eva cet, tadā tenaiva rūpeṇa śabdavikalpayor viṣayībhavantīnāṃ katham atadvyāvṛttipratītiparihāraḥ? atha na vijātīyavyāvṛttaṃ [vyaktirūpaṃ] tathāpratītaṃ vā tadā jātiprasāda eṣa iti katham arthato 'pi tadavagatir ity uktaprāyam | atha jātibalād evānyato vyāvṛttam, sā tarhi pūrvam apy āsīd eveti pūrvaṃ na samarthā, tanniścaye paścād api katham? saṅketasmaraṇasahakāryapekṣā hi nāmayojanāyām eva, vijātīyetarakalpanā tu darśanamātrādhīnā bālādivad iti yat kiñcid etat |

[207.08] yadi vā guṇyate 'bhyasyata iti guṇa upādeyo dharmas tena prādhānyam atra lakṣaṇīyam, tataḥ sa eva guṇo 'poha eva pradhānaṃ teṣu sabdeṣu |[26] tadbhāvenāpoha eva bhāvavāciṣu śabdeṣu gamya ucyate, na vidhiḥ sphurann apy apradhānatvāt[27] | tathā hi vijātīye 'nyatrādṛṣṭyapekṣatvāt, kvacit taddṛṣṭyapekṣaṇād ātmajātīye[28] śrutau saṃbadhyate 'poha iti śāstram | api ca, ubhayāvabhāse 'pi yathāvabhāsa[pra]meyābhāvād anyanivṛttes tu bhāvaniyamān nivṛttir eva pradhānam | yac chāstram, vasturūpasya saṃsparśo vicchedakaraṇe dhvaneḥ | syāt satyaṃ sa hi tatreti |[29] abhāvavāciṣu [11a] punar vastuno 'sattvād eva | yac chāstram, [207.18] rūpābhāvād abhāvānāṃ śabdā rūpābhidhāyinaḥ | nāśaṅkyā eva siddhās te vyavacchedasya vācakāḥ ||[30]

[207.19] iti | yad vā tasminn apohe paryudāsenāpoḍhākāre vā vācye sthito guṇo doṣaniṣedho yeṣāṃ śabdānāṃ tadbhāvenāpoha[31] eva vācya ucyate | yathāha, nivṛtter niḥsvabhāvatvān na sthānāsthānakalpanā[32] | upaplavaś ca sāmānyadhiyas tenāpy adūṣaṇā ||[33] iti | evam apohasya vācyatāvyavasthāyāṃ nimittāny abhidhīyamānāni śāstre 'pohasya śabdān mukhyasphuraṇavirodhīny ūhanīyāni bhāvavāciṣu | abhāvavācakādhikāre cāyam eva mukhyo viveka ity uktam | bhāvavāciṣūpasarjanatayā vivekasyāmukhyatāṃ khyāpayati | viśeṣato hy eṣa boddhavyaḥ | abhāvavāciṣu padārtha evāpohaḥ | bhāvavāciṣu punaḥ padārthasyānyato 'pohaḥ[34], padārthāc[35] cānyasya | enayoś coktimātreṇa bheda iti |

[208.05] yadi tathāvidhanibandhanādhīnā 'pohasya vācyatāvyavasthā, artha eva tu mukhyam ākhyāyate, hanta tarhi sarvadharmānabhilāpyatāsamayo 'stamayam āyātaḥ, tadarthaś ca samārambha iti sūcitam | yac coktaṃ vastuvācyatāropaniṣedhārtham apohasya prādhānyenābhidhānavyavastheti, tatrāpi svayam arthavācyataiva svīkriyate, parasya tv anyathopadiśyata iti mahatī prekṣatety

[208.09] āśaṅkyāha, arthaś caika ityādi | ayam arthaḥ, artho hi dvididhaḥ bāhya āntaraś ca, anyasyābhāvāt | tatraikas tāvad bāhyo 'dhyavasāyād eva vācyo vyavasthāpyate, na svalakṣaṇaparisphūrtyā | katham iti cet? anubhavād eva | yathā hi pratyakṣacetasi deśkālāvasthāniyatāni parisphuṭarūpāṇi svalakṣaṇāni pratibhānty anubhūyante, tathā na vikalpakāle | vikalpakāle hi vijātivyāvṛttam eva parasparākārākīrṇam ivāsphuṭam iva prayakṣāparicitaṃ kiñcid rūpam ābhāsamānam anubhavaviṣayaḥ | yac chāstram, śabdenāvyāpṛtākṣasya buddhāv apratibhāsanāt | arthasya dṛṣṭāv iveti |[36]

[208.19] upāyabhedād ekasyaiva pratibhāsabhedaḥ ekatra hi buddhāv indriyam āśrayo 'nyatra śabdādīti cet? [208.20] atrāpy uktam, jāto nāmāśrayo 'nyonyaś[37] cetasāṃ tasya vastunaḥ | ekasyaiva kuto rūpaṃ bhinnākārāvabhāsi tat ||[38] na hi spaṣṭāspaṣṭe dve rūpe parasparaviruddhe ekasya vastunaḥ staḥ, yata ekenendriyabuddhau pratibhāsetānyena vikalpe, tathā sati vastuna eva bhedaprāpteḥ | na hi svarūpabhedād aparo vastubhedaḥ, na ca pratibhāsabhedād aparaḥ svarūpabhedaḥ | anyathā trailokyam ekam eva vastu syāt |

(209.02) nanu dūrāsannadeśavartinor ekatra śākhini spaṣṭāspaṣṭapratibhāsabhede 'pi na śākhi[39]bhedaḥ, arthakriyāb hedābhāvād ity arthakriyābhedopakṛta eva pratibhāsabhedo bhedakaḥ | [209.04] na cehārthakriyābheda iti katham indriyaśabdābhyāṃ janitajñānaviṣayo gavādir bhedabhāg iti cet? na brūmaḥ pratibhāsabhedo bhinnavastuniyataḥ, kiṃ tu ekaviṣayatvābhāvaniyata iti | [11b] tathā hi, yo yaḥ kvacid vastuni pratyakṣapratibhāsād viparītaḥ pratibhāso nāsau tenaikaviṣayaḥ, yathā ghaṭagrāhakāt paṭapratibhāsaḥ, yathā vā śaṅkhagrāhakāt pītapratibhāsaḥ | tathā ca gavi pratyakṣapratibhāsād viparītaḥ pratibhāso vikalpakāle iti vyāpakaviruddhopalabdhiḥ | ekaviṣayatvaṃ hi pratibhāsābhedena vyāptam, savyetaranayanadṛṣṭavad[40] | avyāptis[41] tu yadi pratyakṣāntaram api viparītapratibhāsaṃ syāt, vastu ca dvirūpaṃ bhavet | tac ca dvayam api nāstīti vyāptir eva | āśrayabhedabhāvini ca jñāne pakṣīkṛte tadviruddhaḥ siddhaḥ | tato yatrārthakriyābhedādisacivaḥ pratibhāsabhedas tatra vastubhedaḥ ghaṭapaṭavat | taṃ punaḥ sahāyaṃ vihāya pravṛtto niyamenaikaviṣayatāṃ pariharatīty eko 'tra bhrānta eva pratibhāsaḥ, śaṅkhe pītapratibhāsavat |

(209.15) tatrāpi saṅkha eva viṣaya iti cet? śuklatām aspṛśantī buddhiḥ śaṅkhaviṣayeti suvyāhṛtam | śaṅkhamātraṃ pratyetīti cet—na, tataḥ parasya śaṅkhamātrasyāsphuraṇāt | pṛṣṭhabhāvini vikalpe sphuratīti cet? astu, na tu nirvikalpaḥ pītapratibhāsaḥ śaṅkhaviṣaya iti siddham | evaṃ dūrataḥ śikhariṇi piṇḍākārapratipattir api na pippalādibhedāvasāyasamarthapatrādiviśeṣavirahiṇī vṛkṣaviṣayeti prakṛtasamam etat | arthakriyābhedādyabhāvāc ca na bhinno 'artha ity ekasyārpite brāntibhāve yadi na pratyakṣapratibhāso bhrāntaḥ, tadānyapratibhāsa eva bhrama iti brūmaḥ | evaṃ pītābhāse govikalpe ca samāno nyāyaḥ | nanu kvacit kasyacid āropaḥ kutaścit sādṛśyād bhavati | na ca vikalpapratibhāsavat saṃbhinnākāraṃ janmāntare 'pi kiñcidupalabdham |

(209.24) tat kutaḥ kasya kva samāropād bhramo 'yam iti cet? ayam aparas tavaiva doṣaḥ, yad ayaṃ vikalpo nādhyakṣagamyagavagocaro[42] nānyagocara iti nirviṣayo 'pi na bhramo 'bhidhātavyaḥ | asmākaṃ tu tadviṣayo na bhavatīty etāvataiva prakṛtasiddhiḥ | tad evānyathākhyātīti tadgocara eveti cet? yathā pratyakṣapuraskṛtena rūpeṇāsti tato 'tiriktasya vastuno' bhāvāt kasyānyathākhyāne kartṛtvaṃ? tat tu na khyāty evety alaṃ bahubhāṣitayā | tasmān na svalakṣaṇapratibhāso vikalpeṣv iti nyāyaḥ |

(210.03) tena yad āha vācaspatiḥ, na ca śābdapratyakṣoyor vastugocaratve pratyayābhedaḥ kāraṇabhedena pārokṣyāpārokṣyabhedopapatter iti, tan nopayogi | parokṣapratyayasya vastugocaratvāsamarthanāt | parokṣatāśrayas tu kāraṇabheda indriyagocaragrahaṇavireheṇaiva kṛtārthaḥ |

(210.06) nanu vastuviṣayatve pratyayābhedaprasaṅgaḥ tvayaivokta iti tatparihāreṇaiva vastuviṣayatvaṃ siddham, na cānyad vastv astīti tadviṣayatvaṃ ceti cet | naivaṃ, yataḥ pratibhāsa-[12a] vaijātyasyātadviṣayatvena vyāptisādhanād asau prasaṅgo 'smadīyaḥ |

asmākam api vyāptivighaṭanāyaiva prayatna eṣaḥ | kāraṇavaijātyakṛte pratibhāsavaijātye saṃbhavini kuto vā tadviṣayatvena vyāptir iti? etad api kadā yujyate? yadi[43] tadviṣayatvamātreṇa vā kāraṇabhedo vyāptaḥ śakyo darśayitum | tat tāvan nāsti, kāraṇabhedasya vastuno 'pratītyaiva caritārthatvāt | atha na tadodbhāvanam[44] etat kāraṇabhedād api saṃbhāvyate pratibhāsabhedas tadviṣayatve 'pīti | saṃbhāvyatāṃ tarhi gāndhāramadhurabodhayor apy ekaviṣayatvaṃ, kāraṇabhedasya tatrāpi saṃbhavāt | nirvik[alpasavi]kalpayor agnitvamātrollekho 'stīty ekaviṣayatāśvāsaḥ | tatra tu na gāndhāratvasya na vā madhuratvasya tadubhayabodhayor ullekha iti cet?

(210.16) aho niruḍhatā mahatī | ātyantikakāraṇavaijātyasya hi phalam etat | ekaviṣayatvāśvāsaḥ punar antato vastuna ullekhād bhviṣyati | sandehe kāraṇavaijātye 'vāntarasyāgnitvāder ullekhaḥ | ātyantike tu sarvāsādhāraṇasya[45] dharmasyeti na tāvataivātadviṣayatvam | asti cāvāntaradharmsya[46] mādhuryasyānuvṛttir gāndhāre 'pi | anyādṛśaṃ tan mādhuryam iti cet? vikalpanyastasyāpy agnitvam anyad eva | na caikarūpe 'py ullikhyamāne 'vāntaradharmapratibhāsayor ekaviṣayatvam, śuktirajatavat | na hi śuktipratibhāso rajataviṣayo rajatapratibhāso vā śuktiviṣayaḥ sādhāraṇadhavalatollekhe 'pi | tasmād yathāgnivikalpe vastusphuraṇe 'py avāntaradharmasya gardabhatvasyāsphuraṇāt na gardabhaviṣayatā, tathāvāntarasyāgnitvasya sphuraṇe 'pi svalakṣaṇākārasya pratiniyatasyāsphuraṇāt nānyadravyasphuraṇam iti nyāyaḥ svalakṣaṇasyaivāgnidravyatvāt | tataḥ kāraṇabhedo jñānapratibhāsasya bhedako 'stu | vastuviṣayatvaṃ tu na dvayor api pratibhāsayor iti sthitam etat | tasmān na svalakṣaṇaṃ viṣayaḥ śabdāder iti siddham |

[211.01] kiṃ caivaṃ vidhiniṣedhayor ayogād uccāraṇam[47] eva na syāt | tau hi dharmiṇo vā syātām, dharmāṇāṃ vā yathā vṛkṣo' sti nāsti vā, vṛkṣo nīlo na vā nīla iti | tatra prathamaḥ pakṣas tāvan nāsti | bhāvābhāvaniyato hi vṛkṣo vṛkṣaśabdena codita iti bhāvaniyamapakṣe 'stīti vyartham, nāstīty asamarthaṃ, virodhāt | abhāvanirūpaṇe tu viparyayaḥ | asti ca vṛkṣapadaśrutau vidhiniṣedhāpekṣeti, bhāvābhāvasādhāraṇo 'yaṃ vṛkṣapadād vṛkṣapratibhāso na bāhyo vṛkṣa iti nyāyaḥ |

(211.07) yat tu nyāyadarśane tātparyaṭīkākāreṇa jātimadvyaktivācyatāṃ svavācaiva prastutyānantaram eva na ca śabdārthasya jāter bhāvābhāvasādhāraṇyaṃ nopapadyate, sā hi svarūpato nityāpi deśakālaviprakīrṇānekavyaktyāśrayatayā bhāvābhāvasādhāraṇībhavanty[48] astināstisaṃbandhayogyā | vartamānavyaktisaṃbandhitā hi jāter astitā | atītānāgatasaṃbandhitā ca nāstiteti | sandigdhavyatirekitvād [12b] anaikāntikaṃ bhāvābhāvasādhāraṇyam anyathāsiddhiṃ veti vilapitam, tāvatā tāvan na prakṛtakṣatiḥ | jātau bharaṃ nyasyatā svalakṣaṇāvācyatvasya svayaṃ svīkārāt | api ca jātir apy astyādipadaprayogāt prāg abhidhīyamānā śabdena vartamāna-vyaktisaṃbaddhā vābhidheyā, atītānāgatavyaktisaṃbaddhā vā, ubhayasaṃbaddhā, asaṃbaddhā veti pakṣāḥ | na caikatrāpi trāṇaṃ prācīnacodyacaturaḥ kṣamate | prathame pakṣe hi bhāvaniyamaḥ dvitīye tv abhāvaniyamaḥ | tṛtīye 'pi yadi sadasadvaktiyogād asyāḥ sattvāsat-tvavyavahāramanorathaḥ, tathā yair yair āśrayair vartamāṇavyaktiyogo 'syā vyavahriyate, yair yair vātītānāgatavyaktiyogaḥ, tān āśrayāṃs tathaiva pratipādayet śabdaḥ | na hy anythobhayavyaktisaṃbaddhā pratipāditā bhavati | tathā ca sati sa evāstyādipadāprayogapra saṅgaḥ ||

(211.21) athaivaṃ matiḥ yat tad ubhayavyaktisaṃbandhi rūpaṃ tad asyāḥ śabdena coditam eva, na tu tatsaṃbandhinīnām ubhay-īnāṃ vyaktīnāṃ pratītiḥ | na hy ekasaṃbandhipratītiḥ saṃbandh-yantarapratītim avaśyam anvākarṣati putrādipratītivad iti cet |evaṃ sati saṃbandhinām apratītau na saṃbandhasyāpi pratītiḥ | yataḥ, dviṣṭha-saṃbandhasaṃvittir naikarūpapravedanāt | dvayasvarūpagrahaṇe sati saṃbandhavedanam ||[49] tato yathā tattvataḥ kasycit putro 'pi pitṛsaṃbandhānavadhāraṇe puruṣamātrarūpaḥ pratīto ghaṭavat svatan-traḥ, tathā sāmānyasaṅkhātam api vastu svatantraṃ pratīyamānaṃ na sāmānyarūpatayā pratītaṃ bhavatīti caturthapakṣapratikṣepaḥ | tadāpi saṃbandhinām anākṣepād astyādipadāprayogaḥ siddhaḥ, svatantre hi tasmin niścīyamāne tasyaiva bhāvābhāvābhyaṃ astyādiprayogeṇa bhāvyam, nānyasya | saṃbandhāvadhāraṇe 'pi hi naikasaṃbandhino bhāvābhāvābhyām itarasyāstyādipadaprayogaḥ | na hi caitrasya bhāvābhāvābhyāṃ tatputratvenāvadhārito 'pi maitro 'sti nāsti veti saṃ-bandham arhati, kiṃ punaḥ saṃbandhābodhi sāmānyaṃ? anyādṛśas tatra saṃbandha iti cet? kīdṛśo 'pi vā bhavatu, pratītim anārūḍhaḥ punar asatkalpa eveti nānyadīyabhāvābhāvābhyām ayaḥśalākākal-pasya pratītasyāstyādipadaprayogo yogam anveti, atiprasaṅgāt | svarūpaṃ cāsya sadāvasthāyi pratipāditam ity astipadavaiyarthyaṃ, nāstipadavirodhaś ca tadavasthaḥ |

(212.11) tasmān nānyathāsiddhaṃ bhāvābhāvasādhāraṇyam aikāntikaṃ ca bāhyaviṣayatvasādhane vikalpapratibhāsasya | niyamavatī hi viṣayavyavasthā nimittavattayā vyāptā | na ca viṣayasadasattāprasādhanād anyat nimittam upapadyate, atiprasaṅgād | tatas tadabhāve vyāpakābhāvād abhavantī viṣayavattā sadasattvaprasādhana eva niyamyamānā tena vyāpteti tadvirodhini katham avatiṣṭhet? yaj jñānaṃ yatra bhāvābhāvasādhāraṇapratibhāsaṃ, na tena tasya viṣayavattvam, [13a] yathā gojñānasyāśvena | bāhye ca bhāvābhāvasādhāraṇapratibhāsaṃ vṛkṣavikalpajñānam iti vyāpakaviruddhopalabdhiḥ | tadviṣayatvavyāpakasya bhāvābhāvaprasādhanasya hi viruddhaṃ tadaprasādhanarūpaṃ sādhāraṇyam | evaṃ jātimadvyaktivacane 'pi doṣa eva | vyakteś cet pratītisiddhiḥ, jātir adhikā pratīyatāṃ mā vā, na tu taddoṣān muktiḥ |

(212.19) yac coktaṃ kaumārilaiḥ, sabhāgatvād eva vastuno na sādhāraṇyadoṣaḥ, vṛkṣatvaṃ hy anirdhāritabhāvābhāvaṃ śabdād avagamyate, tayor anyatareṇa śabdāntarāvagatena saṃbadhyata iti | tatrāpi vṛkṣatvam iti yadi jātir vivakṣitā, tadā taddūṣaṇenaiva nirvṛtiḥ | athāparāmṛṣṭabhedābhedam eva vṛkṣatvam, tadā tad avaśyaṃ bhāve 'bhāve vā niyataṃ, śabdena ca tathaiva khyāpitam iti kim astyādipadenādyāpi?

(212.24) syād etat | tanniyatatve 'pi vṛkṣatvāṅga eva śabdena codito na sattvāsattvāṅga iti cet. tayor aṃśayos tarhi bhedaḥ kālpanikas tāttviko vā? kālpanikatve, iyaṃ gavy avastunīva pratiyatī śābdī buddhiḥ kathaṃ vastuviṣayeti siddhaṃ | tāttvikatve vṛkṣaḥ sann iti sāmānādhikaraṇyānupapattiḥ, ghaṭapaṭavat | ekavastuniyatau dharmāv iti nyāyadarśanavitpratikṣepo vakṣyate | bhedābhedapakṣo 'pi kṣipto 'nyatra |

(213.03) yac cedaṃ na ca pratyakṣasyeva śabdānām arthapratyāyanaprakāro yena taddṛṣṭa ivāstyādiśabdāpekṣā na syāt, vicitraśaktitvāt pramāṇānām iti | tad apy ekārthatve bhinnāvabhāsadūṣaṇena dūṣitaṃ | tato yadi pratyakṣārthapratipādanaṃ śabdena tadvad evāvabhāsaḥ syāt, abhavaṃs ca na tadviṣayakhyāpanaṃ kṣamate | tad asyāpi vicitraśaktitvaṃ pramāṇānāṃ vastusvarūpānubhavādhyavasāyamātrakṛtam eva, naikārthatve 'pi pratibhāsabhedakṛtaṃ[50], tadbhede ekārthatāyāḥ pramāṇabādhitatvād iti | tasmād avasthitam etan na svalakṣaṇābhidhāne dharmiṇo vidhiniṣedhayoga[51] iti kṛtaṃ padaprayogeṇeti |

[213.10] nāpi dharmāṇāṃ, vṛkṣapadena hi dharmiṇo 'dhyakṣavat sarvātmanā pratipāditatvāt ko 'vakāśaḥ padāntareṇa nīlatvādividhiniṣedhayoḥ pramāṇāntareṇa vā? pratyakṣe 'pi pramāṇāntarāpekṣā dṛṣṭeti cet? bhavatu tasyāpy aniścayātmakatvād anabhyastasvarūpaviṣaye | vikalpas tu svayaṃ niścayātmako yatra grāhī tatra kim apareṇa? asti ca śabdaliṅgāntarāpekṣā | tato na vastusvarūpagrahaḥ, kiṃtv ekadharmacchāyānukārivikalpodayasaṃvedanam eveti siddham |

(213.15) na siddham, bhinnā hi jātyādayo dharmāḥ parasparaṃ dharmiṇaś ceti jātyekadharmadvāreṇa pratīte 'pi śākhini dharmāntaravattayā na pratītir iti kiṃ na bhinnābhidhānādhīno dharmāntarasya nīlacaloccaistaratvāder avabodhaḥ? tad ayuktam, yadi hi bhedād dharmiṇaḥ pratītāv api na dharmāṇāṃ śabdaliṅgadvāreṇa bodhaḥ, indriyadvāreṇāpi mā bhūt | athendriyasya saṃyogasamavāyabalāt sannikṛṣṭe dharmini [13b] samavāyādisaṃnikarṣabhājo dharmā api pratītigocarībhavantīty ucyate, liṅgasyāpīyaṃ sāmagrī na khalu kalayāpi hīyate | śabdasya tu yady api na vācyena saha saṃyogasamavāyau, vācyavācakabhāvalakṣaṇā tu pratyāsattir iṣṭaiva, tadabhāve vācyapratīter evābhāvaprasaṅgāt | pratītau vā kīdṛśī saṃyogāder apekṣā? etac ca svābhāvikasaṃbandhāvalambinām api liṅgād vastupratītau tulyam | na ca śabdadvāreṇa pratītau pravṛttinimittarodhinī vyavadhānaśaṅkā | jātimatī hi vyaktiḥ sakṛd eva śabdād avasīyate bhavatām | krameṇa tv ekaikabodhān na kadāpi jātimadvyaktibodhaḥ syāt | na ca niścayakramopalambhaḥ | tasmāt jātir adhikā pratīyatāṃ nāma, vyaktis tu dharmiṇī pratīyamānā na svasamavetaguṇakriyādīn apratipādya svāsthyam āsādayet | anyathā pratyakṣe 'py aparopādhibuddhir anibandhanā syāt |

(214.01) athaivaṃ sati śabdair vyaktibodhanam evāstu kim upādhisāhityasvīkāreṇeti cet? tat kim idānīṃ bhavadupagamavaiyarthyabhayād bhāvaiḥ svabhāvaparityāgaḥ kartavyaḥ? tad ayam aparas tavāstu doṣo na vā, na tu kvacid gocare jñānasādhanais tatsaṃbandhināṃ bodham asādhayitvā sthātavyam indriyavat | athendriyād eva tathā dṛṣṭam iti nānyatra prasaṅga iti cet? evaṃ tarhi tṛṇavahnir indhanavikārakriyānāntarīyakadhūmotpādanasamartho dṛṣṭa iti khādiras tathā na syāt | sāmānyena tu vyāptir ubhayatrāpīti na viśeṣaḥ | tato yadi khādire vikāravirahaḥ tadā nāsau dhūmo 'pi tu vātyāsaṃvalitadhūlinivahaḥ | na vā tatra dhūmadhvajaḥ, kiṃ tu kāntimatpadmarāgaratnarāśiraśmisaṃhatir ucchrāyavatī | yadi punar asau dhūmaḥ sa ca dhūmadhvajaḥ khadire[52] cāvaśyaṃ[53] vikāra iti, tathā yady asau dharmibodhas tatsādhanaś ca śabdo, niyataṃ tadāśrayadharmabodhadoṣaḥ | na cet tadāśrayadharmabodhaḥ, tadā nāsau dharmibodho nāpi dharmibodhanaḥ śabdaḥ | yat kvacit jñānasādhanaṃ tat tadīyadharmāṇāṃ pratītisādhananiyataṃ yathendriyam | tathā ca liṅgaśabdau parokṣābhimatasya pratītisādhanāv iṣṭau taveti svabhāvaḥ prasaṅgahetuḥ | na caivaṃ śabdaliṅgāntarāpekṣaṇāt | yan na yatsamavetadharmabodhasādhanaṃ na tat tasya svarūpajñānajanakam, yathā gośabdas turage, turago vā gardabhe, na bodhayataś ca godhvanidhūmau[54] svaviṣayābhimatasamavetadharmāntaram iti viparyaye vyāpakānupalabdhiḥ | jātiguṇakriyādirahitasya svapne 'pi darśanaśaṅkāvirahād vastudarśanaṃ tatsattāmātrabhāvinā dharmāntarajñānena vyāpyata ity ubhayor api prayogayor nānekāntaḥ | bheda eva hi jātyādīnāṃ vivādaḥ | samavetaśabdas tv abhedapakṣe 'pi kalpanābuddhau bhinnavadābhāsamānānām apṛthakprathanaparaḥ | tad varam abheda eva dharmāṇām astu, [14a] sarvathā vastupratītisvīkāre dharmāṇāṃ pratīticodyasya duṣpariharatvāt, kim anubhavabhraṣṭabhedābhyupagamena? svabhāvā eva bhāvasya jātyādayaḥ |

(214.22) yat tu bhāṣaṇaṃ bhūṣaṇasya, na yat svabhāvasaṃbandhi sa svabhāvaḥ, tathā saty asaṃbandhitvam eva, na hi tad eva tena saṃbadhyata[55] iti | tad asat | svabhāvasaṃbandhīty atraiva svabhāvaḥ kasyacid vastuno vivakṣitaḥ, na ca tayor bhedaḥ | bhede hi svabhāvatvam ity alaukikam etat | tat kathaṃ tad eva tena saṃbaddham iti parihṛtam, anyathāsya svabhāva iti ṣaṣṭhīnirdeśānupapatteḥ | atha svabhāva iti jātyādir evocyata iti na doṣaḥ | doṣa eva,[56] yadā jātyādikaṃ vivicya vastumātrasvabhāvaparāmarśaḥ | na hy asau vastunaḥ kevalasya svabhāvo na vaktavyaḥ | sa eva ca yat svabhāvasaṃbandhīty atra vivakṣitaḥ, saṃbandhiśabdena jātyāder vivakṣitatvāt | tasmād yato yad abhinnam api kalpanayā bhinnam eva darśitam, tat tasya saṃbandhīti vyavahāro duṣpariharaḥ ||

(215.03) yac ca vācaspatiḥ, na caikopādhinā sattvena viśiṣṭe 'smin gṛhīte upādhyantaraviśiṣṭatadgrahaḥ, svabhāvo hi dravyasyopādhibhir viśiṣyate, na tūpādhayo tair viśiṣṭatvaṃ vā tasya svabhāva iti[57] | tad api plavata eva | na hy abhedād upādhyantaragrahaṇam āsañjitam, ākare 'py upakāryopakārakadvāreṇa[58] bhedaṃ puraskṛtyaiva sarvākāragrahaṇaprasañjanāt | śaktīnāṃ tu śaktimatoḥ abheda uktaḥ | tad anenāpi na spṛṣṭam |

(215.08) yat punas tatra dūṣaṇaṃ bhūṣaṇena, sūryādigrahaṇe tad upakāryāśeṣavasturāśigrahaṇaprasañjanam uktam, tad abhiprāyānavagāhanaphalam, tathā hīdam ākūtam | svayaṃ vakṣyamāṇasamavāyaniṣedhaṃ sthirīkṛtya bhavatā naiyāyikapravareṇa pratyakṣakāle 'kṣasaṃbandham anubhavitari dharmiṇi dharmāṇāṃ jātyādīnāṃ bhedābhyupagamād upakāryatayaiva tadupakārakaśaktyabhedāt pratipattir eṣitavyā | na hy anupakāre kvacit kasyacit pratibandho bhedavata iti śaktyabhedāpādanamukhenāha, ... bhede tās tasya kiṃ yadi |nopakāras tatas tāsāṃ tathā syād anavasthitiḥ ||[59] iti |

(215.16) yat tu śaktir nāma sahajā jātir aupādhikī ca sahakārisākalyam ato bhennaivety ālambanam, tad dūṣayitvā kṣaṇabhaṅgādhyāye kāryakriyāpravṛtta eva svabhāvaḥ śaktir ity eva nirvāhitam | upakāraś ca samānakāryārjanasvabhāvo 'kāryasyāpi saṃbhavatīty api tatraiva dhvastam | kāryopakāryayor api tattvato nāsty eva bhedaḥ, vyavahāre punar apūrvotpattau soktāpohāt[60] kāryatā | pūrvasthitābhimānaviṣaye tu viśeṣānubhavād upakāryatocyate | tattvatas tu pūrvasthitaś cādhunā viśiṣṭaś ceti viruddham eva | tad iha sthirābhimatajātipuraskāreṇa cintāyāṃ kāryatāniṣtha evopakāryavyavahāraḥ, tattvata ekārthatayā veti na doṣaḥ | tad evam avaśyābhyupagantavyāyām upakāralakṣaṇāyāṃ pratyāsattau sūryopakāryādibhir anubhavavyabhicāraḥ [14b] prasajyāyātaḥ sādhāraṇa evāvayoḥ |

(216.01) yat tu vācaspatiḥ, svābhāvikaś ca saṃbandho vyakter jātyā saha nopakāram apekṣata iti | tatra na svābhāviko nāma yathāprasiddhād anya eva kaścit saṃbandhaḥ, kiṃtu saṃyogādisattāyām eva saṃbandhinor vyabhicārāvyabhicāreṇa vṛttibhedād aupādhikaḥ, svābhāvikaś ca sambandha iti vyavasthāmātram | etadvicāraś ca vyāpticarcāyām apekṣitavyaḥ | yathā ca jātyā saha vyaktes tadavyabhicārāt svābhāvikaḥ saṃbandhas tathā jāter api vyaktyā sahāvyabhicārād eva, nirviśeṣaṃ na sāmānyaṃ bhavet śaśaviṣāṇavat[61] iti nyāyāt | tad anayoḥ pratyāsattyantarābhāvāt samavāyasya ca kalpanāmātratvād yady upakāryopakārakabhāvo 'pi parasparam asann avanibījādivat, avyabhicāraniyama eva bhedābhyupagamavyasaninām atiprasaṅgād anupapannaḥ | upakāre hi svabhāvas tadviśeṣo vā tannāntarīya[ka] ity evāvybhicārārtho nānyatreti nātiprasaṅgaḥ |

(216.12) tadabhāve tu dvidhā tatparihāraḥ svabhāvavādaṃ samavāyabalaṃ vāvalambya | nādyaḥ pakṣaḥ, sarvasya yatra kvacana dṛṣṭaśakter viparyāsanaprasaṅgāt | dṛṣṭaś copakāro vahniśilpijalādau[62] dhūmakumbhabalāhakāder[63] avyabhicārahetuḥ | kevalaṃ kāladeśādyapekṣayeti viśeṣaḥ | tato bhede 'pi svabhāvād evāvyabhicāro nopakāra iti bruvatā niyamena sāmarthyam apohitam | dvitīyapakṣaś cāsambhavī, samavāyasyaivābhāvāt | ihedam iti buddhisādhano hi samavāyo 'bhyupagataḥ, sā ca buddhir na samānasaṅketagrahatimiranikurambakarambitadṛśām upādeyā, sarvasya sarvārthasiddhiprasaṅgāt | icchāmātraparatantrodayatvād vikalpānām | anyasya ca lokasya nāsty eva vivādapade sarvatra sā buddhiḥ, kāraṇābhāvāt | parasparārūpāsaṅkīrṇavastudvayapratibhāso hi kāraṇam ihedam iti saptamīprathamārthavibhāgam utkalayato vikalpasya, kumbhe 'mbhaḥsaṃbhave 'pi kumbhamātropalambhinaḥ sakalānyakāraṇakalāpavatas tadabhāvāt | tādṛgavasthasya ca paścād dvitīyopalambhamātre bhāvāt | na cāsau dvayapratibhāsaḥ kvacid api samavāyaviṣaye 'stīti saṃyogakalpanāviṣaya eva tadvikalpaviṣayaḥ | yatrānātmarūpaparihāreṇa nobhayopalambho na tatredam iheti pratītir anunmattasya, yathā pātrabadarayor ekānupalambhe | nāsti cātmātmīyarūpapratibhāsabhedena jātitadvator anubhava iti kāraṇānupalabdhiḥ | dhūmāgnivat kāryakāraṇabhāvasya vivakṣitayoḥ sādhanān nānekāntaḥ | tad amī svayaṃkṛtaśabdenārthāntaram upakalpayantas turagatulām anupatantīty etad eva vakṣyati, paṭas tantuṣv ihetyādiśabdāś ceme svayaṃkṛtāḥ |[64] iti |

[217.01] nanu nirvikalpakabodhena dvyātmakasyāpi vastuno grahaṇam ity uktam, tat kathaṃ na svarūpadvayapratibhāsa [15a] ity asiddhā kāraṇānupalabdhiḥ? tad etat pāpīyaḥ | na hi pratyakṣagamye 'rthe paropadeśo garīyān | pratibhāso 'pi tatheti cet ? tad etad āyātam, etāsu pañcasu avabhāsinīṣu pratyakṣabodhe sphuṭam aṅgulīṣu | sādhāraṇaṃ ṣaṣṭham ihekṣate yaḥ śṛṅgaṃ śirasy ātmana īkṣate saḥ || iti | vayaṃ hi tāvac carmacakṣuṣaḥ cakṣuṣī sudūram unmīlya śatakṛtvo nirūpayanto 'pi nāparam upalabhāmahe, bhavatas tv adṛṣṭadevatāprasādāt tathā pratibhāse 'pi netarasya tathā bodhasiddhiḥ |

(217.09) tena pratyakṣam eva draṣṭavyaṃ yad ekam anekasādhāraṇaṃ draṣṭṝṇāṃ darśayatīty ācakṣāṇaḥ trilocano 'py anyalocaneneva vīkṣata iti lakṣyate | yac cāha dṛśyamānāpi jātir apṛthagdeśavartitvād vyaktito bhedena vyaktyantaravan na dṛśyata iti | tatrāpi dṛśyate jātir na tu bhedeneti bruvatā niyamād abhedena pratyakṣagocara ity uktaṃ bhavati | yathā ca pratykṣeṇa gṛhītaṃ tavaiva samastaṃ vastu na khalu tatra bādhakasādhakayor yogaḥ | tataś ca pratyayānuvṛttis tu vyakteḥ sāmānyaṃ bhetsyatīty upapattivarṇanam anavakāśam | yathā spārśanaḥ pratyayo gandhādibhyaḥ sparśaṃ bhinattīty api na yuktam uktam | na hi gandhasparśayor apy abhedagrāhi pratyakṣam | evaṃ tarhi bhedena na dṛśyata iti bhedena na vyavasīyata iti vyākhyāyatām, tadāpi dṛśyamānāpi jātir iti kiṃ bhedenābhedena veti vivakṣitam? yady abhedena, tadā vyavasāyo bhedenābhedena vāstu, kim asya cintayā, pratyakṣeṇābhedasya siddhatvāt? atha bhedena dṛśyamāneti vivakṣitam? tat punar aśakyam, pratibhāsabhedābhāvasyoktatvāt | yuktyā sādhyate pratibhāsabheda iti cet? tad etat lajjākaram | yataḥ, [217.22] kasyacit pratibhāsena sādhyate 'pratibhāsi yat | pratibhāso 'sya nāsyeti nopapattes tu gocaraḥ ||[65] iti vivecitam asmābhir ahetukābhāvaprastāve | kiṃ ca yady ekākārapratibhāse 'pi pratibhāsāntaraṃ yuktisādhyam abhyupeyate, tadānuṣṇo vahnir iti na pratyakṣabādhyam abhidheyam, anuṣṇapratibhāsasyāpi tatra saṃbhavāt, vyaktau jātipratibhāsavat |

(218.05) anuṣṇapratibhāsasya citrabhānau sādhanābhāvān na sāmyam iti cet? tathāpi saṃśayo 'stv iti katham anuṣṇasya bādhakam adhyakṣam, kathaṃ ca sādhanābhāvaḥ, prameyatvasya vidyamānatvāt? avyabhicārī hetur iti cet? vyabhicāro 'pi sākṣāt paramparayā vā pratyakṣād eva | tatra ca viparītapratibhāso niṣeddhum aśakya ity uktam | yadi cānaikāntikatayā prameyatvān na siddhir anuṣṇatāyā hetudoṣāt tarhi dṛṣṭam anuṣṇo 'gnir iti nāyaṃ pakṣadoṣaḥ, tato 'nuṣṇatvābādhanāt | sādhanam api nādhyakṣam | uṣṇam eva hi uṣṇam | na punar uṣṇānuṣṇam | tasmān niyatapratibhāsasaṃvedanam anyapratibhāsasya niyamena bādhakam abhyupagantavyam akāmakenāpi, anyathā pravṛttisaṅkaraprāpteḥ | tathā ca, na hy ayam analaṃ [15b] paśyann ityādi | tato yad oghapatitair udghuṣyate, jātimatīṣu vyaktiṣu saṅkete kṛte yatra yatra jātidarśanaṃ tatra tatra tacchabdavācyatāpratītir iti, tad asūtram ambaraṃ viḍambayati, svalakṣaṇavilakṣaṇasya svapne 'py anupalakṣaṇāt | ata eva svarūpamātreṇa gṛhītāv upādhitadvantau yojayato vikalpasya prāmāṇyam iṣṭaṃ yat tat pratyādiṣṭam, pūrvaṃ dvayadarśanasyaivābhāvāt | tasmān na kāraṇānupalabdher asiddhiḥ | asiddhiḥ punar iheti pratyayasyeti kva samavāyavārtā? vārtaṃ caitad vyakter jātyā saha svābhāvikaḥ saṃbandha iti? tataś ca yady adyāpy upādhitadvatāṃ[66] bhedavādo duṣpariharaḥ, tadopakāralakṣaṇāyām api pratyāsattau samānadeśasyaiva grahaṇe vastugrāhiṇaḥ śaktir iti samānaḥ sūkṣmopakāryavyabhicāraparihāraḥ |

(218.22) tasmād ekadharmadvāreṇāpi vastusvarūpapratītau sarvātmapratīteḥ kva śabdāntareṇa vidhiniṣedhāvakāśa iti kim adyāpi kevalavṛkṣapadena? tataś ca kva sāmānyasāmānādhikaraṇyaviśeṣaṇaviśeṣyabhāvavyavasthā? yadā tu, vācyaṃ vastu na kiñcana ||[67] yasyābhidhānato vastusāmarthyād akhile gatiḥ | bhaven nānāphalaḥ śabda ekādhāro bhavaty ataḥ ||[68] vastuni hi vācye sarvātmanā pratipatter vidhiniṣedhayor ayogaḥ | yadā punar anādivitathavikalpābhyāsavāsanāvaśād ekavyāvṛttyākāraśekharā buddhir eva kutaścid vāsanāprabodhād udayam āsādayati, tadā vastugrahaṇasāmarthyabhāvinām uktadoṣāṇāṃ kvāvakāśaḥ? tathā hi vṛkṣa ity ukte dhavakhadirādisādhāraṇa rūpapratibhāsavaśāt sāmānyam avṛkṣāpohaparamārtham avasthāpyate | tac ca rūpam apratikṣiptānupāttasattāsattvādibhedatayā[69] padāntaraprayogasāpekṣam ity ekatra dharmiṇi dharmyantaranibandhanair iva sannīlacalādipadaiḥ sāmānādhikaraṇyaṃ ca, tadā buddhyanurodhataḥ ekabhedacodanāpekṣāyāṃ vṛkṣasya sattvam iti bhedanirdeśaś ceti dvividho 'pi viśeṣaṇaviśeṣyabhāvaḥ siddhaḥ |

(219.10) evaṃ ca sati yathā pṛthvīruhe pātho'gnisaṅgamād upacayāpacayau dṛṣṭau, ekatvāropāc ca sa evāyaṃ pādapa īdṛśo jāta iti pratītiḥ, sa ca dharmāṇāṃ tatsaṃbandhayogyānām anudaye 'pi tadyogya iva vyavasīyate, tathā vikalpe 'pi vṛkṣākāro dharmāntarāpratibhāse 'pi tadyogyo nīlo na phalina ityādiprayoge copacayāpacayabhāg iva bhāsate sa eveti cāvasīyate, na tathā bāhyo jalādisamparkavac chabdoccāraṇakāle 'py upacayāpacayavān | etac ca na bāhyaviṣayatve yuktam yathāpratibhāsam atattvāt, yathātattvaṃ cāpratibhāsanāt | ata eva caitrasya gaur gomān maitro nāśvavān iti bhinnaviśeṣaṇāpekṣayāpi na padāntaraprayogayogaḥ, tadkṛtopacayāpacayapratibhāsasya bahir abhāvāt |

(219.19) tasmād buddhivilāsa evaiṣaḥ | yatra cāyaṃ viplavaḥ paramparayā parāpoḍhavastunāntarīyakaḥ [16a] tatrābhimatārthakriyākṛtārtho janas tādṛśaṃ viśeṣam ūhituṃ na prayatnavān, nāpi kṣama ity anavacchinno vyavahāraḥ visaṃvāde 'pi mṛṣedam iti na vyavasthāpayati | na punar anyadāpi bāhyenāviṣayatvam iti śāstrakārāṇām apy abhyūhasaṃbhavāt |[70] kā parasya kathā? tasmān na svalakṣaṇsya śabdādigocaratvam iti sthitam ||

ekaṃ dharmiṇam ākalayya vividhavyāvṛttidharmāśrayaṃ tatraikaikavidhānabādhanavidhāv apy avyayābhāsinam[71] | mukhyā buddhir iyaṃ yathā bhramayati bhrāmyaṃs tathāyaṃ janas tattvāṃśena kṛtārthatām upagato nopaplavaṃ manyate || iti saṃgrahaślokaḥ ||

[220.02] nāpi sāmānyalaṣaṇasya | tathā hi uttaratīre saritaś caranti gāva iti vākye gavādiśabdāt sāsnāśṛṅgalāṅgūlādayo 'kṣarākāraparikarāḥ sajātīyabhedāparāmarśāt saṃpiṇḍitaprāyāḥ pratibhāsante, na ca tad eva sāmānyam, varṇākṛtyakṣarākāraśūnyaṃ gotvaṃ hi kathyate |[72] na cāparam ākāśavat kiñcit pratibhāti | anyathā gotvāśvatvavikalpayor aviśeṣaprasaṅgāt | tad eva hi jvaladbhāsurākāramātram akhilavyaktāv atyantavilakṣaṇam api svalakṣaṇena ekīkriyamāṇaṃ sāmānyam ity ucyate | na tu tat sāmānyam eva tāsām, buddhyākāratvenānyatrānugamāt | śāstraṃ hi, buddher[73] avyatiriktaṃ ca katham arthāntaraṃ vrajet |[74] na cālocanānantarajanmanīndriyārthajanyatayābhimate so 'yaṃ, tādṛśo 'yaṃ, gaur ayam iti vā vikalpe 'rthāntarapratibhāsaḥ | yathā tu saṃpiṇḍitākāram alaukikam ātmani pratibhāsamānaṃ puraḥ pratibhāsini piṇḍe yojayati, tathā tasya bāhyasyābhāvād brāntir evāsau, keśaprakāśavat |

(220.15) bādhakād evam iti cet? nanu prayatnapraṇihitapāṇipratighātādyabhāvāt keśapāśe visaṃvādaḥ, prastute tu yadi paribhāvako bhavati sa eva vaktavyaḥ | vyaktyanubhavo[75] bādhakaḥ kim apareṇa? janasya tu vivecanāsāmarthyam ity uktam eva | kathaṃ vā karapratighātādiviraho 'dyāpi na bādhakaḥ? ta eva hi śṛṅgādayo yathāsthānaniveśino 'spaṣṭarūpā apratiṣṭhitadeśadaśāviśeṣā deśakālādibhedād anantamūrtayaḥ saṅkīryamāṇā ivādyāpi bhāsante, teṣāṃ pratighātādiniyatatvāt kīdṛśaḥ keśādibhyo bhedaḥ, yato nātra bādhakam iti syāt?

(220.21) tasmād vāsanāvaśād buddher eva tadātmanā vivarto 'yam astu, asad eva vā tad rūpaṃ khyātu, vyaktaya eva vā sajātīyabhedatiraskāreṇānyathā bhāsantām, anubhavavyavadhānāt smṛtipramoṣo vābhidhīyatām, sarvathā bhrāntir eveyaṃ bahirapekṣayā sāmānyavārtā, idaṃtayā ca purovartivastvanubhavaprabhavatayā bhavituṃ yuktaiva |

(221.02) nanu bhrāntihetavas timirāśubhramaṇādaya indriyavikārakāriṇaḥ parigaṇitā eva | na ca tatraikasyāpi sannidhir iti katham iyam ākasmikī bhrāntiḥ? atha nirvikalpakabhrānter eva hetavas te, iyaṃ ca mānasī bhrāntir iti manyase. [16b] sāpy ārōpyāropaviṣayayoḥ sādṛśyadarśananibandhanaiveti tādṛgavibhāgābhāvāt kathaṃ mānasy api bhrāntiḥ? sarvā ca bhrāntiḥ sādṛśyanibandhanaiva, na khalu janmāntare 'pi sadṛśadarśanam antareṇa bhavitum arhati | na ca saṃbhinnākāraṃ kiñcij janmāntare 'pi dṛṣṭam iti kathaṃ tadāropaḥ? aho mahat pauruṣam | tathā hi nirviṣayatvaṃ tāvad uktena krameṇa na cet parihartuṃ śakyate, bhrāntivyavahāraṃ kuryā[76] mā vā, tāvataiva prakṛtasiddheḥ kim atra nirbandhena?

(221.11) yat punar ākasmikatvam uktaṃ tad ayuktam | janakasāmagrībhedasya bhavatāpy avaśyasvīkaraṇīyatvāt | katham anyathā indriyārthau nirvikalpakajñānajananiyatau dṛṣṭau vikalpam utpādayataḥ? tasmāt pūrvapiṇḍadarśanasmaraṇasahakāriṇātiricyamānasāmarthyeyaṃ sāmagrī vikalpam utpādayatīti nirviṣayaṃ jñānam utpādayatīty evārthaḥ,[77] nirviṣayatāniṣṭhatvād vikalpatāyās tadaṃśena | tad varaṃ vijātīyavikalpavad vispaṣṭapratibhāsād anubhavād bhinna eva sajātīyavikalpo 'pīty eva sādhu, tasmān na jātisiddhir adhyakṣāt |

(221.17) nāpy anumānāt, adhyakṣagocaratayaiva kenacid agnidhūmavat kāryakāraṇabhāvasya grahītum aśakyatvāt | sāmānyena tu jñānajanmani yathā paridṛṣṭakāraṇebhyaḥ kāraṇāntaram apekṣaṇīyam indriyavat kadācit sidhyet yadi sakalānyakāraṇasannidhau kadācid abhimatajñānakāryābhāvaṃ vibhāvayet | na caivaṃ prastute śakyam | yadā hi piṇḍāntare 'ntarāle vā gobuddher abhāvaṃ darśayet, tadā gopiṇḍasyaivābhāvāt abhāvo gobuddher upapadyamānaḥ katham arthāntarāpekṣām ākṣipet, yatas tad eva gotvam iti pratyāśā syāt?

(221.22) nanu gopiṇḍa iti gotvād eva sāmānyād anyathā turagapiṇḍo 'pi gopiṇḍaḥ syāt | yady evaṃ gotvam api sāmānyaṃ gopiṇḍād eva, anyathā turagatvam api gotvaṃ syād iti samānam | na cādṛśyasya sāmānyasya bhāvābhāvau kvacit niścetuṃ śakyau piṇḍavad iti na kiñcid etat | athāpi syād yadi bāhuleyapiṇḍābhāvāt turage na gobuddhiḥ, śābaleye 'pi mā bhūt, svalakṣaṇasya kvacid ananvayāt | satyam ananvayi svalakṣaṇam, yathā tu svajātīyapiṇḍāntaradarśanasmaraṇavati prattipattari tadākārapratyavamarśajananasāmarthyaṃ bāhuleyasya tathā śābaleyasyāpi | tato naika eva gopiṇḍo 'pi tu tādṛgvikalpārohiṇaḥ sarva eva piṇḍāḥ | atas turage na gopratyayaḥ |

(222.03) nanu sāmarthyaṃ śaktir iti jātir evocyate | sā hi śaktir bhinnā vā syād abhinnā vā? yady abhinnā, tadā svalakṣaṇavad ananugāminīti netaraḥ śaktaḥ | atha bhinnā, anyasādhāraṇo ca, tadā jātir evāsāv iti nāmni vivādaḥ | atrocyate | abhinnaiva sā prativastu, yathā tv ekaḥ śaktasvabhāvo bhāvas tathānyo 'pi bhavan kīdṛśaṃ [17a] doṣam āvahati? yathā hi bhavatāṃ jātir ekāpi samānadhīdhvaniprasavahetur anyāpi svarūpeṇaiva jātyantaravirahāt, tathā 'smākaṃ vyaktir api nirapekṣā svarūpeṇaiva bhinnāpi hetuḥ | tat tu svarūpaṃ vyakteḥ kāraṇaparamparāpratibaddham |

(222.10) yat tu trilocanaḥ, aśvatvagotvādīnāṃ sāmānyaviśeṣāṇāṃ svāśrayeṣu samavāyaḥ sāmānyam ity abhidhānapratyayayor nimittam iti | tat samavāyanirākaraṇenaivāpahastitam | samavāya eva vā svarūpeṇaiva nimittam iti na dṛṣṭāntakṣatiḥ | na ca jātisamavāyayoḥ sahakriyākalpanenānyonyaśaktitvam, tadā hi svarūpeṇaikasyāpi janakatvam iti sāmānyābhidhānadhiyor datto jalāñjaliḥ | svarūpeṇa janakānām eva hi bījādīnāṃ sahakārisākalyam aupādhikī śaktir iti svarūpeṇa janakatvam avaśyavācyam iti samavāyāvalambanaṃ viḍambaḥ | na ca tadvyāpāravirahe tadākāravedanodayaḥ kāraṇāntaramātrāt, anyathānuvṛttākārasyāpi pratyayasya janmani svalakṣaṇair eva kiṃ na nirvṛttir iti cintāpi jāteḥ samūlakāṣaṃ kaṣitā syāt | ākasmikatve 'pi sa eva doṣa iti gale pādikayā jātisvīkāriṇo 'nuvṛttapratyaye svarūpeṇaiva jātivyāpāram anavasthābhayāt svayam evānāropitajātyantarāḥ svīkārayitavyā iti kathaṃ samavāyena parihāraḥ? sa punar adhikaḥ sahakārī bhavatu mā vā bhūt, jātis tu jātinirapekṣā svarūpeṇa śaktimatī anuvṛttapratyayaṃ janayati, svabhāvasyāparyanuyojyatvān na vyaktir iti na rājñām ājñām antareṇa śakyam abhidhātum |

(222.23) etena seyaṃ pratyayānuvṛttir anuvṛttavastvanuyāyinī katham atyantabhedinīṣu vyaktiṣu vyāvṛttapratyayaviṣayabhāvānupātinīṣu bhavitum arhatīty apy ūhapravartanam asya pratyākhyātam, jātiṣv eva parasparavyāvṛttatayā vyaktīyamānāsv anuvṛttapratyayena vyabhicārāt |

(222.25) atha jātīnām adarśanāt kvānuvṛttaprayayo yato vyabhicāra iti cet—na, abhyupagamavirodhasya anena krameṇa pratipādanāt | tathā hi pratyayānuvṛttir anuvṛttavastusādhanāyopanīyate, sā cānuvṛttavastvabhāvanāntarīyikā yady anuvṛttavastusiddhir iti ka imaṃ vyāghātam udvoḍhuṃ śakto 'nyatra jāḍyāt? kiṃ ca kalpitāsv api jātiṣu vyabhicāras tadavastha eva kim atra darśanena?

(223.05) atha dṛśyamāneṣv artheṣu niyama ucyate—na, tatrāpi viparyayabādhakābhāvāt pratibandhānupapatteḥ | sāmānyena ca vyabhicāradarśanād anytrāpi śaṅkābījam | yadi ca dṛśyaviśeṣāpekṣayā sāmānyavyabhicāraparihāraḥ, tadā na vaktavyaṃ yā bhinneṣv abhidhānapratyayānuvṛttir asāv anuvṛttavastunimittā, yathā kusumeṣu sūtram ity abhidhānapratyayānuvṛttis tathā ca goṣu bhinneṣu gaur ity abhidhānapratyayānuvṛttir iti | dṛśyamānanimittatāyām evābhidhānaprayayānuvṛtter anuvṛttavastunimittatayā vyāpter viśrāmaniyamāt | yuktaṃ caitat | na khalu sūtre 'pi [17b] darśanā viṣayīkṛteṣu sūtrapratyayānuvṛttiḥ | savastuko hi vikalpo 'numānaṃ vinā vastudarśanakāryaḥ siddha iti viparyayāt kāraṇānupalabdhyā nivartamānānuvṛttavastunā pratyayānuvṛttivyāptir dṛśyanimittatāyām eva viśrāmyati, sati vastuviṣayatve | vastuviṣayatvavivāde tu nāyaṃ niyamaḥ |

(223.15) yat punar anena viparyayabādhakam uktam, abhidhānapratyayānuvṛttiḥ kutaścin nivṛttya kvacid eva bhavantī nimittavatī | na cānyan nimittam ityādi | tan na samyak | anuvṛttam antareṇāpy abhidhānapratyayānuvṛtteḥ svarūpaviśeṣād[78] avaśyaṃ svīkārasya sādhitatvāt | tasmād yathā svalakṣaṇān nivṛttya gotvāśvatvādāv eva sāmānyaṃ sāmānyam ity abhidhānapratyayānuvṛttiḥ kayācit prayāsattyā bhavati, tathā vyaktiṣv api bhavatu, etenānuvṛttavastuni sādhye 'bhidhānapratyayānuvṛttiḥ tenāsyā vyāptau ca viparyayabādhikā vyāpakānupalabdhir ity ubhayam anaikāntikam iti veditavyam | pratyāsattir ity api nāsty anyavyāvṛtter[79] anyā | yathā hi gotvam asāmānyād[80] vyāvṛttaṃ tathāśvatvadravyatvādikam api, evaṃ yathaikā govyaktir agotaḥ parāvṛttā tathā 'nyāpi | asyā api bhedābhedacintāmaukharye śaktivad evottaram | tataś ca ye 'rthā atadrūpaparāvṛttyā parasparaṃ pratyāsannās te teṣv ekadarśanānantaram aparadṛṣṭau anuvṛttapratyayam utpādayanti nānye | saiva ca śaktiḥ, na jātyātmā | anyathā ātmaikatrāpi so 'stīti vyarthāḥ syuḥ sahakāriṇaḥ |[81] etac ca kṣaṇabhaṅge sahakārivādād avadhāryam | sā ca pratyāsattiḥ kāraṇaparamparāyātety anantaram uktam eva | avaśyaṃ ca hetukṛtaḥ pratyāsattiviśeṣa eṣitavyaḥ, yataḥ kāścid eva vyaktayo jātyadhiṣṭhānabhājanībhavanti netarāḥ | anyathā hetusāmagrīniyamāc[82] ca niyatajātimat kāryam[83] bhavatīti uktam aparitrāṇaṃ bhūṣaṇasya syāt | tathā ca sati, tulye bhede yayā jātiḥ pratyāsattyā prasarpati | kvacin nānyatra saivāstu śabdajñānanibandhanam ||[84] kim atra jātyā?

(224.09) yat punar atra tenoktam aparam[85] api kucodyam, na hy evaṃ bhavati, yayā pratyāsattyā daṇḍasūtrādikaṃ prasarpati kvacin nānyatra, saiva pratyāsattiḥ puruṣasphaṭikādiṣu daṇḍisūtritvādivyavahāranibandhanam astu kiṃ daṇḍasūtrādineti? etat kadā śobhate? yadi pramāṇasiddhaṃ sāmarthyaṃ kiñcit kvacid apalapyeta | yathā hi, upasarpaṇapratyayādyāśrayā pratyāsattir daṇḍsūtrayoḥ puṃsi sphaṭike ca prasarpaṇahetuḥ pratyakṣādipramānasiddhā, tatsaṃpṛktapuruṣaspha ṭikānubhavaś ca daṇḍisūtribuddher nibandhanaṃ siddhaṃ samayasmaraṇavataḥ pratipattuḥ, tathā na gotvabhāvābhāvāv anuvidhīyamāneyaṃ gobuddhir upalabdhā, kiṃ tv andhakāre karāmarṣamātram etad īdṛśā kenacid bhavitavyaṃ gobuddhinibandhaneneti | tatra yady avaśyābhyupagantavyena prakārāntareṇa tatsiddhau na [18a] bādhas tat kiṃ gurvitarayā parikalpanayety ucyate? anyathā tad api kalpayitvānarthakārthaśatakalpanam anivāryam | yadi tu yathopasarpaṇapratyayādeḥ puruṣādau daṇḍādisannidhir bhāvābhāvam anuvidadhāno dṛṣṭaḥ dṛṣṭaś ca puruṣādau daṇḍādisannidhānānubhavabhāvānuvidhāyī daṇḍyādipratyayas tathā kāraṇakalāpasya niyatajātikatāyām eva paraṃ vyāpāraḥ | naikāmarśe[86] | ekāmarśe punar iyam asau jātir eva saṃprati vyāpāravatīty anubhūyeta, syāt tadapavaditur aparādhaḥ, yāvatā samayamātram etat, jāter anubhavātikrāntipratipādanāt iti kutas tadvaiyarthyacodanaṃ daṇḍādikam api viṣayīkuryāt? evam anyatrāpīdṛśi pratividhau bādhanam ūhyam |

(225.02) athaivam anumānam, yad viśiṣṭajñānaṃ tad viśeṣaṇagrahaṇanāntarīyakam, yathā daṇḍijñānam | viśiṣṭajñānaṃ cedaṃ gaur ayam iti pratyaya ity arthataḥ kāryahetuḥ | viśeṣaṇānubhavakāryaṃ hi dṛṣṭānte viśiṣṭabuddhiḥ siddheti | atrānuyogaḥ viśiṣṭabuddher bhinnaviśeṣaṇagrahaṇanāntarīyakatvaṃ vā sādhyam, viśeṣaṇamātrānubhavanāntarīyakatvaṃ vā? prathamapakṣe pakṣasya pratyakṣabādhā sādhanāvadhānam anavakāśayati, vastugrāhiṇaḥ pratyakṣasyobhayapratibhāsābhāvāt | viśiṣṭajñānatvaṃ ca sāmānyaṃ hetur anaikāntikaḥ, bhinnaviśeṣaṇagrahaṇam antareṇāpi darśanāt | yathā svarūpavān ghaṭaḥ, gotvaṃ sāmānyam iti vā | dvitīyapakṣe tu siddhasādhanam, svarūpavān ghaṭa ityādivat gotvajātimān piṇḍa iti kalpitaṃ bhedam upādāya viśeṣaṇaviśeṣyabhāvasyeṣṭatvād agovyāvṛttānubhavabhāvitvād gaur ayam iti vyavahārasyeti | tad evaṃ śābdādibuddhau na bāhyasya svalakṣaṇasya sāmānyalakṣaṇasya vā pratibhāsaḥ | na ca sāmānyaṃ pramāṇasiddhim iti pratipāditam | tadvat upādhyantarāṇi cintyāni ||

[225.12] yady evaṃ kathaṃ tarhi, śabdais tāvan mukhyam ākhyāyate 'rthaḥ | iti śāstraṃ saṅgatiyuktam? na hi tac ca tena pratipādyate, na ca tajjñāne tatprakāśa iti saṅgatiḥ kācid [225.16] ity āha, adhyāsata iti | dvidhā viṣayavyavahāraḥ pratibhāsād adhyavasāyāc ca | tad iha pratibhāsābhāve 'pi parāpoḍhasvalakṣaṇasyādhyavasāyamātreṇa viṣayatvam uktam | tathā ca tato 'pi vikalpāt tadadhyavasāyena vastuny eva pravṛtter iti |

[225.19]]atha ko 'yam adhyavasāyo nāma vikalpād anyaḥ, vikalpitam adhyavasitam ity anarthāntaratvāt? tat kathaṃ vikalpād adhyavasāyeneti bhedanirdeśaḥ? anyāpoḍhaṃ ca svalakṣaṇaṃ na vikalpe parisphurati | adhyavasiteḥ pratipādyata[87] iti ka eṣa nyāyaḥ, yato 'dhyavasāyāpekṣatayā tad api vikalpasya viṣaya iti vyavasthāpyate? kiṃ ca vikalpasyāviṣayaś ca bāhyam, grahaṇaṃ cāsya śabdena saṃyojyeti vikalpakatvam api[88] duryojam | ātmani ca tan nāstīti vikalpo nāma nāsty eva, [18b] tat kasya viṣayacintā? agṛhīte ca svalakṣaṇe śabdāt pravṛttir iti sarvatrāviśeṣeṇa prasajyeta, sarvasyāgṛhītatvena viśeṣābhāvāt | tataḥ prāptir api nābhimatasya niyamenety anumānasyāpi viplava iti |

[226.01] atrocyate, satyam ekārthau vikalpādhyavasāyau kevalaṃ vikalpaśabdaḥ śabdādiyojanānimittakaḥ | adhyavasāyas tv agṛhīte 'pi pravartanayogyatānimittaḥ | [226.02] yady api ca viśvam agṛhītam, tathāpi niyataviṣayā pravṛttir niyatākāratvād vikalpasya | niyataśaktayo hi bhāvāḥ pramāṇapariniṣṭhitasvabhāvā na śaktisāṅkaryaparyanuyogabhājaḥ, asadutpattivat | sarvasya tatrāsattve 'pi hi bījād aṅkurasyaivotpattiḥ, tatraiva tasya śakteḥ pramāṇena nirūpaṇāt | tathehāpi hutavahākārasya vikalpasya hutavahārthakriyārthinaḥ, tatsmaraṇavato hutavahaviṣayāyām eva pravṛttau sāmarthyaṃ pramāṇapratītaṃ katham atiprasaṅgabhāgi? pratyāsatticintayā ca tāttivakasyāpi vahner jvaladbhāsurākāratvaṃ vikalpollekhasyāpīti, tāvatā tatraiva pravartanaśaktir jvalanavikalpasya na jalādau | [226.09] na ca sādṛśyāropeṇa pravṛttiṃ brūmaḥ, yenākāre bāhyasya bāhye vākārasyāropadvāradūṣaṇāvakāśaḥ | kiṃ tarhi? svavāsanāparipākavaśād upajāyamānaiva sā buddhir apaśyanty api bāhyaṃ bāhye pravṛttim ātanotīti viplutaiva | yacchāstram,

na jñāne tulyam utpattito dhiyaḥ |
tathāvidhāyā[89] iti |

(226.16) tasmān na rūpyādivad āropadvāreṇa pravṛttir api tu tathāvidhākārotpattipratibaddhaśaktiniyamāt, yathā śālitvena śālibījam upādānaṃ niranvayodaye 'pi śālyaṅkura upādeye, śalitvādisthiteḥ sthairyadūṣaṇena nirastatvāt | [226.18] na ca vicārakasya vastvadarśanaṃ niścinvataḥ apravṛttiprasaṅgaḥ saṅgacchate 'darśane[90] 'pi hi pravṛttir arthakriyayānvitayā, arthakriyāprāptiś ca vastusattāniyame | sa ca niyamo yathā darśanād vastupratibandhakṛtas tathā vikalpaviśeṣād api pāramparyeṇeti, nānumānam anavasthitam | śabdāt tu kvacid arthasaṃśayeneti prāpter api tatrāniyamaḥ | tasmād adhyavasitam ity apratibhāse 'pi pravṛttiviṣayīkṛtam ity arthaḥ |

(226.23) tato vikalpabuddhāv apratibhāse 'py adhyavasitatvaṃ na bāhyasya bādhyate | ayam eva cārtho dṛśyavikalpayor ekīkaraṇasyābhedapratipattyādeś ca | [226.25] tataś ca tac ca na pratīyate tena cābhedabhāsanam ity upālambho 'saṃbhavīti darśitam, tadarthaniṣṭhāyāḥ kṛtatvāt | [226.26] sa cāgniratreti vyavasāyo yathā kāyikīṃ pravṛttiṃ tathāgnir mayā pratīta iti vācikīm api prasūte | [227.01] etadākārānuvyavasāyarūpāṃ mānasīm api prasavati | evaṃ sati yathā vikalpenāyam artho gṛhīta iti niścayas tathā śabdena saṃyojyety api, arthākāraleśavac chabdākārasyāpi sphuraṇāt | tasmād yāvad arthagrahaṇābhimānavān mānavaḥ [19a] tāvad abhidhānasaṃyuktagrahaṇābhimānavān apīty avasāyānurodhād eva vikalpavyavasthā na tattvataḥ | āha ca,

na śabdaiḥ saṃsargaḥ kvacid api bahir vā manasi vākṣarākārākīrṇaḥ sphurati punar arthākṛtilavaḥ | ubhāv apy ātmānau yad api dhiya evādhyavasitir nidhatte tau bāhye vacasi ca vikalpasthitir ataḥ ||

[227.10] ata eva ca tadabhimānamlānamānasaṃ prati pratyakṣalakṣaṇe kalpanāpoḍhaviśeṣaṇam upādīyate, sūtrato 'pi vikalpād adhyavasāyeneti bhedanirdeśaḥ | tatrāpi nāyam adhyavasāyadhvanir dharmiṇa eva vikalpasyābhidhāyakaḥ prayuktaḥ, kiṃtu tadgatasyādhyavasānalakṣaṇasya dharmasya | tad ayam arthaḥ, adṛṣṭe 'pi pravartanayogyatā nāma yo dharmas tayā vikalpāt pravṛttir iti | jñātaś ced artho vyavasthāpito 'dhyavasāyāt saṃvṛtyā, tato viṣayavyavahāro 'pi labdha ity avasāyamātreṇa viṣayatvam iti yuktaṃ | [227.16] ata uktam, arthaś caiko 'dhyāsato vācya iti | yad āha bhāṣyakāraḥ, kathaṃ tadviṣayatvaṃ tatra pravartanād iti |[91]

(227.20) yas tu katham dṛṣṭe pravartanam ity āśaṅkyādṛṣṭa eva sarvatra pravartanam ityādi siṃhanādaḥ, sa na vipañcito 'smābhir granthagauravabhayāt |

[227.22] evaṃ svapratibhāse 'narthe 'rthādhyavasāyena pravṛtter[92] ity atrāpy anarthe svapratibhāse sati adhyavasāyaḥ pūrvavat, arthas tv arthakriyāsamartho bāhya uktaḥ | tatparyudāsenānartho buddhyākāraḥ | evaṃ sa vastv iti asann iti ca draṣṭavyam | etac ca vārttikavācaiva sphuṭīkṛtaṃ sākārasiddhau | arthādhyavasāyena pravṛttir anumānasyety api hi arthādhyavasāyo 'numānam[93] ity arthaḥ | ṭīkākārasya tu yathā 'tra vyākhyānaṃ svāpohasiddhau tad dheyam eva, vistaraprasaṅgabhītyā nodbhāvitam asmābhiḥ |

[228.04] yadi tarhi bāhyasyādhyavasāyena vācyatā, kathaṃ buddhyākārasya? yac chāstram, anādivāsanodbhūtavikalpapariniṣṭhitaḥ | śabdārthaḥ[94] ityādi | vikalpapratibimbeṣu tanniṣṭheṣu nibadhyate |[95] vyatirekīva yaj jñāne bhāty arthapratibimbakam | śabdāt[96] iti | na hi buddhyākāre 'py adhyavasāyaḥ śakyo 'bhidhātum, pravṛttiviṣaye tasya vyavasthāpanāt | sa cārthakriyārthino bāhya evety āha, bhāsato[97] 'nyo 'rtho vācya iti | bāhyād anyo buddhyākāra ity arthaḥ | śabdādijanyāyāṃ buddhāv ākāramātrasya pratibhāsanāt sa eva viṣaya ucyate, cakṣuṣa iva rūpaṃ viṣayaḥ, na punar adhyavasāyād iti bhāvaḥ | uktaṃ ca, yathāpratīti kathitaḥ śabārtho 'sāv[98] iti |

[228.19] asann iti tu yathāpratibhāsaṃ bahirabhāvāt, bahirmukhāpekṣayā ca cintāyāḥ prakramāt | ayam evārtho yathādhyavasāyam atattvāt, yathātattvaṃ cānadhyavasāyād iti adhyavasāyasya vikalpaparyāyatvād yathāvikalpasphuraṇaṃ ity arthaniṣṭhānāt | asadarthaprakāśanāder api yathāpratīti bahirasattvam evārthaḥ | bhrāntitvam api bahirapekṣayaiveti sarvam anākulam | na tu svasaṃvedanagocarasya jñānarūpatayārthatvāt keśādyākārasyevāsattābhidhānaṃ [19b] sādhu | ata eva vācyatve 'pi,

> [229.03] nākārasya na bāhyasya tattvato vidhisādhanam |
> bahir eva hi saṃvṛtyā saṃvṛtyāpi tu nākṛteḥ ||

na hy asandehasya viṣayasya svasaṃvedyasyākārasya śabdādinā vidhiniṣedhayogaḥ vaiyarthyād asāmarthyāc ca | nāpi vikalpāpratibhāsino bāhyasya | viṣayāpratipatter hi kasya vidhir niṣedho vā syāt? tasmād yathā vṛkṣaśabdena bāhyo vṛkṣo 'dhyavasāyād abhideyo vyavasthāpitaḥ, tathādhyavasāyād eva bāhyasya vidhir niṣedho vā vyavahriyate | [229.08] yadāpi kutaścit prakaraṇād buddhyākāraṃ kañcid vikalpāntareṇādāya parīkṣā, tadāpi tadvikalpād bāhya eva vidhiniṣedhau | taṃ hi pataty arthe vivecayan |[99] iti hi śāstram | tasmāt tattvato nobhayor api vidhiniṣedhau, saṃvṛtyā hi bāhyasyaiva duṣpariharau ca | anyathā saṃvyavahārahāniprasaṅgāt |

[229.14] etena yaṭ ṭīkākāraḥ āropitasya bāhyatvaviṣayau vidhiniṣedhāv ity alaukikam anāgamam atārkikīyaṃ kathayati, tad apahastitam | na hi saṃvṛtiparamārthasatyadvayam anāśritya kācid vyavasthā | tatra na tāvad iyaṃ saṃvṛtiḥ, lokābhimānarūpatvāt tasyāḥ, lokasya ca bāhya eva padasyārtho vihitaḥ pratiṣiddho vety avigānena vyāpī pravṛttinivṛttyāśrayo 'bhimānaḥ, nāropitasya bāhyatvādikaṃ spṛśati lokaḥ | nāpy eṣa paramārthaḥ | na hy avācyasya vidhiniṣedhau | na ca vācyaṃ kiñcit tattvata ity āgamaḥ | tarkasyāpi nānyā dik | kiṃ ca nānadhyavaseyasya vidhiniṣedhau, na ca śabdād adhyavasāyaḥ svalakṣaṇād anytreti svayam apy udghuṣyate | ataḥ kim āyātam āropitabāhyatvavidhiniṣedhayoḥ? pratibhāsādhyavasāyadvārā ca sarvā vyavasthitis tattvam aspṛśatī | tatrāropitam āropitabāhyatvaṃ vā na pratibhāsasya viṣayo, nāpy adhyavasāyasya | tatrāropitaṃ tāvan na pratibhāsasparśi, yat svayam evāha, ullekhānubhavasamānakālaṃ samāropaṇam apratibhāsarūpam evāvastu vikalpaviṣaya iti | ata eva tadbāhyatvam api na pratibhāsi, taddharmatvāt | adhyavasāyas tu[100] bāhyasvalakṣaṇaniyamād eva nainayor ity alam enām utthāpya |

āropitam ity api kalpitam evocyate, kalpanākarma ca pratibhāsam avasitaṃ ceti dvayam | tat kutastyo'yam āropitākhyo rāśir aparaḥ? tasmād buddhyākārabāhyāśrayaiva saṃvṛtiparamārthābhyāṃ cintociteti | tathāvidhārthakriyāvivakṣāyāṃ ca kiṃ vakradurgamārgāśrayeṇety alam atinirbandhena | sthitam etad adhyavasāyena bāhyasya buddhyākārasya tu pratibhāsena śabdavācyatvam ucyate iti |

[230.08] nanv evaṃvyācakṣāṇena bhavatobhayārtharāśer aśeṣasya vācyatā svīkṛteti kathaṃ sarvadharmānabhilāpyatāsamarthanār tham idam avatāritam ity āha, sthāpya[101] iti prayojanāntaram uddiśya vyavasthāmātram etat, adhyavasāyamātreṇa pratibhāsamātreṇa [20a] vā vācyatvam iti | tathā[102] bahirviṣayīkaraṇaṃ tattvavyavasthānamātraṃ gṛhṇataḥ tāvad anyāpoḍhaṃ svalakṣaṇam eva viṣaya ity ucyate upādhirāśinirasanaparaṃ,[103] evam anyāpoḍhākāro vikalpasyātmā viṣaya iti samastabāhyanirasanaparam, na tu svasmin viṣayatvasya viśrāmāyeti na virodhaḥ |

[230.16] kutaḥ punar etat? tatra tatra viṣayatāpratipādane 'pi na viśrāmo vivakṣitaḥ, kiṃtv anyanirasane tātparyam ity āha, vācyas tattvato naiva kaścid arthaḥ | iti | adhyavasāyasahāpohipratibhāsaḥ sāṃvyavahārikāpekṣayā tattvato jñeyasya jñānaviṣayatām upanayati pratyakṣavat | na hi pratibhāsamātram avasāyaśūnyam anyāvasāyākrāntavyāpāraṃ vā pravṛttikāmasya viṣayavyavasthām arthe kṣamate, gacchattṛṇasparśavat, marīcāv udakāropavat | nāpy avasāyamātram apetapratibhāsam, udakāropavad eva | tasmāt pravṛttiyogyatayā vyāptaṃ viṣayavyavasthānam ubhayābhāve[104] vyāpakābhāvena paribhūyamānam ubhayasaṃbhavapratibaddham ekaviveke svīkriyamāṇaṃ sāṃvṛtam eva | yatra jñāne yan na pratibhāsate yena vā yan nāvasīyate sa na tasya viṣayo yathā gojñānasyāśvaḥ | na pratibhāsate ca śābdajñāne svalakṣaṇaṃ, nāvasīyate cānena buddhyākāra iti vyāpakānupalabdhiḥ | pratibandhasādhanāt nānekāntaḥ | yady api cātyantābhyāse pratibhāsamātreṇāpi pravṛttiviṣayatvaṃ[105] ca dṛṣṭam, tathāpi sa evābhyāso nāvasāyād vinety avasāyasyaiva tat pauruṣam, tato yena yan nāvasīyate 'saty abhyāsa iti viśeṣaṇam apekṣyam |

[231.03] nanu pratyakṣe 'pi na gṛhītakṣaṇasyāvasāyaḥ, kiṃ tu santateḥ, na cāsyāḥ pratibhāsa iti kenāsyāpi saviṣayatvaṃ, kṣaṇe santatau cobhayābhāvāt | anumāne tu parīkṣaiva vartate | na cānyat pramāṇam asti, yasyobhayasaṃbhavena viṣayaḥ kaścid ity asaṃbhavam etat | tad ekaikena viṣayatve sthitam akhilasya[106] bāhyasyāntarasya vā vācyatvam iti | atrocyate | tattvavyavasthām āha ubhayasaṃbhavenaiva viṣayatvaṃ, kevalaṃ sāṃvyavahārikāpekṣayā saṃvṛtir[107] evādharasaṃvṛtim apekṣya tattvam iti vyavahriyate, kṣaṇabhedāvatāre saṃvyavahāravilopāt vyāvahārikaṃ prati pratikṣaṇakṣīṇatāyā abhāvāt, tattvataḥ pratyakṣeṇobhayasaṃbhavābhāvaḥ, iti na doṣaḥ |

(231.10) atha pṛthagjanasya dṛśyavikalpyayor apy abhedagraho niyata evetyavasito vahniḥ pratibhāsita eveti cet—na, pratibhāsāntarasmaraṇena tatpratibhāsabhramabhraṃśasya kṛtatvāt | yathā ca vikalpapratibhāsād anya eva vastupratibhāso darśayitum adhyakṣe śakyaḥ, tathā cādhyakṣapratibhāsād[108] anyo 'stīti tatraiva vastupratibhāsaviśrāmāt tadvijātīyasya vastupratibhāsatāvyudāsaḥ śreyān | tasmād yuktam uktam, sthāpyo vācyas tattvato naiva kaścit | iti |

[231.16] [20b] athavā vastvantarāvācyatve 'pi tatrāpohas tadviśeṣaṇatvena gamya iti apohasya vācyatā svīkṛtaiva | tathāpi kathaṃ sarvadharmānabhilapyatvam ity āha, vācyas tattvato naiva kaścid artha iti | ayam abhiprāyaḥ | paryudāsapakṣe tāvad vasturūpavat tasyāpy adhyavasāyamātrakṛtaṃ vācyatvam, na pratibhāsād adhyakṣavat | prasajyapakṣe punar anyanivṛttimātrasyānyadāpi na viśeṣaḥ, tathāpy asau nārtha iti noktadoṣaḥ | yad vā yaḥ śāstre, tasmāt siddham etat sarvaśabdā vivekaviṣayā vikalpāś cety upasaṃhāraḥ, tasyārthaniṣṭhām upasṃhāreṇaiva darśayati, vācyas tattvato naiva kaścid artha iti | saṃvṛtau pratibhāsādhyvasāyamātreṇa vācyatāyā darśitatvāt, tattvata ity āha | tad ayam arthaḥ | yad etac chāstre viveka eva vācya ity upasaṃhṛtaṃ tasya na kiñcid vācyam ity[109] evārthaḥ, yathābhāvo bhavatīti bhāvo na bhavatīty evārthaḥ, tathāpohasya vācyateti vācyatāyā evāpoha ity arthaḥ | etac ca hetutrayavibhāgakaraṇādinā svayam eva sphuṭīkṛtam ity upapāditam |

[232.05] tad evaṃ katham apohaḥ śabdavācya iti praśne tadguṇatvena yathoktārthenety uttaram | atha buddhyākāraḥ svalakṣaṇam upādhayo vā kasmān na vācyā iti praśnaḥ, tadadhyavasāyasya pratibhāsasya ubhayasya cābhāvād iti krameṇa visarjanāni | yadā tu śabdaiḥ kiṃ vācyam ity anuyogaḥ, tadā pratibhāsād arthādhyavasāyāt, yad vā tattvata iti vikalpya vikalpastho[110] 'nyāpoḍhākāraḥ, anyāpoḍhasvalakṣaṇaṃ na kiñcid iti prativacanāni krameṇaivety uktaṃ bhavati | tasmāt śabdaliṅgayor apohaviṣayatāsthitiprasādhanaṃ sarvadharmāvācyatvapratipādanaparam iti prathamaślokārthopasaṃhāraḥ ||

[232.12] bhavatv apohe kṛtināṃ prapañco vastusvarūpāsphuraṇaṃ tu marma |
tatrādṛḍhe sarvam ayatnaśīrṇaṃ dṛḍhe tu sausthyaṃ nanu tāvataiva ||
samarthane[111] tasya diśaḥ prakāśaḥ kṛto 'yam asmābhir avistareṇa |
tadvistaras tv ākara eva cintyaḥ paroditaṃ tūlam iva kṣipadbhiḥ ||

|| apohaprakaraṇaṃ samāptam ||

ABBREVIATIONS

AP	*Apohaprakaraṇa* (Jñānaśrīmitra) in JNĀ.
AP-Dh	*Apohaprakaraṇa* (Dharmottara) in Frauwallner 1937.
AS	*Apohasiddhi* (Ratnakīrti) in Thakur 1975.
ĀTV	*Ātmatattvaviveka* (Udayana) in Dvivedin and Dravida 1986.
BKNCT	*Bulletin of Kochi National College of Technology.*
DhPr	*Dharmottarapradīpa* (Durvekamiśra) in Malvania 1971.
HB	*Hetubindu* (Dharmakīrti) in Steinkellner 1967.
HBṬ	*Hetubinduṭīkā* (Arcaṭa) in Sanghavi and Jinavijayji 1949.
HBṬĀ	*Hetubinduṭīkāloka* (Durvekamiśra) in Sanghavi and Jinavijayji 1949.
IPVV	*Īśvarapratyabhijñāvivṛtivimarśinī* (Abhinavagupta) in Śāstri 1987.
Jms	*Apohaprakaraṇa* (Jñānaśrīmitra), manuscript. The scanned photocopy that we used was kindly provided by H. Krasser from the manuscript collection of the Department of South Asian, Tibetan, and Buddhist Studies at the University of Vienna. For more on this manuscript, see Kellner 2007.
JNĀ	*Jñānaśrīmitranibandhāvali* (Jñānaśrīmitra) in Thakur 1987.
KBhA	*Kṣaṇabhaṅgādhyāya* (Jñānaśrīmitra) in JNĀ.
LPrP	*Laghuprāmāṇyaparīkṣā* (Dharmottara) in Krasser 1991.
MD	*Mīmāṃsādarśana* in Gosvāmi 1984.
MīKo	*Mīmāṃsākośa* in Kevalānandasarasvati 1992.
MS	*Mīmāṃsāsūtra* in Gosvāmi 1984.
NB	*Nyāyabindu* (Dharmakīrti) in Malvania 1971.
NBṬ	*Nyāyabinduṭīkā* (Dharmottara) in Malvania 1971.
NBṬṬ	*Nyāyabinduṭīkāṭippaṇa* in Shastri 1984.

NBṬVi	*Nyāyabinduṭīkā* (Vinitadeva) in Gangopadhyaya 1971.
NBh	*Nyāyabhāṣya* (Vātsyāyana) in Thakur 1997a.
NBhū	*Nyāyabhūṣaṇa* (Bhāsarvajña) in Yogindrananda 1968.
NKaṇ	*Nyāyakaṇikā* (Vācaspatimiśra) in Stern 1988.
NKu	*Nyāyakusumāñjali* (Udayana) in Gosvāmi 1972.
N1	*Apohasiddhi* (Ratnakīrti), Manuscript nos. 5–256 from the National Archives of Nepal.
N2	*Apohasiddhi* (Ratnakīrti), Manuscript nos. 3–696 from the National Archives of Nepal.
N3	*Apohasiddhi* (Ratnakīrti), Manuscript no. 764d running number from the National Archives of Nepal.
NSū	*Nyāyasūtra* (Gautama) in Thakur 1997a.
NV	*Nyāyabhāṣyavārttika* (Uddyotakara) in Thakur 1997b.
NVTṬ	*Nyāyavārttikatātparyaṭīkā* (Vācaspatimiśra) in Thakur 1996.
PS 1	*Prāmāṇasamuccaya* (Dignāga) in Steinkellner 2005.
PSṬ	*Prāmāṇasamuccayaṭīkā* (Jinendrabuddhi) in Steinkellner, Krasser, and Lasic 2007.
PSV	*Prāmāṇasamuccayavṛtti* (Dignāga) in Steinkellner, Krasser, and Lasic 2007.
PV	*Pramāṇavārttika, Parārthānumāna* (Dharmakīrti) in Miyasaka 1971/72; Tillemans 2004.
PV	*Pramāṇavārttika, Prāmāṇasiddhi* (Dharmakīrti) in Miyasaka 1971/72.
PV	*Pramāṇavārttika, Pratyakṣa* (Dharmakīrti) in Miyasaka 1971/72.
PV	*Pramāṇavārttika, Svārthānumāna* (Dharmakīrti) in Gnoli 1960.
PVA	*Pramāṇavārttikālaṅkāra* (Prajñākaragupta) in Sāṃkrtyāyana 1953.
PVin 1	*Pramāṇaviniścaya* 1 (Dharmakīrti) in Vetter 1966.
PVin 2	*Pramāṇaviniścaya* 2 (Dharmakīrti) in Steinkellner 1973.
PVinṬ	*Pramāṇaviniścayaṭīkā* (Dharmottara) in Steinkellner and Krasser 1989.
PVSV	*Pramāṇavārttikasvavṛtti* (Dharmakīrti) in Gnoli 1960.
PVV	*Pramāṇavārttikavṛtti* (Manorathanandin) in Sāṃkrtyāyana 1938–40.
RNĀ	*Ratnakīrtinibandhāvali* (Ratnakīrti) in Thakur 1975.

SāmDū	*Sāmānyadūṣaṇa* (Paṇḍit Aśoka) in Shastri 1910.
ŚBh	*Śabarabhāṣya* (Śabara) in Gosvāmi 1984.
SBNT	*Six Buddhist Nyāya Tracts* in Shastri 1910.
SRK	*Subhāṣitaratnakośa* (Vidyākara) in Kosambi and Gokhale 1957.
SSS	*Sākārasiddhiśāstra* (Jñānaśrīmitra) in JNĀ.
ŚV	*Ślokavārttika* (Kumārila) in Ray 1993.
SVR	*Syādvādaratnākara* (Vādidevasūri) in Motilal 1926–30.
TBh	*Tarkabhāṣā* (Mokṣākaragupta) in Iyengar 1952.
TV	*Tantravārttika* (Kumārila) in Abhyankar and Joshi 1980–94.
VC	*Vyāpticarcā* (Jñānaśrīmitra) in Lasic 2000a; Thakur 1987.
WSTB	*Wiener Studien zur Tibetologie und Buddhismuskunde.*
WZKM	*Wiener Zeitschrift für die Kunde des Morgenlandes.*
WZKS	*Wiener Zeitschrift für die Kunde Südasiens.*
WZKSO	*Wiener Zeitschrift für die Kunde Süd- und Ostasiens.*

NOTES

INTRODUCTION

1. See, e.g., Dravid 1972; Mookherjee 1935; Sharma 1969; and Stcherbatsky 1984, which was originally published in 1930/32. For an accessible introduction to the history of Buddhist thought and philosophy in India, see Siderits 2007 and Williams 2000.
2. For some exceptions to this, see Dunne 2004; Hayes 1986; and Patil 2003, 2009.
3. Dignāga (ca. 480–540), who is considered by many to be the founder of the Buddhist epistemological text tradition, is thought to have been born into a Brahmin family in Kāñcī and to have lived and worked for a time at the Buddhist monastic and educational complex of Nālanda, which was established in the fifth century CE and located in what is now the modern Indian state of Bihar. For what we know of Dignāga's life and works, see Hattori 1968 and Hayes 1988. For a useful discussion of Nālanda, see Mullens 1994, 49–68.
4. "Conceptual awareness" (*vikalpa*/ *kalpanā*) refers to awareness events in which an object is constructed as something in association with one or more concepts, classes, or labels. This is contrasted with "nonconceptual" (*nirvikalpa*), awareness in which an object is directly apprehended without being associated with any concepts, classes, or labels. For more on this issue and Dignāga's thought more generally, see Hattori 1968; Hayes 1988; and Taber 2005.
5. Dharmakīrti (ca. 600–660) is arguably the most important Buddhist philosopher in Indian philosophical history and among the most important Sanskrit philosophers. For a short but useful introduction to Dharmakīrti's life and works, see Steinkellner 1998. For recent book-length studies of Dharmakīrti, see Dreyfus 1997; Dunne 2004; Eltschinger 2007; Franco 1997; Tillemans 2004; and van Bijlert 1989.

6. For the earlier history of the theory, see Dunne 2004; Frauwallner 1959; Hattori 1977; Hoornaert 2001; Katsura 1991; Pind 1991, 1999; Raja 1986; Saito 2004; and Siderits 1991. For the later history, see Akamatsu 1983; Dravid 1972; Dunne 2004; Frauwallner 1937; Hattori 2006; Katsura 1986a; McCrea and Patil 2006; and Patil 2003 and forthcoming.
7. See, e.g., Katsura 1986a, which is discussed in McCrea and Patil 2006. This tendency is not confined to the study of the Buddhist epistemological tradition but extends to the Sanskrit philosophical tradition more generally. See, e.g., Frauwallner 1973, vii, who suggests that the history of Indian philosophy effectively ended in the fifth century.
8. Jñānaśrīmitra's views are discussed, e.g., in the work of the Jaina philosopher Vādidevasūri (ca. twelfth c.) in his *Syādvādaratnākara*, the Naiyāyika Udayana (ca. eleventh c.), in his *Ātmatattvaviveka*, and Gaṅgeśa (ca. fourteenth c.), in his *Tattvacintāmaṇi*, and the Vedāntin, Sāyana-Mādhava's (ca. 1350) *Sarvadarśanasaṃgraha.* Interestingly, a modern commentator on Vedāntadeśika's *Tattvamuktākalāpa*, Srimad Abhinavaraṅganātha-brahmatantraparakālayati, who was the head of one of the Viśiṣṭādvaita religious/educational centers, seems to know of Jñānaśrīmitra's and Ratnakīrti's work, from Shastri's *Six Buddhist Nyāya Tracts* (H. P. Shastri 1910). In his commentary, he says that Vedāntadeśika refers to the views of Jñānaśrīmitra and Ratnakīrti.
9. In his commentary on Udayana's *Ātmatattvaviveka* (ĀTV), Śaṅkaramiśra names both Jñānaśrīmitra and Ratnakīrti as targets of Udayana's critique, although Udayana himself names only Jñānaśrīmitra, and there is nothing specific in his arguments to indicate that he was familiar with Ratnakīrti's work. In this text, Udayana himself mentions Jñānaśrīmitra. For a translation of the ĀTV, see Dravid 1995. Sections of the ĀTV are also translated in Laine 1993 and 1998. For an excellent study of another of Udayana's works, the *Nyāyakusumāñjali* (NKu), and an introduction to his life, works, and thought, see Chemparathy 1972. For a translation of the NKu, see Dravid 1996.
10. The body of Jñānaśrīmitra's work available to us comes primarily from a single manuscript found in Tibet. It contains *A Study of Moment by Moment Destruction, Investigation of Pervasion, Examination of "Difference and Non-Difference," The Secret of Non-Apprehension, Investigation of the Absence of All Sound, Monograph on Exclusion, Debating God, Proof of Cause-Effect Relationship, Monograph on the Discernment of Yogis, Monograph on the Drop Non-Duality, A Treatise Proving That Awareness*

Contains an Image, and *A Verse Summary on the Possession of an Image*. In addition to these texts, Jñānaśrīmitra also wrote a work on poetic meter. For more on Jñānaśrīmitra's work, see Hahn 1971 and Thakur 1987. For a discussion of metrics at Buddhist Universities in India, see Hahn 1989.

11. SRK vv. 19–22, pp. 4–5.
12. See Thakur 1987. A tantric work, the **Vajrayānāntadvayanirākaraṇa* (*rDo rje theg pa'i mtha' gñis sel ba*), also is attributed to him. For a discussion of this text, see Kyuma 2009 and Tanemura 2009.
13. For more on Vikramaśīla, see Asher 1975 and Vidyabhusana 1921, 519–20. For bibliographical material on these philosophers, see Steinkellner and Much 1995; and the online bibliography maintained in Vienna, at http://www.istb.univie.ac.at/cgi-bin/suebs/suebs.cgi.
14. "Yogācāra" is one of the four canonical "schools" of Buddhism. The foundational figures are said to be Vasubandhu and Asaṅga. This is often referred to as the "mind-only" (*cittamātra*) school, since its adherents generally held that there are no mind-independent objects. For Bhāviveka's interesting sixth-century Buddhist perspective on this "school" (and Buddhist epistemology), see Eckel 2008.
15. The "*sākāra*" (with an image) position is that the images in our awareness are ultimately real, while the "*nirākāra*" (without an image) position is that the images in our awareness, like the putatively extra-mental objects they are taken to represent, are illusory and ultimately unreal. For an early discussion of this debate, see Kajiyama 1965.
16. For an edition, translation, and brief study of Ratnākaraśānti's work on logic and epistemology, see Kajiyama 1999 and Mishra 2002. For his work on Tantra, see Isaacson 2001, 2002a, 2002b, 2007.
17. RNĀ (ISD: 32.3). For Ratnakīrti's work, see Patil 2009 and Thakur 1987.
18. While Dignāga is really the founder of the Buddhist epistemological tradition, Dharmakīrti largely supplanted him as the principal figure in this text tradition, and it is mainly his work that later Buddhist epistemologists comment on and refer back to in formulating their own positions.
19. Ratnakīrti follows him in this respect. Monographs seem to have been generally preferred to commentaries in Vikramaśīla around this time. Other than Ratnakīrti, prominent figures such as Jitāri and Ratnākaraśānti (who did, however, write extensive commentaries on tantras and "perfection of wisdom" literature) also wrote monographs. For Ratnakīrti's work, see Thakur 1975; and for Jitāri's, see Bühneman 1985 and Eltschinger 2003.

For an excellent bibliographic outline of the Buddhist epistemological tradition, see Steinkellner and Much 1995.

20. Śubhagupta and Dharmottara accepted the existence of mind-independent objects, but Jñānaśrīmitra and Ratnākaraśānti did not (see McCrea and Patil 2006; and n. 51 in this introduction). Ratnākaraśānti and Jñānaśrīmitra differ with each other on the reality of the contents of our awareness (see the preceding note). Jñānaśrīmitra defended the idea of a maximally adequate philosophical description of reality, in contrast to those such as Jitāri who interpreted Dharmakīrti from a Madhyamaka perspective (Dreyfus 1997, 21, 467, n. 19).
21. See section 4.
22. For a comparative discussion of "scholasticism" that includes the work of Buddhist philosophers, see Cabezón 1998 and, more generally, Cabezón 1994 and Griffiths 1999.
23. By the term "root text," we mean the foundational texts on which later members of the text tradition directly or indirectly commented. In most Sanskrit text traditions, these texts take the form of *sūtra*s, which are brief aphoristic works outlining the traditions' basic positions.
24. For a comparative discussion of "commentaries," see Griffiths 1999; for an interpretation of Sanskrit commentarial practices, see Patil 2006; and for a historically grounded discussion of commentaries in the Nyāya text tradition, see Preisendanz 2008.
25. The origin of this mode of argumentation seems to lie in the Sanskrit grammatical tradition, and it is found fully developed in the commentaries of Kātyāyana and Patañjali on Pāṅini's grammar.
26. The literature on Buddhist, Mīmāṃsā, and Nyāya polemics is extensive. See, e.g., Arnold 2005; Dravid 1972; Dreyfus 1997; Eckel 2008; Ganeri 2001; Krasser 2002; Matilal 1986; Mookherjee 1935; Patil 2009; Phillips 1997; and Taber 2005.
27. The only notable exception seems to be the materialist skeptic, Jayarāśi. See Franco 1994.
28. Similar arguments were made for analogy (*upamāna*), necessary presumption (*arthāpatti*), and absence (*abhāva*) as independent sources of knowledge. Again, when they accepted them as valid at all, the Buddhist epistemologists regarded them all as varieties of inference.
29. Followers of the Mīmāṃsā and Nyāya text traditions, respectively.
30. For a discussion of Kumārila's critique of Dignāga, see Taber 2004; and for

a discussion of some of the most philosophical issues from the perspective of the Naiyāyikas, see Chakrabarti 1992, 1998, 2000, 2003, and 2004.

31. The position of the early Naiyāyikas is that we become aware of pervasion between two things through repeated observation (*bhūyodarśana*) of their copresence. Dharmakīrti, in contrast, argued that the repeated observation of copresence is neither necessary nor sufficient for becoming aware of pervasion. Rather, he contended that one becomes aware of pervasion only after establishing either a causal relation (*tadutpatti*) or an identity relation (*tādātmya*) between two things. The later Naiyāyikas, reformulating their own position in response to Dharmakīrti, claimed that what underwrites pervasion is a "natural connection" (*svābhāvikasambandha*) between two things and that to be aware of pervasion is to be aware of this connection. The secondary literature on this is extensive. See, e.g., Krasser 2002; Lasic 2000a, 2000b; Patil 2009 and forthcoming; and the references contained therein. Also see JNĀ 216. For an introduction to inferential reasoning in classical India, see Ganeri 2001; Matilal 1998 et al.; and Potter 1991.
32. ŚBh on MS 1.1.2, see MD vol. 1:15. For a translation of the ŚBh, see Jha 1973/74.
33. In the case of the word "cow," e.g., the universal would be its "cow-ness"; the particular would be any given cow; and the characteristic structure would be those features distinguishing a cow as a cow, e.g., dewlap, horns, and tail. See NBh and NV ad NS 2.2.66. For more on NV ad NS 2.2.66, see Much 1994. For a translation of the NS corpus with extracts from the commentaries, see Chattopadhyaya and Gangopadhyaya 1992; and Jha 1985.
34. NVTṬ ad NS 2.2.66.
35. For a useful discussion of testimony as a source of knowledge, see Chakrabarti 1994; and Taber 1996, 2002.
36. PS 1, in Steinkellner 2005.
37. Particulars (*svalakṣaṇa*) are utterly unique and ontologically basic entities that only appear to share elements with other particulars on the basis of conceptualization, a form of error. These are contrasted with "universals" (*sāmānyalakṣaṇa*), which we discuss later. For two very useful discussions of "particulars," see Dunne 2004 and Keyt 1980.
38. PS1, in Steinkellner 2005.
39. Buddhist philosophers typically distinguish between "two truths": "conventional" (*saṃvṛti*) and "ultimate" (*paramārtha*). Statements that are conven-

tionally true are convenient fictions that enable us to function successfully in our ordinary lives but that cannot withstand full philosophical scrutiny, e.g., the acceptance, for pragmatic purposes, of persisting objects whose ultimate reality most Buddhists deny. For more on "two truths," see Newland 1999.

40. In Sanskrit, many of the words used to describe "awareness," e.g., *jñāna*, *buddhi*, and *pratyaya*, function as "count nouns" rather than "mass nouns." That is, unlike the English term "awareness," they are used to refer to individual episodic awareness-events rather than to persisting or dispositional mental states. Therefore, in the Introduction and Translation in this book, we often speak of "awarenesses," meaning individual episodic awareness-events.
41. PSV ad PS 1.7; also see PSṬ 58. For our translation practices, see section 5.
42. Universals (*sāmānyalakṣaṇa*) are conceptually constructed objects that give us our sense of recurrent properties on the basis of which things are classified and labeled. Such objects do not have mind-independent existence and are said to be only "conventionally real" (*samvṛtisat*), which we discuss later. For a book-length discussion of this, see Mookherjee 1935.
43. For a discussion of this issue, see NBh ad NS 1.1.3.
44. See NBh ad NS 1.1.3.
45. Recall that for Dignāga, testimony is reducible to inference.
46. Uddyotakara NV ad 2.2.66 in Thakur 1997b, 314; and Kumārila ŚV *Apohavāda* 1–10, ad MS 1.1.5 in Ray 1993, 400.
47. PV *Pramāṇasiddhi* 1, 5/7 and HB 1.7.
48. For a discussion of this concept in Dharmakīrti's work, see Dunne 2004; Franco 1997; Katsura 1984; McCrea and Patil 2006; Mikogami 1979; and Nagatomi 1967.
49. See PV *Pramāṇasiddhi* 1 on *arthakrīyāsthitiḥ*. For translations, see Dunne 2004; Franco 1997; Katsura 1984; Kellner 2001, 507; Nagatomi 1967; van Bijlert 1989; and Vetter 1964. Dharmakīrti's use of the word *sthitiḥ* in this much discussed passage is significant. It does not mean simply the "existence" of pragmatic efficacy but its persistence or consistency. Also see PV *Pratyakṣa* 1–3. The test for the validity of awareness is that its object continues to behave within the expected parameters as defined by our interests. This is not limited to cases in which we actually want this object and obtain it but also includes cases in which we wish to avoid a particular object or, according to some, cases in which we are indifferent. This

is recognized by authors in the tradition who take *arthakrīyā* to include avoidance (*hāna*) as well as obtaining (*upādāna*). An awareness is said to be valid, therefore, if the object that we come to know on the basis of it behaves in conformity with the expectations that we form on the basis of that awareness. Note that others in the tradition such as Vinītadeva, NBṬ-Vi: 39.4ff, but not Dharmottara, NBṬ: 30.2, add to "avoidance" and "obtaining/acquisition," "neglect/indifference" (*upekṣā/upekṣaṇīya*). For a short but interesting discussion of this point, see Kellner 2001, 511, n. 32; and Krasser 1997.

50. See HB 2*15–3*16, discussed in McCrea and Patil 2006.
51. See McCrea and Patil 2006, esp. 307–25.
52. In this context, the word "object" translates the term *viṣaya*, by which Dharmakīrti means the (real or imagined) extra-mental referent of either conceptual or nonconceptual awareness.
53. For a discussion of this, see Dreyfus 1997; Dunne 2004; Kellner (forthcoming); Kyuma (forthcoming); and McClintock 2002. On Dignāga specifically, see Dreyfus 1997, 104ff.
54. Compare, e.g., the discussion in Dreyfus 1997, in which these various views are presented as being "unstructured," with the discussion in Dunne 2004, in which these views are presented as being "hierarchically structured."
55. PS/PSV ad PS 1.8cd-1.9.
56. Many of the features of his epistemology—e.g., the triple conditions that define a good inference—may be intended to be shared more broadly and in fact were largely accepted, at least tacitly, by almost all Sanskrit philosophers of his time.
57. PVin 1.44–58, PV *Pratyakṣa* 209ff, 388–422.
58. Śubhagupta is widely acknowledged as being a Buddhist realist, and we argue elsewhere that Dharmottara—who is said to have been his pupil—should likewise be seen as such. See McCrea and Patil 2006, 332–33. Jñānaśrīmitra, as we shall see, unmistakably falls into the idealist camp.
59. See, e.g., Eckel 2008; Kang 1998; Matilal 1987; Matilal et al. 1998; Meuthrath 1996; Prets 2000, 2001; Randle 1930; Ruben 1928; Solomon 1976; and Vidyabhusana 1921.
60. See, e.g., Katsura 1986a and 2000.
61. For a brief but useful comparison of Dharmakīrti's views with those of the Naiyāyaikas see Gokhale 1993, which also contains an English translation

of Dharmakīrti's *Vādanyāya*. For the standard edition and German translation of this text, see Much 1991.

62. Note that this second condition rules out inferences based on unique properties for which there is no similar case. The secondary literature on these three conditions is extensive. See, e.g., Franco 1990; Ganeri 2001; Katsura 2000, 2004; Oetke 1994, 1996, 2003a; Patil (forthcoming); Taber 2004; and the references contained therein.

63. For very useful discussions of "pseudoinferential reasons," see Gokhale 1992; Hayes 1988; and Matilal et al. 1998.

64. For a discussion of Dharmottara's views on validity, see his LPrP, whose Tibetan translation is edited and translated in Krasser 1991. For an excellent summary and analysis of this text, see Krasser 1995. For Dharmottara's discussion of validity in his PVinṬ, see Steinkellner and Krasser 1989. For a general discussion of his views, see Dreyfus 1997; and for more focused work on specific aspects of Dharmottara's thought, see Kellner 1997b, 1999, and 2004.

65. It is worth highlighting just how radical Dharmottara's position is here. Never before had anyone connected with the Buddhist epistemological tradition even suggested that perception has more than one object. What Dharmakīrti himself says is simply that the object of perception is a particular. By importing the term "grasped" (*grāhya*) into his gloss on Dharmakīrti's text, without any clear basis in either the *Nyāyabindu* or any of Dharmakīrti's other works, Dharmottara introduces into his account of perception precisely what Dharmakīrti sought to avoid: a bifurcation between two different kinds of objects, which creates a gap between them that needs to be bridged by determination. Sanskrit commentaries on Dharmottara's text try to minimize his break with Dharmakīrti by suggesting that he did not mean to literally claim that perception itself has both a grasped and determined object. The author of the anonymous Ṭippana (NBṬṬ: 3) comments as follows:

> [Objector:] But how is the continuum an object of perception, since it is [in fact] the object of conceptualization? [Reply] We say that it is due to figurative usage. Because it is made into an object in such a way that it is determined by that conceptualization, which is the functional output [*vyāpāra*] of perception, it is called the "object of perception" on the basis of figurative usage; thus there is no problem [*nanu ca kathaṃ pratyakṣasya santāno viṣayaḥ, yato vikalpasyāsau viṣayaḥ?*

ucyate, upacārāt | *pratyakṣavyāpāreṇa vikalpenādhavaseyatayā viṣayīkṛtatvāt pratyakṣaviṣaya ity ucyate upacārād ity adoṣaḥ* ||].

In his commentary, Durveka Miśra (DhPr [1955: 71.21]) says, "Since the judgment that follows perception functions only with respect to what was grasped in perception, adding nothing to it, therefore, what is determined by that [judgment] is [said to be] "determined by perception itself"—this is the idea [*pratyakṣapṛṣṭhabhāvino niścayasya pratyakṣagṛhīta eva pravṛttatayā 'natiśayādhānena yat tenādhyavasitaṃ tat pratyakṣeṇaivāvasitam iti bhāvaḥ* ||].

66. Here Dharmottara's phrasing closely parallels Dharmakīrti's description of inference in PVin 2.8–10 and HB 3*14–15. Both passages are quoted and discussed in McCrea and Patil 2006.

67. NB 1.12: *tasya viṣayaḥ svalakṣaṇam.* NBṬ ad NB 1.12: *tasya caturvidhasya pratyakṣasya viṣayo boddhavyaḥ svalakṣaṇam* | *svam asādhāraṇaṃ lakṣaṇam tattvaṃ svalakṣaṇam* | *vastuno hy asādhāraṇaṃ ca tattvam asti sāmānyaṃ ca* | *tatra yad asādhāraṇam tat pratyakṣasya grāhyam* | *dvividho hi viṣayaḥ pramāṇasya grāhyaś ca yadākāram utpadyate, prāpaṇīyaś ca yam adhyavasyati* | *anyo hi grāhyo 'nyaś cādhyavaseyaḥ* | *pratyakṣasya hi kṣaṇa eko grāhyaḥ* | *adhyavaseyas tu pratyakṣabalotpannena niścayena santāna eva* | *santāna eva ca pratyakṣasya prāpaṇīyaḥ* | *kṣaṇasya prāpayitum aśakyatvāt* | *tathānumānam api svapratibhāse 'narthe arthādhyavasāyena pravṛtter anarthagrāhi* | *sa punar āropito 'rtho gṛhyamānaḥ svalakṣaṇatvenāvasīyate yataḥ, tataḥ svalakṣaṇam avasitaṃ pravṛttiviṣayo 'numānasya* | *anarthas tu grāhyaḥ* | *tad atra pramāṇasya grāhyaṃ viṣayaṃ darśayatā pratyakṣasya svalakṣaṇaṃ viṣaya uktaḥ* |.

68. Beginning with Dharmottara's work, the status of the mental image (*ākāra*), as distinct from the putatively real external object that it is sometimes taken to represent and from those conceptual or determined objects that we construct on the basis of it, assumes great importance in Buddhist epistemology. It is only the mental image that actually appears in our awareness, as a result of which many later Buddhist epistemologists, including Jñānaśrīmitra, use the term "appearance" (*pratibhāsa*) as a synonym. The term "object" (*viṣaya*) is used generically for mental images, putatively real external objects, and determined objects. The term "thing" (*vastu*) is generally used to refer to only putatively real mind-independent objects. As we shall see, however, the semantic range of all these terms is subject to much debate in the post-Dharmottaran Buddhist epistemological tradition. For a discussion of "images" in Buddhist epistemology,

see Kajiyama 1965; McCrea and Patil 2006; and the discussion in Patil (forthcoming).

69. The standard Buddhist argument for momentariness is based on a particular understanding of causality. To explain briefly, experience tells us that after some time, a seed that has been planted and properly cared for will produce a sprout. Buddhists argue that at the moment of producing a sprout, the seed has to be different in some way from the seed in previous moments, since the seed at just that moment produces a sprout, while the seed in previous moments did not. But if this is the case, one must also admit that the seed that existed just before (and therefore produced) the sprout-producing seed is itself somehow different from the seeds in each of the moments that preceded it: It produced the sprout-producing seed, and they did not. A similar argument can be made about the seed at the moment before that (i.e., the seed that produced the seed that produced the sprout-producing seed), and the moment before that, and so on. Thus, the single observed event—the production of the sprout from the seed—requires that we accept that each moment in the history of the seed is different from any other. If the seed were the same at each and every moment, then it would produce its effect, the sprout, in each and every moment of its existence. Thus, the continuity of the seed over time is not based on the persistence of a single entity. The "continuity" is only apparent, and it is this appearance of continuity over time that Buddhists designated by the term "continuum" (*santāna*). By analogy, all pragmatically effective objects must be momentary in this way. For more on this, see Stcherbatsky 1984, vol. 1, 79–118. For a discussion of the early history of this idea, Steinkellner 1969 and von Rospatt 1995. For a discussion of Dharmakīrti's famous *sattvānumāna*, the inferential proof of momentariness from "existence," see Yoshimizu 1999 and Oetke 1993. For an edition and German translation from the Tibetan of Dharmottara's *Kṣaṇabhaṅgasiddhi* (*Proof of Momentariness*), see Frauwallner 1935. For an analysis of this text, see Tani 1997. And for a discussion of this theory in the work of later Buddhist epistemologists, see Mimaki 1976; Tani 1999; and Woo 1999.
70. For an extended defense of the claim that Dharmakīrti introduced determination only in the context of inferential/verbal awareness and not in the case of perception, see McCrea and Patil 2006, 307–25.
71. While there has been some disagreement about whether Dharmottara is a "Sautrāntika," in the sense that he accepts the ultimate reality of external objects (cf. Hattori 1968), or whether he is a "Yogacārin/

Vijñānavādin," in the sense that he does not accept the ultimate reality of external objects (cf. Matsumoto 1981), we think that there are good reasons to believe that Dharmottara believed in the reality of external, mind-independent objects. Both Vācaspatimiśra and Mokṣākaragupta, e.g., treat Dharmottara as a Sautrāntika and quote his texts in support of a Sautrāntika position. See Vācaspatimiśra's remarks in his NKaṇ: 256–7, translated in Stcherbatsky 1984, vol. 2, 360ff, and Mokṣākaragupta's remarks in his TBh 1944:66.18f, translated in Kajiyama 1966, 144. Apparently, Dharmottara was the pupil of Śubhagupta, who seems to have been the classical exponent of a realist position in post-Dharmakīrtian Buddhist philosophy in India. See Frauwallner 1961, 147; Krasser 1991, introduction, n. 1, quoting from PVinṬ 3.209b1; and Steinkellner and Much 1995. Furthermore, Abhinavagupta tells us that Dharmottara was the author of a text entitled *Bāhyārthasiddhi* (*Proof of External Objects*) in which he defended a Buddhist realist position. This text is not referred to elsewhere, as far as we know, and its existence seems to have passed unnoticed in contemporary secondary literature. See the IPVV, vol. 2: 128, 394.

72. The Sanskrit version of this text is lost. For an edition and German translation of the Tibetan translation, see Frauwallner 1937, 233–87. For one of the few secondary articles, see Steinkellner 1976.
73. Sanskrit fragment quoted in the NVTṬ 444.22 and JNĀ 332.14–16: *yac ca gṛhyate yac cādhyavasīyate te dve apy anyavyāvṛttī na vastunī.* Cf. Frauwallner 1937, 277.
74. NVTṬ 444.18–19: *adhyavasīyamānam api svalakṣaṇaṃ na paramārthasat. api tu tad api kalpitam.*
75. On the issue of implicative negation (*paryudāsa*), see, e.g., JNĀ 205; on imposition (*āropa*), see JNĀ 228; on causality (*kāryakāraṇabhāva*), see JNĀ 332; on supernormal perception (*yogipratyakṣa*), see JNĀ 332; and see the references in Woo 2001 to Jñānaśrīmitra's *Kṣaṇabhaṅgādhyāya*, and the references in Kellner 1997b and 2007 to his *Anupalabdhirahasya*.
76. See JNĀ (VC166.13–15) and Lasic 2000a:13*2–13*.6. Note that Lasic 2000a: 13*5 corrects Thakur: *adhyavaseya for adhyavasāya. asmākaṃ tāvad ubhayam api pramāṇam ubhayaviṣayam, grāhyādhyavaseyabhedena. yad dhi yatra jñāne pratibhāsate, tad grāhyam. yatra tu yat pravartate, tad adhyavaseyam. tatra pratyakṣasya svalakṣaṇaṃ grāhyam, adhyavaseyaṃ ca sāmānyam. anumānasya tu viparyayaḥ.* Also see JNĀ (AP 225.17): *dvidhā viṣayavyavahāraḥ pratibhāsād adhyavasāyāc ca* ["There are two

ways of talking about objects: On the basis of appearance and on the basis of determination"].

77. Jñānaśrīmitra, unlike Dharmottara, explicitly identifies the determined object of perception as a universal (*sāmānya*) in order to provide a basis for distinguishing between the two different sorts of universals that can be constructed from the grasped moment in the perceptual process. In explaining how we come to know that there is pervasion (*vyāpti*) between an inferential reason and a property to be proved, Jñānaśrīmitra points out that when we come to know the pervasion of, e.g., smoke by fire, we construct not simply a single smoke continuum (*santāna*)—as in the typical cases of perception discussed by Dharmottara—but the entire class of smoke continua, in order to arrive at the determination that "wherever there is smoke there is fire." Thus, while we always construct a universal as the determined object of perception, we sometimes construct what post-Dharmottaran Buddhist and Jaina philosophers call a "vertical universal" (*ūrdhva-sāmānya*), i.e., an individual object continuum. At other times we construct a "horizontal universal" (*tiryak-sāmānya*), i.e., the class comprising all, e.g., individual smoke continua. See JNĀ (VC 166.14–166.21) and Lasic 2000a, 13*6–14. JNĀ (VC 166.16–19) also is discussed and translated in Balcerowicz 1999, 212. For more on these two kinds of universals and the use of the terms *ūrdhva* and *tiryak* in Buddhist philosophical texts, see Balcerowicz 1999, 2001, 180–82, n. 158; and Patil 2003.
78. JNĀ (SSS:367.09): *vijñaptimātram akhilaṃ sthitam etaj jagattrayam*. Also see JNĀ (SSS: 365.16).
79. See NBṬ 52.06, (*nirvikalpaka*); *Apohaprakaraṇa* (in Frauwallner 1937,277), (*anyavyāvṛtti*); PVin (in Steinkellner and Krasser 1989, 31), (*āropita, paramārtha*); NBṬ 71–72 (*anartha*).
80. JNĀ (AP 226.01–226.03).
81. For a similar sort of "relativization" in the work of Dharmakīrti, see Dunne 2004, 275.
82. JNĀ (AP 220.02–220.04).
83. JNĀ (AP 220.07–220.09).
84. JNĀ (AP 226–227): "And just as the determination 'there is fire here' produces bodily activity, in the same way it produces verbal [activity] as well: 'Fire has been apprehended by me.' It also produces mental activity, that is, a reflective awareness having the same form [as the verbal statement]."
85. For a general discussion of these concepts, see Eckel 1987 and Newland 1999; and for a specific discussion of these concepts in the Buddhist

epistemological tradition, see the references in Dreyfus 1997 and Dunne 2004.

86. But Jñānaśrīmitra qualifies this (as discussed later). Verbal awareness cannot affirm or deny its own mental image, but we can affirm or deny prior mental images in subsequent verbal awareness. But when we do so, the mental image that we affirm or deny is thereby "external" to the awareness event in which it is affirmed or denied.
87. JNĀ (AP 229.03–06).
88. JNĀ (AP 229.06–07).
89. JNĀ (AP 229.07–229.10).
90. See JNĀ (AP 201.08–202.04).
91. The secondary literature on the types of inferential reasons is extensive. For a discussion of inferences based on effect-cause relations, see Gillon 1991; Kajiyama 1989; Lasic 1999, 2003; and Steinkellner 1991. For a discussion of inferences based on identity, see Hayes 1987; Iwata 2003; and Steinkellner 1974, 1991, 1996. For those based on nonapprehension, see the references to Kellner cited earlier. For a more general discussion, see the references in Dunne 2004 and Oetke 1991.
92. See JNĀ (AP 202.12–202.23).
93. JNĀ (AP 202.20–21), quoting from the introductory verse of the *Apohaprakaraṇa: apohaḥ śabdaliṅgābhyāṃ prakāśyate.*
94. JNĀ (AP 202.21–203.05).
95. While the verse mentions only what is "expressed by words," in explaining it, Jñānaśrīmitra makes clear that the verse applies equally well to inference and conceptual awareness in general. JNĀ (AP 203.08–203.09): "And the expression 'by words' is a metonym (*upalakṣaṇam*): What is made known by inferential reasons and what is made into an object by conceptual awarenesses, should also be seen [to be included]."
96. For a discussion of this "complex object" in the work of Jñānaśrīmitra's student Ratnakīrti, see Patil 2003 and 2009.
97. JNĀ (AP 206.13–206.14). "If at the time of hearing the word, the exclusion of others were not apparent, how could one act by avoiding what is other? And therefore, having been told 'Tie up the cow,' one would also tie up horses and so on."
98. For the classification of exclusion theorists as "negativists," "positivists," and "synthesists," see Mookherjee 1935, 132. For discussions of this typology, see Katsura 1986b; Patil 2003; and Siderits 1986, 1991.
99. JNĀ (AP 204.24–204.25).

100. JNĀ (AP 204.26–205.03).

101. Sāṃkhya was an early philosophical movement that focused on the enumeration of material and immaterial elements that make up the world. The Sāṃkhya understanding of material causation held that all effects preexist in their causes, for example, the yogurt that forms when milk ferments is thought to have already existed in the milk itself and only to have been manifested (*abhivyakta*) through the process of fermentation. Through the generalization of this basic principle, they conclude that all material things are simply the manifestation of what already existed in the primordial matter (*pradhāna*) that makes up the universe. For much more on Sāṃkhya, see Larson 2001.

102. One of the most characteristic and widely held tenets of Buddhists is that people do not have an enduring self/soul (*ātmā*). All that exists is an aggregate of ever-changing psychophysical components. Our mistaken impression that we have such a self/soul is the result of ignorance and is the principal cause of our inability to be released from the otherwise endless cycle of death and rebirth. For a very accessible discussion of debates about this issue, see K. K. Chakrabarti 1999 and Watson 2006.

103. JNĀ (AP 205.03–205.09).

104. See JNĀ (AP 225.19ff) and Katsura 1993.

105. JNĀ (AP 226.01–226.03).

106. The conceptual awareness that immediately follows perception classifies the grasped object by picking out one aspect of it. Thus, in conceptualizing the smoke that one sees as "smoke" rather than as "gray" or "wispy," the awareness contains just an aspect or part of what was grasped by the preceding nonconceptual awareness (in conjunction with the memory of prior instances of smoke, the word "smoke," and the like). For a discussion of selectivity in conceptualization, see Dunne 2004; Kellner 2004; and Patil 2003.

107. While we usually translate the term "*vyavasthā*" as "conditionally adopted position," it could be more literally rendered as "setting something (√*sthā*) down (*ava*) as distinct (*vi*)." In adopting the position that something is a certain way, one always implicitly adopts the position that it is distinct from what is not that way.

108. JNĀ (AP 227.01–227.04).

109. JNĀ (AP 227.10–227.11). The reference is to HB 3*14–15, quoted in JNĀ (AP 225.18–225.19).

110. For a brief but useful discussion of this tenet, see Hattori 1968, 82–85, nn. 1.25–1.27. For more detailed analysis, see Funayama 1992 and the discussion in Franco 1997.
111. JNĀ (AP 223.24–223.25): *ye 'rthā atadrūpaparāvṛttyā parasparaṃ pratyāsannās te teṣv ekadarśanānantaram aparadṛṣṭau anuvṛttapratyayam utpādayanti nānye . saiva ca śaktiḥ.*
112. JNĀ (AP 207.01–207.03): *yato jāter adhikāyāḥ prakṣepe 'pi vyaktīnāṃ rūpam atajjātīyavyāvṛttam eva cet, tadā tenaiva rūpeṇa śabdavikalpayor viṣayībhavantīnāṃ katham atadvyāvṛttipratītiparihāraḥ.*
113. JNĀ (AP 204.13): *saṃketakaraṇam ayam gaur iti.*
114. JNĀ (AP 225.18–225.19): *tathā ca "tato 'pi vikalpāt tadadhyavasāyena vastuny eva pravṛtter" iti* (quoting Dharmakīrti's *Hetubindu* 3*14–3*16).
115. JNĀ (AP 218.19–218.20): *tataś ca yady apy upādhitadvatāṃ bhedavādo duṣparihāraḥ, tadopakāralakṣaṇāyām api pratyāsattau samānadeśasyaiva grahaṇe vastugrāhiṇaḥ śaktir.*
116. JNĀ (AP 222.10–222.13): *yat tu trilocanaḥ, aśvagotvādīnāṃ sāmānyaviśeṣāṇāṃ svāśrayeṣu samavāyaḥ sāmānyam ity abhidhānapratyayayor nimittam iti. tat samavāyanirākaraṇenaivāpahastitam. samavāya eva vā svarūpeṇaiva nimittam iti na dṛṣṭāntakṣatiḥ. na ca jātisamavāyayoḥ sahakriyākalpanenānyonyaśaktitvam, tadā svarūpeṇaikasyāpi janakatvam.*
117. JNĀ (AP 226.17): *yathā śālitvena śālibījam upādānaṃ niranvayodaye 'pi śālyaṅkura upādeye.*
118. JNĀ (AP 215.05–215.06): *ākāre 'py upakāryopakārakadvāreṇa bhedaṃ puraskṛtyaiva sarvākāragrahaṇaprasañjanāt.*
119. JNĀ (AP 201.05–201.06): *ubhayathāpi sarvadharmānabhilāpyatvapratipā danaparam apohavyavasthāpanam ity uktaṃ bhavati.*
120. JNĀ (AP 204.03–204.06): *yadā tu puraḥsthitaṃ piṇḍam ekam upadarśya deśakālāntaraviprakīrṇāśeṣa vyaktisādhāraṇarūpavikalpasthāyinaṃ prakaraṇādeḥ pratipattāram avadhāryāyaṃ gaur iti saṃketaḥ, tadā yatraivāsau tat sādhāraṇaṃ rūpaṃ nirūpayati tam eva gośabdena vyavaharati.*

JÑĀNAŚRĪMITRA'S *MONOGRAPH ON EXCLUSION*

1. See Introduction, sec. 2, "The Elements of Inferential Reasoning."
2. By the term "property" (*dharma*), Jñānaśrīmitra, following standard Buddhist usage, means anything that can be located, e.g.; the red color of a piece of cloth is a "property" of the cloth in that it is "located" in it.

Similarly, a fire located on a mountain is a "property" of that mountain and the quality "being a cow"—that by virtue of which all cows are cows—is a "property" of each and every cow. For more on this "property-location model" in Sanskrit philosophy, see Matilal 1968, 16–18; and Matilal 1998 et al., 143–52.

3. "Conditionally adopted position" (*vyavasthā*) is a technical term that Jñānaśrīmitra explains at JNA 204.26ff. Also see Introduction, sec. 4, "Conditionally Adopted Positions."
4. Jñānaśrīmitra uses a variety of terms synonymously to refer to the "form" or "nature" of a thing (e.g., *rūpa, svabhāva, ātmā, svarūpa*). But in employing these terms, he makes use of what he himself acknowledges to be a fictitious distinction: The "form" or "nature" of a thing is just what the thing is. It is not anything that it has. Following Dharmakīrti, Jñānaśrīmitra takes it to be the case that the distinction between properties (*dharmas*)—such as "form" and "nature"—and property bearers, such as the things that have them (*dharmins*)—is fictitious.
5. The "means of valid awareness" are the "sources of knowledge" discussed in the introduction. For more on this, see Introduction, sec. 1, "Sources of Knowledge."
6. Here "experience" is used as a synonym for "perceptual awareness."
7. For a discussion of pragmatic efficacy (*arthakrīyā*). See Introduction, sec. 2.
8. Here and throughout the text, *italics* are used to indicate the voice of an opponent who is arguing against Jñānaśrīmitra's positions. These arguments sometimes express the views of actual opponents and sometimes of hypothetically constructed ones.
9. See Introduction, sec. 2, 3, and 4.
10. This argument was originally made by the Mīmāṃsakas in defense of their claim that a universal is the semantic value of a word. See *Tantravārttika* (TV) ad MS 1.3.33 in MD 2.247–2.248, and *Ślokavārttika* (ŚV) *Apohavāda* 88cd in Ray 1993, 516. The argument, however, is not Kumārila's. In these passages, Kumārila cites an old and often quoted Mīmāṃsā verse that makes the same point. See Mīmāṃsākośa (MīKo) 2309–2310.
11. On "image" and "appearance," see Introduction, sec. 3.
12. Here the opponents are principally the Mīmāṃsakas and Naiyāyikas, who believe that all members of a class such as "cows" must share a real common property, which they refer to as a universal, e.g., "cow-ness." For them, when one sees some thing and recognizes it as a "cow," one is aware

that that thing possesses the universal "cow-ness," regardless of whether or not one thinks of oneself as being aware of a universal.

13. An awareness that has a positive form (*vidhi-rūpa*) presents to us an object in terms of what it is, e.g., "This is a cow," while one that has a negative image or form (*abhāva-ākāra*) presents an object to us in terms of what it is not, e.g., "This is not a horse."
14. To "ascertain" something means to be aware of it as belonging to a particular class, e.g., "This is a cow" or as possessing a certain property, e.g., "It has horns." Ascertaining awareness (*niścaya*) is contrasted with doubtful awareness (*saṃśaya*), in which an object is presented as possibly, but not definitively, belonging to a particular class, e.g., "That is either a real person or a statue" or as possibly, but not definitively, possessing a certain property, e.g., "That is either blue or black."
15. This quotation is from Dharmakīrti's Pramāṇavārttika (PV), *Svārthānumāna* 57.
16. As generally understood by Buddhist epistemologists up to Jñānaśrīmitra's time, exclusion is the object of inferential/verbal awareness but not perceptual awareness. See Introduction, sec. 2, 3, and 4.
17. These two grammatical analyses of the word "exclusion" both lead to the conclusion that "exclusion" is a positive entity. In the first case, it is "that which is excluded from other things," i.e., an external object, such as a cow that is excluded from things that are not cows. In the second case, it is "that in which other things are excluded," i.e., a mental image, in which an object such as a cow is presented as something that is excluded from things that are not cows.
18. The term "authoritative text" (*śāstra*) can be used to refer to individual statements or passages from a foundational text recognized by the tradition as well as to the entire text.
19. Dharmakīrti's *Nyāyabindu* (NB) 2.21. Dharmakīrti and his followers divide inferential reasons into three types: (1) an effect (*kārya*), from which we can infer its cause (e.g., smoke, from which we can infer fire); (2) an essential property (*svabhāva*) of a thing, from which we can infer another essential property of that thing that is necessarily copresent with it (e.g., the fact that something is an oak, from which we can infer that it is a tree); and (3) failure to apprehend (*anupalabdhi*) something under conditions when it should be apprehensible (e.g., the failure to apprehend a pot on the floor, given proper lighting, healthy eyes, and the like, from which we can infer that there is not a pot on the floor). Only the third

type of inferential reason can establish the absence/negation of a thing. The opponent's point here is that if exclusion is a kind of negation and all inferential reasons reveal an exclusion, all inferential reasons would be of type 3. Also see Introduction, sec. 2, "The Elements of Inferential Reasoning."

20. Dharmakīrti's Pramāṇavārttika (PV) *Parārthānumāna* 262. Drawing on the resources of the Sanskrit grammatical tradition, the Buddhist epistemological tradition distinguishes between two types of negation: non-implicative negation *(prasajya-pratiṣedha)*, e.g., "There is no cow in the room" and implicative negation (*paryudāsa*), e.g., "There is a non-cow in the room." For more on this distinction, see Kajiyama 1989, 155–70.
21. Here we translate the Sanskrit term "*guṇa*" (quality, subordinate element, positive quality, etc.) with the very generic term "element," since Jñānaśrīmitra goes on to provide six different interpretations of the term. See Outline.
22. The point here is that we all agree that the content of the negation of a predicate such as "not a cow" is not a positive entity but an absence.
23. A "partial indicator" (*upalakṣaṇa*) is a member of a class that is mentioned in order to indicate other unspecified members of the same class.
24. Dharmakīrti's Pramāṇavārttika (PV), *Svārthānumāna* v. 124.
25. The term "conventional association" (*saṅketa*) refers to the relation between a word and what it is taken to refer to on the basis of general agreement (either implicit or explicit) among speakers of a language. The object with which a word is conventionally associated is generally taken to be its "primary" (*mukhya*) referent, in contrast to those objects that are picked out when a word is used figuratively. There was a long running debate in Sanskrit philosophy about whether the relation between a word and its primary referent/meaning is "conventional" or "natural." While Nyāya and Buddhist philosophers take the relation to be "conventional," the Mīmāṃsakas argue that the relation between a word and its primary referent is natural and eternal.
26. For the "circularity argument" in Uddyotakara and Kumārila, see Introduction, sec. 2.
27. Mīmāṃsakas take the primary referent of a word to be a universal. For them, the word "cow" refers literally only to the universal "cow-ness." It can be used to refer to individual cows only metonymically, owing to their connection with the universal "cow-ness." In contrast, Naiyāyikas (at least from the time of the tenth-century philosopher Vācaspatimiśra) take the

position that a word generally refers to an individual as a possessor of a certain universal. For them, the word "cow" refers literally to an individual as qualified by the universal "cow-ness."

28. "Reflective awareness" (*pratyavamarśa*) is a second-order awareness, i.e., an awareness that takes as a part of its object one or more awarenesses.
29. This account of term "acquisition" presupposes that the language learner has (to some extent) already individuated and grouped the objects within his sensory sphere, even before the language teacher prompts him to associate a specific group of such objects with a specific term. The "reflective awareness" (*pratyavamarśa*) referred to here is the language learner's preexisting awareness in which certain objects are seen as similar. The language teacher prompts the language learner on the basis of context to pick out one set of "similar" objects from the many such preexisting sets. He then teaches him to associate the new term with that group.
30. See Introduction, sec. 4.
31. For more on class-properties/universals, see Introduction, sec. 2, 3, and 4.
32. Jñanaśrīmitra uses the Sanskrit term "*vidhi*" (here rendered as "positive verbal content") to refer both to affirmation, saying that something exists rather than saying that it does not exist, and to "positive entities," i.e., things that exist, as opposed to nonentities, i.e., absences.
33. This is the third interpretation of "element." The first interpretation is at JNĀ 203.11 and the second at JNĀ 203.15.
34. This quotation is from Vācaspatimiśra's commentary on *Nyāyasūtras*, *Nyāyavārttikatātparyaṭīkā* (NVTṬ) ad *Nyāyasūtra* (NS) 2.2.66. The full passage is as follows: "And an exclusion, which is other than the particular, does not make the false construct (which is excluded from what is other) similar to the particular: If that were the case, then a donkey could make an elephant and a mosquito similar as well. *Furthermore, you do not accept that exclusion is a property (dharma) of a particular (svalakṣaṇa).*" NVTṬ 444.16–17: *na ca svalakṣaṇād anyā vyāvṛttir alīkam anyavyāvṛttam svalakṣaṇena sarūpayati tathā sati hastimaśakāv api rāsabhaḥ sarūpayet | na ca svalakṣaṇadharmo vyāvṛttir bhavadbhir abhypeyate.* We are emending the printed text by removing the word "*dharma*" which appears before "*na*." This reading is also attested in several manuscripts. See NVTṬ2 684. We also are emending "*anyavyavṛttir*" to "*anyā vyāvṛttir*."

In this passage, Vācaspatimiśra is responding to the position of the Buddhist philosopher Dharmottara. Dharmottara argues that the semantic value of a word can only be an exclusion because an exclusion is the only kind of thing that can belong to both the internal mental image that is produced upon hearing the word and the real external objects that we take that word to refer to. Given the ontological commitments of the Buddhist epistemologists, there can be no real, positive, similarity between any two things (including the mental image and its external referent). But even two utterly distinct things can be "alike" in what they are not, e.g., both the mental image "cow" and a real, external, cow, are "alike" in that they are excluded from what is non-cow.

Vācaspatimiśra rejects the claim that any "third form" (i.e., an exclusion) that is distinct from both the internal image and the external referent can create similarity between these two utterly distinct things. Furthermore, he argues that it is contrary to the ontological commitments of the Buddhist epistemologists to say that exclusion (which is nothing but a conceptual construct) can be a property of a real particular.

35. Here the word "real" (*bhāvikī*) clearly refers to exclusion (*vyāvṛtti*), as it does when Vācaspatimiśra uses the same term at *Nyāyavārttikatātparyaṭīkā* (NVTṬ) 444.09.
36. Jñānaśrīmitra rejects Vācaspatimiśra's criticism. In his view, the Buddhist epistemologists do in fact accept that exclusion is a property of particulars. Moreover, this property is not simply a fictitious mental construct but is in fact constitutive of the particular. There is no problem with claiming that exclusion is a "property" of particulars, since the distinction between properties and property possessors is a conceptually constructed fiction. See JNĀ 227.11–227.15.
37. Sanskrit philosophers usually divide absences into four types: (1) "prior absence," the absence of something that does not exist now but will exist later; (2) "absence after destruction," the absence of something that previously existed but no longer exists; (3) "absolute absence," the absence of something that never has and never will exist; and (4) "mutual absence," an absence that is entailed by what is present, e.g., the fact that a pot is not a cloth.
38. This is referring to the view of Sāṃkhya authors who argued that nothing truly new can ever be produced and that all apparently new effects are simply the manifestations of preexisting elements. See Larson 2001, 10ff.

39. Buddhists deny the existence of a persisting "self," yet like most Sanskrit philosophers, they accept a theory of karma. They argue that a person will experience in the future positive or negative karmic consequences for actions performed in the present while at the same time also arguing that there is really no such "person" who persists between now and then.
40. See JNĀ 203.06ff.
41. The point of this seems to be that in the case of inferential reasons that establish positive entities and affirmative statements, both the positive and negative contents of the inferential/verbal awareness, i.e., the positive component and the exclusion component have as their object the positive entity. Such an awareness simultaneously tells us what the object is and what it is not. This appears to be a quotation or variant reading of Dharmakīrti's *Hetubindu* (HB) 26*23–24.
42. Jñānaśrīmitra's account of conceptual awareness requires that all conceptual awarenesses have both a positive and a negative component. Here he explains why it nevertheless seems to us that some conceptual awarenesses have "positive" content while others have "negative" content. A conceptual awareness is considered to have positive content when the activity pursued on the basis of it and the reflective awareness that we form regarding it are taken to involve a positive object. It is considered to have negative content when the activity pursued on the basis of it and the reflective awareness that we form regarding it are taken to involve an absence. This answers the objection raised by the opponent, at JNĀ 202.12–202.22, that accepting the theory of exclusion undermines the division of inferential reasons into those that establish positive entities and those that establish absences.
43. For the distinction between "implicative" and "nonimplicative" negation, see n. 20.
44. Appears to be a quotation, with some variants, of either *Pramāṇavārttika* (PV), *Svārthānumāna* vs. 125 or *Pratyakṣa* vs. 30d.
45. Dharmakīrti's *Pramāṇaviniścaya* (PVin) 2.8 in Steinkellner 1973, 29; and Steinkellner, Krasser, and Lasic 2007, 49.
46. I.e., Dharmottara's commentary on Dharmakīrti's *Pramāṇaviniścaya*, the *Pramāṇaviniścayaṭīkā* (PVinṬ).
47. Trilocana was the teacher of Vācaspatimiśra. His work, which is no longer extant, is known to us from references in later works.
48. Dharmottara's *Apohaprakaraṇa* (AP-Dh) 251.11–12. See Akamatsu 1983, 196–97, n. 55, and note his correction of Frauwallner's translation.

49. Both these examples are cases in which an expression presupposes a qualifier/qualified relation between two things that are in fact identical. Rāhu, e.g., is the being thought to be responsible for eclipses. He is a disembodied head that swallows the sun or moon, only to have it reappear from his neck. Thus to say "Rāhu's head" implies a distinction where none exists; Rāhu simply is a head. In this and similar expressions, the possessive term ("Rāhu's") is taken to be a qualifier (*viśeṣaṇa*) of the thing qualified by it (*viśeṣya*), i.e., the head. Sanskrit-language theorists generally recognize two types of qualifiers: Those that are co-referential (*samānādhikaraṇa*) with what they qualify and those that are non-co-referential (*vyadhikaraṇa*) with what they qualify. The term "Rāhu's" in "Rāhu's head" is an example of the non-co-referential type. Examples of the first type include adjectives as well as nouns used in apposition to other nouns, as in "The universal, cow-ness." Jñānaśrīmitra chooses the latter example because his Nyāya opponents, as discussed later, do not accept that universals themselves possess universals and therefore that in this expression the terms "cow-ness" and "universal" do not refer to a type and its token but refer to one and the same thing.
50. For a Nyāya discussion of *viśeṣya-viśeṣaṇa-bhāva*, see *Nyāyavārttika* (NV) *ad Nyāyasūtra* (NS) 1.1.4 and *Nyāyavārttikatātparyaṭīkā* (NVTṬ) *ad Nyāyasūtra* (NS) 1.1.4.
51. We are supplying this sentence from a few lines earlier. The text simply says, "in this very sentence."
52. I.e., Vācaspatimiśra's objection that taking exclusion to be a "property" contradicts the standard Buddhist view.
53. This is the fourth explanation of the term "element."
54. This refers back to the introductory verse.
55. Because the claim here is that exclusion is not an element of the external object itself but an element of the assertion about the external object, it is necessarily understood as a part of our awareness of that assertion.
56. Dharmakīrti's *Pramāṇavārttika* (PV), *Svārthānumāna* vs. 96ab.
57. Dharmakīrti's *Pramāṇavārttika* (PV), *Svārthānumāna* vs. 1.23c.
58. This is apparently a reference to the *Nyāyavārttika* (NV) ad *Nyāyasūtra* (NS) 1.2.66. See *Nyāyavārttika* (NV) 687, in which Uddyotakara argues that it is not possible for every word to have the exclusion of what is other as its meaning, since for words such as "everything," there is nothing other than it to be excluded.

59. This example appears in Uddyotakara's *Nyāyavārttika* (NV) ad *Nyāyasūtra* (NS) 1.1.33. See *Nyāyavārttika* (NV) 104.21.
60. I.e., other things going toward Śrughna.
61. I.e., one says only what does not go without saying.
62. This is either a paraphrase or variant reading of Vācaspatimiśra's *Nyāyavārttikatātparyaṭīkā* (NVTṬ) *ad Nyāyasūtra* (NS) 2.2.66 in Thakur 1996, which is quoted in n. 34.
63. I.e., the capacity referred to earlier, namely, the capacity to attain a state in which it is not mixed up with what is other.
64. A "class property" is whatever marks an individual as belonging to a particular class, e.g., "cow-ness" as a class property of cows.
65. *Nyāyavārttikatātparyaṭīkā* (NVTṬ) 443.23–444.02.
66. This is the fifth interpretation of the term "element."
67. This interpretation is based on the etymology of the term used for "element" (*guṇa*), which can be derived from the verbal root "to repeat or multiply" (√√*guṇ*).
68. Jñānaśrīmitra is here glossing the word "*tatra*" (literally, "there") from the summary verse—which we translated earlier as "this being the case"—as "in these" (*teṣu*).
69. This is a quotation with inserted explanatory material from Dharmakīrti's *Pramāṇavārttika* (PV), *Pratyakṣa* vs. 172.
70. Here the term "distinction" (*viccheda*) is being used as a synonym for exclusion.
71. Dharmakīrti's *Pramāṇavārttika* (PV), *Svārthānumāna* vs. 133.
72. Dharmakīrti's *Pramāṇavārttika* (PV), *Svārthānumāna* vs. 185cd–186ab.
73. This is the sixth and final interpretation of the term "element."
74. Dharmakīrti's *Pramāṇavārttika* (PV), *Svārthānumāna* vs. 169cd–170ab.
75. By "section on words expressing absences" (*abhāvavācikādhikāra*), Jñānaśrīmitra is referring to Dharmakīrti's *Pramāṇavārttikasvavṛtti* (PVSV) *Svārthānumāna* 185cd–186ab.
76. A slight variation of PVSV 92.21 ad *Pramāṇavārttika* (PV), *Svārthānumāna* 185 in *Pramāṇavārttikasvavṛtti* (PVSV) 92. See Akamatsu 1983:11.
77. JNĀ 205.03–205.06.
78. JNĀ 203.03–203.04.
79. For "determination," see Introduction, sec. 3 and 4.
80. Dharmakīrti's *Pramāṇaviniścaya* (PVin) 1.15, in Steinkellner, Krasser, and Lasic 2007, 16; and Vetter 1966, 84.

81. Dharmakīrti's *Pramāṇavārttika* (PV), *Pratyakṣa* vs. 235.
82. For "pragmatic effect" (*arthakriyā*), see Introduction, sec. 2.
83. This refers to a standard example of perceptual error, that of a person who has jaundice and therefore sees even white objects, e.g., a conch shell, as if they were yellow.
84. Here, "having the same object" is said to be pervaded by "having the same appearance." Therefore, if it can be established that the two awarenesses do not have the same appearance, it follows that they cannot have the same object. This "apprehension of something that precludes a pervading factor" (*vyāpakaviruddhopalabdhi*) is one of the eleven types of absence-establishing inferential reasons in Dharmakīrti's *Nyāyabindu* (NB) 2.38 in Malvania 1971, 135.
85. This refers to the tree example at JNĀ 209.02ff. Jñānaśrīmitra takes this argument to imply an inference, which he here refutes. In this inference, the subject (*pakṣa*) is a difference in appearance between two awarenesses; what is to be established (*sādhya*) is that the object of these awarenesses need not be different; the inferential reason (*hetu*) is the absence of any difference in their pragmatic effect; and the similar case (*sapakṣa*) is the tree, which looks different to near and distant observers but is nevertheless considered to be a single object.
86. I.e., when one sees that a tree looks less clear at a distance than it does close up, one does not conclude that the tree itself has two distinct forms, one clear and one less clear. Rather, we conclude that the clear awareness that we have when we are up close more accurately captures what the tree looks like, and therefore we reject the less clear appearance as a kind of misperception.
87. I.e., the conch shell independent of its color.
88. The "question begging response" (*prakṛta-sama* or *prakaraṇa-sama*) is one of the standard forms of "sophistical rejoinders" listed in the Nyāyasūtra (NS)1.2.10. For a discussion of "false rejoinders," see Matilal 1998 et al., chap. 3.
89. The opponent has argued that the difference in appearance between the perceptual and conceptual awarenesses of a cow is like the difference in appearance between distant and up-close perceptions of a tree. But Jñānaśrīmitra has just shown that if this is so, one of these appearances (the less clear one) must be rejected as erroneous. But this cannot be explained on the Nyāya view that conceptual awarenesses have real extra-mental particulars for their objects. The conceptual awareness "cow" cannot have a real particular cow as its object for the reason just stated,

but there is nothing else that could be its object. Hence, the conceptual awareness cannot even be properly described as an error, since there is nothing for it to be in error about.

90. "That thing," i.e., the real cow.
91. *Nyāyavārttikatātparyaṭīkā* (NVTṬ) ad *Nyāyasūtra* (NS) 1.1.4 in Thakur 1996, 119. The term "remote" (*parokṣa*) literally means beyond the range of the senses.
92. This refers back to JNĀ 209.09–209.11. See JNĀ 209.02ff.
93. Jñānaśrīmitra's point is that Vācaspatimiśra's argument can establish that perceptual and conceptual awarenessess have the same object only if it is claimed that all differences in appearance between awarenesses are due to differences in their causes (rather than differences in their objects).
94. Vācaspatimiśra's *Nyāyavārttikatātparyaṭīkā* (NVTṬ) in Thakur 1996, 444.02–06. For a discussion of "inconclusive," see Introduction, sec. 2, "The Elements of Inferential Reasoning." "Otherwise Established" (*anyathāsiddha*) is recognized as a subtype of the fallacy "Unestablished" (*asiddha*) by some Naiyāyikas. See Gokhale 1992, 116–18.
95. This is a quotation from Prajñākaragupta's commentary on Dharmakīrti's *Pramāṇavārttika* (PV) at *Pramāṇasiddhi* vs 1. See *Pramāṇavārttikālaṃkāra* (PVA) 4.
96. "Overextension" (*ativyāpti*) exists when a definition or description is formulated in such a way that it applies to cases other than those to which it is intended to apply. In this case, if the claim that the particular exists or does not exist is conditioned by the existence of something other than the particular itself, there is no basis for restricting its reference. The existence or nonexistence of any other thing could just as well govern it.
97. This goes back to JNĀ 211.12, to the section before the four alternatives are discussed.
98. I.e., in something that is not restricted.
99. See n. 84.
100. See n. 49.
101. It is unclear who is being referred to here. See Akamatsu 1983, 219–20, n. 113.
102. It is not clear whether this is meant to refer to a later passage in his *Monograph on Exclusion* or elsewhere in Jñānaśrīmitra's works. In either case, we have not been able to identify the relevant passage.
103. I.e., in Jñānaśrīmitra's *Examination of Difference/Non-Difference* (*Bhedābhedaparīkṣā*).

104. It is unclear whose view is being referred to here.
105. For more on determination see Introduction, sec. 2, 3, 4.
106. The term "natural connection" (*svābhāvika-sambandha*) was coined by Vācaspatimiśra to refer to the natural basis for the inference warranting relation of pervasion. See Introduction, sec. 2, "The Elements of Inferential Reasoning."
107. Here, the term "contingent feature" (*upādhi*) refers to any feature that belongs to a particular thing but is not considered to be identical with it.
108. See n. 19, and Introduction, sec. 2, "The Elements of Inferential Reasoning."
109. This refers to JNĀ 213.10–213.15.
110. "Nonapprehension of a pervading factor" (*vyāpakānupalabdhi*) is one of the eleven types of inferential reasons for establishing absences recognized by Dharmakīrti. See Dharmakīrti's *Nyāyabindu* (NB) 2.33. The contrapositive form of the inference is that in which the absence of the inferential reason is said to occur wherever what is to be established by it is absent, e.g., "wherever there is no fire there is no smoke, as in a lake." In this case, the inferential reason is "having the form of the real thing as its object," and what is to be established is "making one aware of the properties of a thing." Therefore, when "making one aware of the properties of a thing" is absent, "having the form of the real thing as its object" is invariably absent as well.
111. The two inferences in this case are the positive inference, "Whatever makes one aware of the form of a real thing makes us aware of its properties," and its contrapositive, "Whatever does not make us aware of the properties of a real thing does not make us aware of the form of that real thing."
112. See n. 4.
113. As Akamatsu 1983, 227, n. 127, has noted, this quotation is not from Bhāsarvajña's *Nyāyabhūṣaṇā* (NBhū) but from Vācaspatimiśra's *Nyāyavārttikatātparyaṭīkā* (NVTṬ) 119.28–120.1.
114. If a thing and its nature are different, there is no basis for connecting the thing and its nature in a possessive-relation.
115. Vācaspatimiśra's *Nyāyavārttikatātparyaṭīkā* (NVTṬ) 115.11–115.13.
116. "Treasury" (*ākara*) is often used to designate the most important foundational text within a text tradition, e.g., the *Mahābhāṣya* (MBh) in Grammar or the *Śābarabhāṣya* (ŚBh) in Mīmāṃsā. It seems to be used here to refer to Dharmakīrti's *Pramāṇavārttika* (PV), specifically *Svārthānumāna* v. 52–55.

117. In the aforementioned section of the *Pramāṇavārttika* (PV), Dharmakīrti introduces the terms "enabler" (*upakāraka*) and "enabled" (*upakārya*) to refer, respectively, to property possessors (*dharmin*) and their properties (*dharma*). He argues that something can be a property only if it belongs to some property possessor and therefore this property possessor is what "enables" that property to be a property. Even if one accepts that properties are distinct from their property possessor, one also must accept that the property possessor's capacities to enable those properties are intrinsic to it. (If this were not the case, then these capacities, too, would be properties and would have to be related to the property possessor by a further enabling capacity, leading to regress.) And since these enabling capacities are intrinsic to the property possessor, it is impossible to grasp it without grasping those capacities as well. Furthermore, one cannot be aware of the property possessor's capacity to enable a specific property without being aware of that property as well. Thus, it follows that one cannot be aware of any property possessor without grasping all its properties, even if it is granted that property possessors and properties are distinct.
118. Bhāsarvajña's *Nyāyabhūṣaṇa* (NBhū) 246.30–247.05. Bhāsarvajña's point here is that the sun has the property of illuminating everything in the world and, in that sense, "enables" them to be illuminated. Thus, whenever we see the sun, we should inevitably see everything illumined by it.
119. It is not clear to what Jñānaśrīmitra is referring there. There is a place where Bhāsarvajña discusses this issue, but it is in the voice of an opponent. See *Nyāyabhūṣaṇa* (NBhū) 267.2ff.
120. This is a partial quotation of Dharmakīrti's *Pramāṇavārttika* (PV), *Svārthānumāna* 54. The full verse is as follows: "If the capacities of the thing to enable its contingent features are different from the thing, then in what sense do they belong to it? If they are not enabled by it, then there would be an infinite regress of capacities." [*dharmopakāraśaktīnāṃ bhede tas tasya kiṃ yadi* | *nopakāras tatas tāsāṃ tadā syād anavasthitiḥ* ||]
121. This appears to refer to JNĀ (KBhA: 19–20), where Jñānaśrīmitra criticizes Bhāsarvajña's argument that "capacity" is different from what has it.
122. The central purpose of Jñānaśrīmitra's *Study of Moment by Moment Destruction* is to defend the well-known Buddhist thesis (accepted by everyone in the Dharmakīrtian text tradition) that there are no things that persist through time, since each and every thing can exist for only a single moment. Objects that appear to persist through time are nothing more than a series of moments that we mistakenly take to be single

objects. Hence, it is impossible for there to be any real thing that lacks a capacity at one moment and acquires it in a subsequent moment. See Introduction, n. 69.

123. Vācaspatimiśra's commentary at *Nyāyasūtra* 2.2.66, *Nyāyavārttikatātparyaṭīkā* (NVTṬ) 443.19–443.20.
124. Jñanaśrīmitra is referring to JNĀ (VC: 162) in Lasic 2000a, 7*, 17*–18*.
125. This is a quotation from Kumārilabhaṭṭa's *Ślokavārttika* (ŚV), *Ākṛtivāda* vs. 10ab.
126. According to Naiyāyikas, "inherence" (*samavāya*) is the relation by which universals, qualities, and the like are located in property possessors.
127. In the absence of any other sort of connection between a property possessor and its properties, one must accept the enabler/enabled relation between them. Otherwise, there would be no way for any specific property to belong to a specific property possessor, and in fact, any property, if it existed anywhere would have to exist everywhere.
128. If "nature" is something ultimately real and not conceptually constructed, it can belong only to unique particulars. Nothing is repeated, and there can be no real patterns. Any "nature" that is relied on to explain observed regularities can do so only in terms of purportedly repeatable properties that cannot really exist. Thus, natural capacity as an account of nondeviation must be a conceptual fiction.
129. On Jñānaśrīmitra's account, visual awareness has two objects, one that is grasped and one that is determined. The latter is a conceptual construction and is dependent on both the conventions through which we have learned to construct objects and on our own desires, expectations, interests, and the like. It is not determined by the grasped object itself. See Introduction, sec. 4.
130. I.e., when we see, e.g., a blue pot, we do not see two distinct things, the pot and its blueness. The argument that a color such as blue "inheres" in an object/locus such as a pot fails because it cannot be convincingly shown that there are two objects in question. It is only when there is a clear distinction between two objects such as the pot and the water that it contains that one can meaningfully say "This is in this."
131. I.e., without the awareness of both fruit and the pot, one would not have the awareness "This fruit exists in this pot."
132. Here Jñānaśrīmitra states his argument in the form of an inference: The inferential reason is the "failure to apprehend two separate things"; what is to be proved is "the legitimacy of saying 'This is in that'"; the site is "our

awareness of a purported universal and what possesses it." For more on inferential arguments, see Introduction, sec. 2.

133. The "nonapprehension of a cause" is another of the eleven types of inferential reasons for establishing absences discussed in Dharmakīrti's *Nyāyabindu* (NB) 2.39. From the nonobservation of the cause, one can infer the absence of the effect.
134. I.e., those who argue that properties inhere in their property possessors.
135. Dharmakīrti's *Pramāṇavārttika* (PV), *Pratyakṣa* v. 149.
136. This verse is also quoted in Paṅḍit Aśoka's *Sāmānyadūṣaṇa* (SāmDū) in SBNT:101–2, but we have not been able to trace the original source.
137. Jñānaśrīmitra's point is that since Trilocana acknowledges that one sees universals, but not as something separate from the individual, he must acknowledge that one sees the universal and the individual as a single object. And if one has already perceived that the universal and the individual are, in fact, one, it would be inappropriate to offer arguments for or against this nondifference.
138. This seems to be another quotation from Trilocana.
139. "Also," i.e., as it does grasp the nondifference between the individual and the universal.
140. "Ascertainment" (*vyavasāya*) refers to a conceptual judgment subsequent to perception, but if perception itself has already established the nonseparation of the individual from the universal, this obviates the need for any further argument.
141. This is a quotation from Jñānaśrīmitra's *Kṣaṇabhaṅgādhyāya*, the *Section on Uncaused Absence* JNĀ (KSA:111).
142. If fire is the only thing that is hot, everything else that, like it, has the property of being knowable, has the property of not being hot, and we therefore could infer that because fire has the property of being knowable, it also would not be hot.
143. If actually feeling that the fire is hot cannot establish that there isn't the absence of heat there, then no argument could possibly establish it.
144. This is a quotation from Dharmakīrti's *Hetubindu* (HB) 25*9–25*.19. The full passage runs as follows:

    For even one who sees fire does not see fire to the exclusion of all other things such that if he desired water, he would not act with respect to that object. If one were to argue that the absence of water is known merely by not perceiving it, then we would ask, "How can an absence be an awareness, or a cause for the awareness, of anything?"

And furthermore, how can there be an awareness of this absence of perception? If the absence of water is apprehended even without the apprehension of that nonperception of water or of anything else, then why is the absence of water not known in states of sleep, intoxication, or delirium or in conditions when something is blocking one's view or one's back is turned? This is analyzed further in the *Pramāṇaviniścaya*. Therefore, this person, although seeing fire, would neither act nor refrain from acting without determining that "this is fire, not water." Thus, he would meet with an intractable dilemma. [*na hi ayam analaṃ paśyann api kevalam analam eva paśyati, yena salilārthī na pravarteta. anupalambhena salilābhāvaḥ pratīyata iti cet, ko 'yam anupalambho nāma. yadi salilopalambhābhāva iti, kathaṃ so 'bhāvaḥ kasyacit pratipattiḥ partipattihetur vā; tasyāpi kathaṃ pratipattiḥ. tasya tato vānyasya kasyacid apy apratipattāv apy abhāvapratipattau satyāṃ svāpamadamūrchāvyavadhānapṛṣṭhībhāvādyavasthāsv apy abhāvaḥ kiṃ na pratīyate. bhūyo 'pi vicāritaṃ pramāṇaviniścaye. tasmād ayam analaṃ paśyann apy analo 'yam na salilam ity anadhyavasyan na tiṣṭhen nāpi pratiṣṭheteti dustaraṃ vyasanaṃ pratipannaḥ syāt.*]

145. This "nonapprehension of a cause" is the one mentioned in JNĀ 216.25. The charge that this nonapprehension of a cause is not established is made in JNĀ 217.04. Jñānaśrīmitra's claim was that one cannot coherently maintain that one thing "inheres" in another if one is not aware of those two things as distinct from each other. The opponent argued that it was possible to establish that one sees two distinct things, an individual and a universal, but Jñānaśrīmitra has now shown that there is no basis for seeing two objects at all and hence has shown that his inferential reason is a good one.

146. This refers to the inferential argument stated in JNĀ 214.11–214.12:

"Whatever produces an awareness of something invariably produces the awareness of its properties, just like a sense faculty." Jñānaśrīmitra has now established that even if one accepts that the property and the property possessor are distinct, one must accept this inferential argument. He has shown that anyone who accepts that the property and the property possessor are distinct must accept that there is an "enabling relation" between them and that one cannot be aware of an enabler, that is, a property possessor, without being aware of everything that is enabled by it, that is, its properties.

147. I.e., the word "tree" by itself still requires a predicate such as "exists" or "does not exist" in order to make a meaningful statement. If the word "tree" caused us to be aware of an actual tree, we would not need to be told further whether or not the tree exists. Since we do need to be told this, it follows that what the word "tree" makes us aware of cannot be a real tree.
148. This is a quotation from Dharmakīrti's *Pramānavārttika* (PV), *Svārthānumāna* 130b–131b.
149. Jñānaśrīmitra wishes to show that his explanation accounts for both sorts of qualification (co-referential and non-co-referential) referred to earlier. See JNĀ 205.21–205.23 and n. 49. Hence, one may refer to the "tree" and its properties co-referentially, e.g., "The tree exists," or non-co-referentially, e.g., "The tree has existence."
150. For Jñānaśrīmitra, because no objects persist through time, the "tree" that changes over time but still remains the "same tree" is a conceptual fiction. Because of this, it is not possible for any real thing such as a tree to acquire or lose properties, since each real tree exists for only a moment.
151. When we hear the word "tree," it produces a generic mental image of a tree. When it is qualified by other words such as "tall" or "green," other mental images are produced in which the generic tree-image is combined with generic images such as "tall" or "green." If someone tells us "The tree in my yard has fruit," our initial image of a generic tree is replaced by an image of a generic "tree in that person's yard that has fruit." Yet we think that the latter part of the sentence tells us something new about the same "tree" that we first thought of, when really a generic image has been replaced by a more specific generic image.
152. This phrase echoes that of Dharmakīrti at *Pramāṇavārttikasvavṛtti* (PVSV) 107.2 and Dharmottara's *Apohaprakaraṇa* (AP-Dh) 239.18–19, as noted by Akamatsu 1983, 258, n. 217.
153. By "separate qualifier," Jñānaśrīmitra means one that is non-co-referential (*vyadhikaraṇa*). See n. 49.
154. People ordinarily think that when they hear an expression such as "there is a tree there," they become aware of a real tree, and when they further hear that "the tree is tall," they believe they have acquired a more specific awareness of that same tree, which is now marked as being "tall" and therefore excluded from trees that are not tall. Similarly, when they hear that the tree is "a pine tree," they believe they have acquired a still more specific awareness of that same tree, which is now excluded from trees that are not pines. As we have already seen, however, for Jñānaśrīmitra,

the second awareness—since it has a different appearance—cannot have the same object.

155. I.e., the distinction between the object of conceptual awareness and the real thing.

156. When we hear the word "cow," what comes to mind is a generic collection of properties, e.g., four legs, two horns, tail, dewlap, and so forth, inextricably mixed up with a set of generic sounds "c"-"o"-"w."

157. This is a quotation from Dharmakīrti's *Pramāṇavārttika* (PV), *Pratyakṣa* v. 147. Dharmakīrti's argument is that those who believe in real universals, e.g., the Naiyāyikas, maintain that these universals do not themselves have sensible properties such as color and shape, but he contends that in the awareness produced, there is nothing but such sensible properties; hence, this awareness cannot be an awareness of a universal.

158. There is nothing in the awareness produced by hearing the word "cow" apart from its sensible content, i.e., the legs, horns, tail, dewlap, and so forth and the sounds "c"-"o"-"w." The "universal" cannot be a component of this awareness because it, like "space," doesn't have any sensible properties of its own.

159. Since it is accepted that "universals" do not have any sensible properties, if universals were the object of inferential/verbal awareness, and if no image containing sensible properties came to mind upon hearing words such as "cow" and "horse," then the awarenesses produced by these two words would be indistinguishable.

160. I.e., when we (mis)identify through conceptualization a mental image with one or more putatively real external particulars.

161. Dharmakīrti's *Pramāṇavārttika* (PV), *Svārthānumāna* v. 73.

162. "Initial sense impression" (*ālocana*) is a term used by Buddhists and others to refer to the first moment of the perceptual process before any conceptualization has taken place. See, e.g., *Ślokavārttika* (ŚV) *Pratyakṣa* 112, *Vākyādhikaraṇa* 116, *Śabdanityatā* 233; *Pramāṇavārttika* (PV) *Pratyakṣa* 310; and *Pramāṇaviniścya* (PVin) 118, 137 in Steinkellner, Krasser, and Lasic 2007, 18, 32.

163. This is a classic example of perceptual error. When one has a particular sort of eye disease, one sees a "clump of hair" in front of one, even though there isn't one there. See, e.g., *Pramāṇavārttika* (PV), *Pratyakṣa* 1–9.

164. A "blocking awareness" (*bādhakajñāna*) is one of the two generally recognized ways of detecting error. When one mistakes a piece of mother-of-pearl for silver and later comes to see that it is a piece of mother-of-

pearl, the awareness of it as mother-of-pearl is said to "block" the earlier awareness of it as silver. The other generally recognized way of detecting error is awareness of a defect in the causes of one's earlier awareness (*kāraṇadoṣajñāna*). E.g., when one is afflicted with jaundice and sees a white conch shell as yellow and then later learns that one's perception is impaired by jaundice, one recognizes that one's awareness of the "yellow" conch is erroneous, even without a blocking awareness. See *Ślokavārttika* (ŚV) *Codanā* 47ff.

165. The reason that we know that the "clump of hair" is not real is that it doesn't behave like a real clump of hair; e.g., when we try to brush it aside we don't feel anything. The opponent's position is that our awareness of a universal as distinct from a particular is never "blocked" or "defeated" in this way, and therefore there is no basis for dismissing it as an error.
166. JNĀ 219.19ff.
167. Here Jñānaśrīmitra accounts for our erroneous belief that there are real universals in terms of the four most widely recognized theories of error in Sanskrit philosophy: "The appearance of the self" (*ātmakhyāti*), according to which the object of an erroneous awareness is not anything external to it but rather is just the awareness itself; "the appearance of something nonexistent" (*asatkhyāti*), according to which what appears in erroneous awareness is something entirely nonexistent; "the appearance of something otherwise" (*anyathākhyāti*), according to which the object of an erroneous awareness is a real thing that appears otherwise than it actually is; and "nonappearance" (*akhyāti*), according to which everything that appears in our awareness is real and that what we call "error" is an awareness that frustrates our expectations, not because anything that appears in it is false, but because something relevant to our expectations fails to appear in it; e.g., when we see a shiny piece of mother-of-pearl and think "this is silver," two real things appear in our awareness: "this," i.e., the mother-of-pearl that is actually in front of us, and "silver," i.e., real silver that we previously experienced. The "error" lies in our failure to be aware of a third relevant thing, namely, that the "this" and the "silver" that appear to us are not identical and that the "silver" is recalled rather than seen. See Schmithausen 1965.
168. I.e., in identifying a unique particular as "this" or "that," our conceptual awareness misidentifies it as belonging to a constructed class of things that are imagined to be alike in some way.
169. This refers to the list of causes of perceptual error listed in Dharmakīrti's *Nyāyabindu* (NB) 1.6.

170. The opponent's point is that one cannot misidentify something as "x" if one has never experienced "x." Therefore, Jñānaśrīmitra cannot explain how one can mistakenly think that one sees a universal when there is really only a particular there, since on his view, one can never have experienced the universal in the first place.
171. As long as words cannot be shown to refer to an *external* universal, Jñānaśrīmitra's primary point is secure whether or not we call our awareness of universals an error.
172. A "set of causal factors" (*sāmagrī*) is the complete set of causal conditions necessary and sufficient for producing a result.
173. Here, Jñānaśrīmitra uses the term "lump" (*piṇḍa*) to refer to a generic object that is considered without regard to any of its supposedly repeatable properties.
174. When we see a cow and think "that is not a horse," we do not imagine that "not being a horse" is something that we actually see when we are looking at the cow. Seeing the cow and thinking "that is a cow" or "that has horns" is really no different. In each case, one is conceptually assigning the thing that one sees to a class, but this assignment of a thing to a class is not something that one sees.
175. I.e., between the universal and our conceptualization of a thing as belonging to a class.
176. One learns that smoke is an effect of fire by observing fire and smoke together in certain circumstances. But this cannot be the case for the universal and our conceptualization of things as belonging to a class, since one can never observe the universal in the first place.
177. No one can ever observe sense faculties, yet we can infer that they exist from the fact that when all of the other awareness-producing factors are present, some people do and other people do not experience the relevant awareness event, e.g., under conditions when most people would hear a sound but a deaf person does not hear it. Hence, even if one cannot perceive it, there must be some faculty that the hearing people possess and the deaf person does not.
178. If there were awareness of the universal "cow" because of the cow lump, then because of the absence of any one cow lump, the awareness of the universal "cow" would be absent.
179. Naiyāyikas do not accept that there is a universal "universalness," yet they believe that it is possible for us to use and understand the term "universal" even given the absence of universalness. Jñānaśrīmitra is simply extend-

ing this point to other sorts of things. If we can use and understand a term such as "universal" without universalness, we should also be able to use and understand the term "cow" without cow-ness. Hence, we cannot infer that the universal cow-ness is a necessary precondition for our ability to use and understand the word "cow."

180. This refers to the discussion in JNĀ 216. 12ff.
181. This is because each universal does what it does by its own nature and not because of some higher-order universal, and there is no reason why each individual cow should not be able to do the same thing.
182. The point is that the causal capacity to produce something cannot jointly belong to two or more things. Each thing either has or does not have the capacity to produce an effect. Even though a seed will produce a sprout under certain conditions, it is still the seed alone that is said to produce the sprout and not the seed, sunlight, and water together. In the same way, even if a universal produced the awareness "universal" only under certain conditions—when inhering in one or more loci—it would still be the universal alone and not the universal and inherence that jointly produced the awareness.
183. A "recurring image" (*anuvṛttākāra*) is one that appears to be repeated in different awareness events; e.g., when we see one, it produces in us the awareness "cow," and when we see another, it produces in us at least what appears to be an awareness with the same "cow" image.
184. I.e., higher-order universals, such as "universalness."
185. This seems to be another quotation from the work of Trilocana.
186. I.e., in the case of the awareness "universal."
187. Since the recurrence of the constructed universals would also have to be explained by recurrent things that don't exist.
188. In order to establish that a connection is in fact "invariable," it is necessary to rule out any counterexamples to it. Thus there needs to be a source of knowledge on whose basis the presence of such counterexamples can be ruled out (*viparyayabādhakapramāṇa*).
189. This seems to be a quotation from Trilocana.
190. See McCrea and Patil 2006, 313–18.
191. This seems to be another quotation from the work of Trilocana.
192. This possibly refers to JNĀ 215.16ff or the passage from JNĀ (KBhA: 19–20) referred to there.
193. Dharmakīrti's *Pramāṇavārttika* (PV), *Svārthānumāna* 164cd. The word that we translate as "cause" (*kāraka*) does not appear in the portion of text

quoted by Jñānaśrīmitra but is understood to be carried over from the previous line in Dharmakīrti's text.

194. Seemingly refers to JNĀ (KBhA: 49–53).
195. See JNĀ 222.03ff.
196. Bhāsarvajña's *Nyāyabhūṣaṇa* (NBhū) 261.7–8. See Akamatsu 1983, 251, n. 86.
197. I.e., given that all particulars are unique and equally distinct from one another.
198. Dharmakīrti's *Pramāṇavārttika* (PV), *Svārthānumāna* vs. 162. This same verse is quoted in Bhāsarvajña's *Nyāyabhūṣaṇa* (NBhū) 261.03–04.
199. With the phrase "stupid objection" (*kucodyam*), Jñānaśrīmitra is echoing Bhāsarvajña, who uses the same term to describe Dharmakīrti's argument in the verse just quoted.
200. Bhāsarvajña's *Nyāyabhūṣaṇa* (NBhū) 261.05–261.07. Bhāsarvajña's point is this: If even though it seems to us that all cows belong to the same class, we can dispense with the idea of a real class property by arguing that each individual cow, though utterly distinct from all others, has the capacity to produce in us the awareness "cow," then using the same argument, we could say that all people who have sticks have the capacity to produce in us the awareness "stick possessor" simply because of their individual causal capacities and not because there is any such thing as a "stick" that they all possess.
201. The point is that we conclude that the word "stick possessor" refers to a person who possesses a certain thing called a "stick" because we have seen both the person and the stick, but in the case of the universal, we do not see, and have never seen, the "cow-ness." Hence we accept that it is the presence of the stick that is the basis for our awareness "stick possessor," since the existence of the stick is established by an independent source of knowledge. The existence of "cow-ness," however, is not established by any other source of knowledge, and we should not postulate the existence of such a thing to account for the awareness "cow" if it can be explained without doing so.
202. The point seems to be that if "cow-ness" were visibly present in the cow, we would see it the very first time that we looked at a cow, just as we see its horns, tail, and so forth. Because the awareness that a cow belongs to a class arises only after we have observed cows on more than one occasion, it cannot be part of what we see when we see a cow. If we did have the awareness of a cow as belonging to the class of cows even upon seeing a

cow for the first time, then it could be argued that we see "cow-ness," just as the first time we see a person with a stick, we see a stick.

203. See Introduction, sec. 2, "The Elements of Inferential Reasoning."
204. I.e., because we do not perceive the cow and "cow-ness," we perceive just the cow.
205. Again, Jñānaśrīmitra gives references to both sorts of qualifiers—co-referential and non-co-referential. See the earlier reference at JNĀ 205.21–205.24 and n. 49.
206. I.e., other supposedly repeatable features of objects, e.g., shape, that might be imagined to provide a real basis for an awareness such as "cow."
207. Quoting Jñānaśrīmitra's own summary verse at JNĀ 202.22.
208. See JNĀ 203.03.
209. Dharmakīrti's *Hetubindu* (HB) 3*14–3*16.
210. It is impossible for a conceptual awareness to conceptually grasp itself. See Dharmakīrti's *Pramāṇavārttika* (PV), *Pratyakṣa* 249. "External" means not just extra-mental but anything other than the awareness in question, including, of course, other awarenesses. See Introduction, sec. 4, "Relativization of Internal and External."
211. Because conceptual awareness can have neither anything external nor itself as its object, it cannot have an object and hence cannot be an awareness at all.
212. A seed produces only a sprout as its effect and not anything else, even though the sprout and all other nonpresent objects are similarly nonexistent just before the sprout produces its effect.
213. This seems to be the position of Dharmottara, who argues that the conceptually constructed "determined particular" is superimposed on the real external particular. See n. 34 and Introduction, sec. 3.
214. This is a quotation from Dharmakīrti's *Pramāṇavārttika* (PV), *Pratyakṣa* 13. Dharmakīrti is arguing against Vaibhāṣikas (another group of Buddhist philosophers) , according to whom "name" (*nāma*) and "causal basis" (*nimittam*) are what words refer to. Dharmakīrti argues that if this were the case, we would never act with respect to external objects, since the referent of the word would be something entirely different. The Vaibhāṣika opponent argues that Dharmakīrti would be faced with the same problem: For him, the referent of a word is a conceptually constructed mental image. And thus for him, the referent of a word and the object that we are prompted to act upon are completely distinct. Dharmakīrti's response is that the same problem does arise if the referent of a

word is an awareness, since this conceptually constructed awareness just is the sort of thing that prompts us to act toward an external object. See Dharmakīrti's *Pramāṇāvārttika* (PV), *Pratyakṣa* 11cd-13, and Manorathanandin's *Pramāṇavārttikavṛtti* (PVV) ad *Pramāṇāvārttika* (PV), *Pratyakṣa* 13.

215. Some, but not all, awarenesses produced by language are properly inferential and therefore valid.
216. These are two ways in which some Buddhist epistemologists describe the relation between conceptually constructed universals and the real particulars that they are taken to bear on.
217. The objector's point is that it makes no sense for Jñānaśrīmitra to claim that the external particular does not appear in awareness, yet the object of our conceptual awareness appears as if it were nondifferent from this external particular. Jñānaśrīmitra's account of determination shows how the external particular can be the object of our intentional activity, with which we mistakenly identify the content of our conceptual awareness, even though the particular itself does not appear in it.
218. See Introduction, sec. 4.
219. See Introduction, sec. 4.
220. The "two" aspects refer to the "little bit of the image of the thing" and "the image of the speech sounds."
221. I.e., the conceit that conceptualizing a thing and apprehending its name are the same.
222. I.e., by Dignāga and Dharmakīrti. See Introduction, sec. 2.
223. See JNĀ 225.20–225.21; and McCrea and Patil 2006, 66, nn. 106ff.
224. See JNĀ 202.22ff.
225. I.e., Prajñākaragupta, the ninth-century author of a commentary on Dharmakīrti's *Pramāṇavārttika* (PV), the *Pramāṇavārttikālaṃkāra* (PVA), sometimes called the *Pramāṇavārttikabhāṣya.*
226. Prajñākaragupta, *Pramāṇavārttikālaṃkāra* (PVA) 221.28–221.29 ad *Pramāṇavārttika* (PV) *Pratyakṣa* 59.
227. Seemingly a misquotation or a paraphrase of Prajñākaragupta's *Pramāṇavārttikālaṃkāra* (PVA) 221.29.
228. This quotation is from Dharmakīrti's *Pramāṇaviniścaya* (PVin) 2.1, Steinkellner, Krasser, and Lasic 2007, 46.
229. Dharmakīrti's *Pramāṇavārttika* (PV), *Pratyakṣa* 321ff; see *Pramāṇavārttikālaṃkāra* (PVA) 349.
230. Dharmakīrti's *Pramāṇavārttika* (PV), *Svārthānumāna* 205abc.

231. Dharmakīrti's *Pramāṇavārttika* (PV), *Pratyakṣa* 164ab. In translating this verse, we have supplied all the words in brackets based on the context. "It [the word] is connected with conceptual images that rest on that [exclusion of what is other]."
232. Dharmakīrti's *Pramāṇavārttika* (PV), *Pratyakṣa* 165abc.
233. This is a quotation from the summary verse at JNĀ 202.22ff.
234. Dharmakīrti's *Pramāṇavārttika* (PV), *Svārthānumāna* 84ab.
235. Dharmakīrti's *Pramāṇavārttika* (PV), *Svārthānumāna* 84b.
236. See n. 150.
237. This appears to be a quotation, but we have been unable to locate the source.
238. This refers to the objection at JNĀ 225.23–225.24.
239. See Dharmakīrti's *Pramāṇavārttika* (PV), *Pratyakṣa* 8–10. The point is that the image of "clump of hair" for a person with some eye disease really does exist as an image. It is only the external clump of hair that does not exist. In the same way, the mental image is not "real" in the sense that it not an extramental object, as we often take it to be, but it is nonetheless a real image.
240. I.e., useless in the case of affirmation and impossible in the case of denial. See JNĀ 211.03ff.
241. Dharmakīrti's *Pramāṇavārttika* (PV), *Pratyakṣa* 220cd.
242. I.e., Dharmottara's *Apohaprakaraṇa* (AP-Dh) 244.3–244.4.
243. Dharmottara's *Apohaprakaraṇa* (AP-Dh) 236.15, as quoted in Akamatsu 1983, 258, n. 222.
244. Dharmottara's *Apohaprakaraṇa* (AP-Dh) 238.19–238.21. See Akamatsu 1983, 258, n. 223.
245. I.e., meant by the "externality of the superimposed." The point is that by saying that what one asserts or denies is the "externality of the superimposed," Dharmottara means that in inferential/verbal awareness, one always superimposes a mental construct on some external locus, e.g., "fire" on that mountain. Sometimes, when one reaches the locus in question, one finds a real pragmatically effective fire that satisfies one's expectations, but sometimes one does not. Dharmottara's real position, as Jñānaśrīmitra understands it, is that when we claim that there is fire on that mountain, what we are really asserting is that the pragmatic effects available for one approaching that locus match up with the expectations generated by the constructed object that one superimposes on it.
246. As Jñānaśrīmitra argues earlier, in both the introductory verse and the summary verse.

247. I.e., universals or other supposedly repeatable features of objects, e.g., shape, that might be imagined to provide a real basis for an awareness such as "cow."
248. See JNĀ 202.22ff.
249. This is apparently a well-known example of sensory perception without determination and is discussed in, e.g., Jain philosophical literature. See Vādidevasūri's *Syādvādaratnākara* (SVR):

    [Sūtra 1.14] "*Without determination*" [which is the third variety of "superimposition" (*samāropa*), SVR 1.8–1.9 in SVR: 102] *is the mere sensation "something."* [Commentary] The mere sensation "something" is the mere awareness of a certain thing that is not clearly specified. "What is this?" He says: This is "*Without determination*," the third type of superimposition. After taking it to be different from determination, i.e., an awareness that depicts a specific thing, he gives an example: [Sūtra 1.15] *Like the awareness of the touch of grass for one who is moving through it.* [Commentary] For a knower, who is "*moving*," i.e., walking, "*the awareness of the touch of grass*," i.e., the awareness that has the touch of grass as its object—i.e., the mere sensation that "I have touched something," which does not pick out any specific features such as "this thing is of this sort and has such a name" because one's attention is directed elsewhere—is just sensation [without determination]—this is the meaning [of the sūtra]. *Syādvādaratnākara* 1.14–15, vol. 1, p. 146. [Sūtra] *kim ity ālocanamātram anadhyavasāya iti* ||14|| [Commentary] *kiṃ ity ālocanamātram aspaṣṭaviśiṣṭaviśeṣajñānamātram* | *kim ity āha* | *anadhyavasāyas tṛtīyaḥ samāropabhedo 'dhyavasāyād viśeṣollekhijñānād anya iti kṛtvā* | *udāharaṇam āha* [Sūtra] *yathā gacchattṛṇasparśajñānam* iti ||15|| [Commentary] *gacchato vrajataḥ sataḥ pramātus tṛṇasparśaviṣayaṃ jñānaṃ tṛṇasparśajñānam anyatrāsaktacittatvād evaṃjātīyakam evaṃnāmakam idaṃ vastv ity ādiviśeṣānullekhi kim api mayā spṛṣṭam ity ālocanamātram ity arthaḥ* |

250. This is referring to a mirage.
251. I.e., between being both manifest in appearance and determined and being an object of awareness.
252. The property to be proven is carried over from the inference stated earlier in JNĀ 230.24–230.25.

253. Cf. Dharmottara *Nyāyabinduṭīkā* (NBṬ) 71, quoted in Introduction, sec. 3.
254. I.e., *appearance and determination.*
255. I.e., *appearance and determination.*
256. "This" refers to the defining characteristic that you propose for being an object.
257. The "one or the other" referred to here is appearance or determination.
258. I.e., the convention that there can be objecthood by virtue of either appearance or determination, separately.
259. Quoting the summary verse; see JNĀ 202.22ff.
260. For more on "implicative" and "nonimplicative" negation, see n. 20.
261. This is because exclusion is a kind of absence and not a positive entity.
262. This is a quotation of Dharmakīrti's *Pramāṇavārttikasvavṛtti* (PVSV) ad *Pramāṇavārttika* (PV), *Svārthānumāna* 185.
263. We have been unable to trace this quotation. It may be a paraphrase of the passage referred to in n. 262.
264. See above JNĀ 205.12ff.
265. See n. 116, on "Treasury."

SANSKRIT TEXT OF THE *MONOGRAPH ON EXCLUSION (APOHAPRAKARAṆAM)*

1. We are reading *sādhyata* in place of manuscript *prasādhya* (Jms 8a.6) and Thakur's suggestion *prakāśyata.*
2. We are reading "*vātatpratibhāse*" in place of the printed "*vā tatpratibhāse.*"
3. Following RNĀ (AS 58.1), we are adding the term "*pratītiḥ*" at Thakur's suggestion.
4. We are reading "*'sphuratas*" in place of the printed "*asphuratas,*" following Jms 8b.5.
5. Correcting the printed *avagrahādhyakṣavad* following Jms 8b.6 and RNĀ (AS: 59.03).
6. Jms 8b.6 confirms Thakur's suggested reading *anya[da]smin.*
7. See NB 2.18.
8. PV *Parārthānumāna* 262.
9. We are correcting the printed "*naňaprayogavat*" to "*naňprayogavat,*" following Jms 8b.7.
10. Following Jms 9a.2 and the printed edition of the RNĀ, and *ms* N1, N2, and N3, we are reading "*bhāsato*" in place of the printed "*bhāsate.*"

11. We are emending the text to read "*gamya*," as in the verse, in place of the printed (and Jms9a.4) "*gamyata*."
12. The printed texts reads "*mukhatvena*." We are correcting it to "*mukhyatvena*" following Jms9a.4.
13. PV *Svārthānumāna* 124.
14. We are emending the printed *īdṛśākāram* to *īdṛśākāram,* parallel to the preceding. The *ms* is unclear.
15. This is a portion of the following passage. NVTṬ 444.16–17: *na ca svalakṣaṇād anyā vyāvṛttir alīkam anyavyāvṛttam svalakṣaṇena sarūpayati tathā sati hastimaśakāv api rāsabhaḥ sarūpayet | na ca svalakṣaṇadharmo vyāvṛttir bhavadbhir abhypeyate.* We are emending the printed text by removing the word "*dharma*," which appears before "*na*." This reading is also attested in several manuscripts. See NVTṬ2 684. We are also emending "*anyavyavṛttir*" to "*anyā vyāvṛttir*."
16. We are adding a sentence break after "*abhidhānam*."
17. We accept Thakur's suggested emendation of "*-pratītir apy apoha*" for Jms 10a.1 "*-pratītir apoha eva*."
18. We are adding a sentence break and changing "*vidhis*" to "*vidhiḥ*." Jms10a.1 is not legible here.
19. This appears to be a quotation or variant reading of HB 26*23–24.
20. We are emending to "*eva | ubhayatra*" from the printed "*evobhayatra*" at JNĀ 205.15.
21. See PV *Svārthānumāna* 125 and PV *Pratyakṣa* 30d. See n. 44 to the translation.
22. PVin 2.8.
23. We are emending the printed *niṣedhe* to *niṣedho*. Jms 10a.5 is not legible here.
24. We are emending the printed text and Jms 10a.5, which reads *ca śakya,* to *cāśakyā*.
25. We are reading *gamya* instead of the printed *gamyata*, in conformity with the portion of the summary verse just quoted. Jms 10a.6 is not legible.
26. We are emending the text to *teṣu* and inserting a sentence break after it.
27. We are correcting the printed *apradhānavat* to Jms 10b.7 *apradhānatvāt.*
28. We are emending *sarvatra* to *anyatra*, following PV *Pratyakṣa* 172, and *apekṣaṇātmajātīye* to *apekṣaṇād ātmajātīye*. We are emending *tu* to *tad* also following PV *Pratyakṣa* 172. See PVA 264 on this verse, where *tad* and *anyatra* are read.
29. PV *Svārthānumāna* 132.

30. PV *Svārthānumāna* 184–85. We are correcting the printed reading, *bodhakāḥ*, to *vācakāḥ*, in conformity with PVV 184–85 and Jms 11a.1.
31. We are emending the printed *apoḍha* to *apoha.*
32. We are correcting the printed *sthānāntarakalpanā* to *sthānāsthānakalpanā*, in accordance with PVV ad PV1.169cd–70ab and with Jms 11a.1.
33. PV *Svārthānumāna* 168–69.
34. Correcting the printed *anyataḥ apohaḥ*, following Jms 11a.2.
35. We are correcting *padārtha[va]cc* to *padārthācc*, following Jms 11a.2.
36. PVin 1.15.
37. We are emending the printed *nāmāśrayonyānyaś* to *nāmāśrayo 'nyonyaś* following Pandeya 1989.
38. PV *Pratyakṣa* 235.
39. We accept Thakur's insertion of *śākhi*, following RNĀ (AS: 61).
40. We are emending the text by eliminating *dṛṣṭam.*
41. We are correcting "*avyāptitas*" to "*avyāptis*" following Jms 11b.1.
42. Following Jms 11b.5, we are reading "*vikalpo nādhyakṣagamyagavagocaro*" in place of the printed "*vikalpenādhyakṣagamya eva gocaro*" (in Thakur 1987) and "*vikalpenādhyakṣagamyagavagocaro*" (in Thakur 1959).
43. On the basis of Jms 12a.1, we are restoring the *yadi* that is printed in Thakur 1959 but omitted from Thakur 1987.
44. We are emending the printed *gavodbhāvanam* to *tadodbhāvanam* in place of Thakur's suggested emendation *satyodbhāvanam*. Jms 12a.1 is unclear at this point.
45. We are emending the printed *sarvasādhāraṇasya* to *sarvāsādharaṇasya.*
46. We are correcting *avāstava* to *avāntara*, on the basis of Jms 12a.3 and in conformity with JNĀ 210.21.
47. We are emending the printed *apo[hatvādu]ccāraṇam* to *ayogād uccāraṇam.* Jms12a.5 is unclear at this point.
48. We are correcting Thakur's reading of "*bhāvābhāvasādhāraṇī bhavati*" to "*bhāvābhāvasādhāraṇībhavantī*" on the basis of Jms 12a.7 and are re-spacing Thakur's printed "*bhāvābhāvasādhāraṇī bhavantī.*"
49. PVA on PV *Pramāṇasiddhi* 1. See PVA 4.
50. We are emending *kṛte* to *kṛtaṃ.*
51. We are correcting *vidhiniṣedhāyoga* to *vidhiniṣedhayoga*, following Jms 13a.5.
52. We are correcting the printed *khādire*, following Jms 13b.5.
53. We are correcting the printed reading *vāvaśyam* to *cāvaśyam*, following Jms 13b.5.

54. We are correcting *godhulidhūmau* to *godhvanidhūmau*, following Jms 13b.6.
55. We are emending *sādhyate* to *sambadhyate* on the basis of JNĀ 214.25, where the word *sambaddham* is used, and on the printed text of NVTṬ ad NS 1.1.4 (115.13–115.14).
56. We are following the reading of JNĀ 1959 (where *na doṣa* | *doṣa eva* is printed in place of JNĀ 1987, which reads *na doṣaḥ* |), following Jms 14a.2.
57. NVTṬ ad NS 1.1.4 (115.11–115.13) *na caikopadhinā sattvena viśiṣṭe gṛhīte upādhyantaraviśiṣṭatadgrahaprasaṅgaḥ* | *svabhāvo hi dravyasyopadhibhir viśiṣyate na tūpādhayo vā tair viśiṣṭatvaṃ vā tasya svabhāvaḥ* | We are emending the printed reading "*viśeṣyatvaṃ vā*" to "*tair viśiṣṭatvaṃ vā*" following NVTṬ.
58. We are correcting the printed *upakāryopakāradvāreṇa* to *upakāryopakārakadvāreṇa*, following Jms 14a3.
59. PV *Svārthānumāna* 53.
60. We are emending the printed *sohāpohāt* to *soktāpohāt*.
61. ŚV *Ākṛti*, 10.
62. Jms 14b.3 reads "*vahnijalaśilpijalādau*," but following Thakur's emendation, we read "*vahniśilpijalādau*."
63. We are emending the printed *balāka*, also Jms 14b.3, to *balāhaka* = cloud.
64. PV *Pratyakṣa* 149.
65. In the printed edition at JNĀ 111, the second line reads slightly differently: "*pratibhāso 'sya nāsyeti sādhyate nopapattibhiḥ*." See JNĀ (KBhA 111).
66. Following Jms 15b2, we are correcting the printed reading *yady api* to *yady adyāpi*.
67. Thakur 1959 prints the first three *pādas* of this verse, PV *Svārthānumāna* 129cd–130a, in brackets, but Thakur 1987 prints the same verse without brackets. This portion of the verse is not found in Jms 15b.3, and there is no reason to believe that Jñānaśrīmitra meant to include it.
68. PV *Svārthānumāna* 130b–31b.
69. We are emending the printed text and Jms 15b to *sattāsattva* from *sattāsādvala*.
70. Following Thakur, we adopt the reading "*śāstrakārāṇām*" in place of Jms 16a.1, "*śāstrakāraṇām*," and the conjectural reading "*abhyūha*" for the partly illegible reading of Jms 16a.1 at this point. We also insert a sentence break after "*sambhavāt*."
71. We are reading *vidhāvapyavyaya* in place of the printed *vidhāvāyavya*.

72. PV *Pratyakṣa* 147.
73. PVV reads "*jñānād*" in place of "*buddher*."
74. PV *Svārthānumāna* 71.
75. In place of printed "*vyaktavyaktyanubhavo*" and Jms 16a.5, we are emending to "*vaktavyaḥ | vyaktyanubhavo*."
76. We don't accept Thankur's suggested emendation, *kuryā*[*t*] and retain the reading of Jms 16b.1.
77. We are reading *utpādayatītyevārthaḥ* in place of the printed *utpādayatyevārthaḥ*, following Jms 16b.2.
78. Here we follow Jms 17b.2 and reject Thakur's insertion on the basis of RNĀ 64.20 of *atadrūpaparāvṛtta*.
79. We accept Thakur's emendation "*anyavyāvṛtter*" in place of Jms 17b.3 "*avyāvṛtter*."
80. Following Jms 17b.3, we are reading "*asāmānyād*" in place of Thakur's suggested reading "*aśvasāmānyād*."
81. PV *Svārthānumāna* 164.
82. Following Nyāyabhūṣaṅa (NBhū) 261.07–8, we read "*anyathā hetusāmagrīniyamāt*" in place of the printed "*anyathātve tu sāmagrīniyamāt*." Jms 17b.5 is illegible at this point.
83. Following Thakur 1959 and Jms 17b.5, we are reading *kāryaṃ* instead of Thakur 1987, which reads *kārya* at JNĀ 224.04.
84. PV *Svārthānumāna* 162.
85. We are accepting Thakur's conjectural reading of *tenoktam aparam api*. Jms 17b.5–6 is unclear at this point.
86. We are emending the printed "*vyāpāro naikāmarṣe*" (and Jms 18a.1) to "*vyāpāraḥ | naikāmarṣe*."
87. In place of Thakur's conjectural reading "*adhyavasite* [*vikalpi*]*ta*" (for the illegible Jms 18a.7), we conjecturally read "*adhyavasiteḥ pratipādyata*" on the basis of JNĀ 225.14.
88. We are adding "*vikalpakatvam api*" on the basis of Jms 18a.7. It is not found in the printed edition of the text.
89. PV *Pratyakṣa* 13.
90. We are emending the printed "*saṅgacchate, darśane*" (and Jms 18b.5) to "*saṅgacchate 'darśane*."
91. PVA ad PV *Pratyakṣa* 59. See PVA 221.
92. In place of printed "*svapratibhāse 'narthādhyavasāyena*" and Jms 19a.3 "*svapratibhāse 'narthe 'rthā'dhyavasāyena*," we read "*svapratibhāse 'narthe 'rthādhyavasāyena*," following Steinkellner 1973 (PVin 2.8–10) and

Steinkellner, Krasser, and Lasic 2007, 46 i.e., PVin 2.1 Also as quoted in PVV 25.10–12 and NBhū 140.25–26.

93. We are emending the printed (and Jms 19a.4) reading "*adhyavasāyānumānam*" to read "*adhyavasāyo 'numānam.*"
94. PV *Svārthānumāna* 205.
95. PV *Pratyakṣa* 164ab.
96. PV *Pratyakṣa* 165abc.
97. We are correcting the printed reading *bhāsate* to *bhāsato*, following Jms 19a.6, confirmed by the preceding JNĀ 203.01–4, as well as MSS N1, N2, and N3 of Ratnakīrti's *Apohasiddhi* and H. P. Shastri 1910.
98. PV *Svārthānumāṇaa* 84.
99. PV *Pratyakṣa* 220.
100. We are reading *adhyavasāyas tu* as in Thakur 1959 and not *adhyavasāvastu* as in Thakur 1975 (as confirmed by Jms 19b.6).
101. We are emending the reading *sthāpyate* (of Thakur's text and Jms 19b.7) to *sthāpya* in accordance with JNĀ 203.04.
102. Following Jms 20a.1, we omit the "*ca*" following "*tathā*" in Thakur 1987.
103. Following Jms 20a.1, we are correcting the printed "*niraśana*" to "*nirasana.*"
104. Following Jms 20a.3, we are correcting the printed "*ubhayābhāvo*" to "*ubhayābhāve.*"
105. We are emending the reading of Thakur and Jms 20a.4, "*pravṛttirviṣayatvaṃ,*" to "*pravṛttiviṣayatvaṃ.*"
106. Following Jms 20a.5 (and rejecting the marginal gloss "*viṣayakasthiti*" that Thakur includes here), we read "*ekaikena viṣayatve sthitam akhilasya*" in place of the printed "*ekaikena vidheyatve sthitaviṣayakasthitir akhilasya.*"
107. Following Jms 20a.6, we are correcting the printed reading "*samvṛter*" to "*saṃvṛtir.*"
108. We are emending the reading of Thakur (and Jms 20a.7) from "*na*" to "*ca.*"
109. Following Jms 20b.2, we read "*vācyam ity evārthaḥ*" in place of the printed "*vācyam evārthaḥ.*"
110. Following Jms 20b.4, we are correcting the printed reading "*vikalpasthe*" to "*vikalpastho.*"
111. Thakur reads "*samarthanaitasya,*" which we are emending to "*samarthane tasya.*" This reading is confirmed by Jms 20b.5.

BIBLIOGRAPHY

Abhyankar, K.V., and G. Joshi. 1980–94. *Mīmāṃsādarśanam*, 3rd ed., vols. 2–7; 4th ed., vol. 1. Pune: Ānandāśrama Press.

Akamatsu, A. 1983. *L'évolution de la theorie de l'Apoha*. PhD diss., Université de la Sorbonne Nouvelle.

Arnold, D. A. 2005. *Buddhists, Brahmins, and Belief: Epistemology in South Asian Philosophy of Religion*. New York: Columbia University Press.

Asher, F. M. 1975. *Vikramaśīla Mahāvihāra*. Lalitkala: Dhaka.

Balcerowicz, P. D. 1999. "How Could a Cow Be Both Synchronically and Diachronically Homogenous, or On the Jaina Notions of *Tiryak-Sāmānya* and *Ūrdhva-Sāmānya*." In *Approaches to Jaina Studies: Philosophy, Logic, Rituals, and Symbols*. South Asian Studies Papers no. 11, 211–35. Toronto: University of Toronto, Center for South Asian Studies.

Balcerowicz, P. D. 2001. *Jaina Epistemology in Historical and Comparative Perspective: Critical Edition and English Translation of Logical-Epistemological Treatises: Nyayâvatara, Nyayâvatara-vivrti and Nyayâvatâra-tippana with Introduction and Notes*. Stuttgart: Franz Steiner Verlag.

Bronkhorst, J. 1999. "Nagārjuna and Apoha." In *Dharmakīrti's Thought and Its Impact on Indian and Tibetan Philosophy: Proceedings of the Third International Dharmakīrti Conference*, ed. S. Katsura, 17–24. Vienna: Verlag der Österreichischen Akademie der Wissenschaften: Beiträge zur Kultur—und Geistesgeschichte Asiens.

Bühneman, G. 1985. *Jitāri; Kleine Texte*. Vienna: Arbeitskreis für Tibetische und Buddhistische Studien Universität Wien.

Cabezón, J. I. 1994. *Buddhism and Language: A Study of Indo-Tibetan Scholasticism*. Albany: State University of New York Press.

Cabezón, J. I., ed. 1998. *Scholasticism: Cross-Cultural and Comparative Perspectives*. Albany: State University of New York Press.

Chakrabarti, A. 1992. "I Touch What I Saw." *Philosophy and Phenomenological Research* 52, no. 1:103–16.

Chakrabarti, A. 1994. "Testimony: A Philosophical Survey (Review Essay)." *Philosophy and Phenomenological Research* 54, no. 4:965–72.

Chakrabarti, A. 1997. *Denying Existence: The Logic, Epistemology, and Pragmatics of Negative Existentials and Fictional Discourse*. Synthese Library no. 261. Dordrecht: Kluwer Academic.

Chakrabarti, A. 1998. "Experience, Concept Possession, and Knowledge of Language." In *The Philosophy of P. F. Strawson*, ed. L. E. Hahn, 315–24. Chicago: Open Court.

Chakrabarti, A. 2000. "Against Immaculate Perception: Seven Reasons for Eliminating Nirvikalpaka Perception from Nyaya." *Philosophy East and West* 50, no. 1:1–8.

Chakrabarti, A. 2003. "Perception, Apperception and Non-Conceptual Content." In *Perspectives on Consciousness*, ed. A. Chatterjee, 89–107. New Delhi: Munshiram Manoharlal.

Chakrabarti, A. 2004. "Seeing Without Recognizing? More on Denuding Perceptual Content." *Philosophy East and West* 54, no. 3:365–67.

Chakrabarti, A., et al., eds. Forthcoming. *Apoha Semantics and Human Cognition*. New York: Columbia University Press.

Chakrabarti, K. K. 1999. *Classical Indian Philosophy of Mind: The Nyāya Dualist Tradition*. Albany: State University of New York Press.

Chattopadhyaya, D., and M. Gangopadhyaya. 1992. *Nyāya Philosophy*. Calcutta: Indian Studies Past and Present.

Chemparathy, G. 1972. *An Indian Rational Theology: Introduction to Udayana's* Nyayakusumañjali. Publications of the de Nobili Research Library, no. 1. Vienna: Gerold.

Dravid, N. S. 1995. Ātmatattvaviveka *of Udayanācārya with Translation, Explanation, and Analytical-Critical Survey*. Shimla: Indian Council of Philosophical Research.

Dravid, N. S. 1996. Nyāyakusumāñjali *of Udayanācārya, vol. 1, with Translation and Explanation*. New Delhi: Indian Council of Philosophical Research.

Dravid, R. R. 1972. *The Problem of Universals in Indian Philosophy*. Delhi: Motilal Banarsidass.

Dreyfus, G. 1996. "Can the Fool Lead the Blind? Perception and the Given in Dharmakīrti's Thought." *Journal of Indian Philosophy* 24:209.

Dreyfus, G. 1997. *Recognizing Reality: Dharmakīrti's Philosophy and Its Tibetan Interpretations*. Albany: State University of New York Press.

Dunne, J. D. 1998."Nominalism, Buddhist Doctrine of." *Routledge Encyclopedia of Philosophy*, vol. 7, ed. E. Craig, 23–27. New York: Routledge.

Dunne, J. D. 2004. *Foundations of Dharmakīrti's Philosophy*. Boston: Wisdom Publications.

Dvivedin, V. P., and L. S. Dravida. 1986. *Ātmatattvaviveka: With the Commentaries of Śaṅkara Miśra, Bhagīratha Thakkura, and Raghunātha Tārkikaśiromaṇī*. Calcutta: Asiatic Society.

Eckel, M. D. 1987. *Jñānagarbha's Commentary on the Distinction Between the Two Truths: An Eighth Century Handbook of Madhyamaka Philosophy*. Albany: State University of New York Press.

Eckel, M. D. 2008. *Bhāviveka and His Buddhist Opponents*. Harvard Oriental Series no. 70. Cambridge, Mass.: Harvard University.

Eltschinger, V. 1999. "Śubhagupta's Śrutiparīkṣākārikā, vv. 10cd–19 and Its Dharmakīrtian Background." *Dharmakīrti's Thought and Its Impact on Indian and Tibetan Philosophy: Proceedings of the Third International Dharmakīrti Conference*, ed. S. Katsura, 47–62. Vienna: Verlag der Österreichischen Akademie der Wissenschaften: Beiträge zur Kultur—und Geistesgeschichte Asiens.

Eltschinger, V. 2003. "Le Vedāprāmāṇyasiddhi de Jitāri: Introduction et traduction." *Journal asiatique* 291, nos. 1/2:137–72.

Eltschinger, V. 2007. *Penser l'autorité des écritures: La polémique de Dharmakīrti contre la notion brahmanique orthodoxe d'un Veda sans auteur.* Vienna Verlag der Österreichischen Akademie der Wissenschaften.

Franco, E. 1990. "Valid Reason, True Sign." *Wiener Zeitschrift für die Kunde Südasiens* 34:189–208.

Franco, E. 1994. *Perception, Knowledge and Disbelief: A Study of Jayarāśi's Scepticism*. Stuttgart: Steiner.

Franco, E. 1997. *Dharmakīrti on Compassion and Rebirth*. Vienna: Arbeitskreis für Tibetische und Buddhistische Studien Universität Wien.

Frauwallner, E. 1935. "Dharmottaras Kṣaṇabhaṅgasiddhih. Text and Übersetzung." *Wiener Zeitschrift für die Kunde des Morgenlandes* 42:217–58.

Frauwallner, E. 1937. "Beitrage zur Apohalehre. II. Dharmottaras." *Wiener Zeitschrift für die Kunde des Morgenlandes* 44:233–87.

Frauwallner, E. 1959. "Dignāga, sein Werk und seine Entwicklung." *Wiener Zeitschrift für die Kunde Süd- und Ostasiens* 3:83–164.

Frauwallner, E. 1961. "Landmarks in the History of Indian Logic." *Wiener Zeitschrift für die Kunde Süd- und Ostasiens* 5:125–48.

Frauwallner, E. 1973. *History of Indian Philosophy*. Vols. I and II. Delhi: Motilal Banarsidass.

Funayama, T. 1992. "Study of Kalpanāpoḍha: A Translation of the *Tattvasaṃgraha* vv. 1212–1263 by Sāntarakṣita and the *Tattvasaṃgrahapañjikā* by Kamalaśīla on the Definition of Direct Perception." *Zinbun* 27:33–128.

Ganeri, J. 2001. *Philosophy in Classical India: An Introduction and Analysis*. New York: Routledge.

Gangopadhyaya, M. 1971. *Vinītadeva's* Nyāyabindu-ṭīkā. *Sanskrit Original Reconstructed from the Extant Tibetan Version with English Translation and Annotations*. Calcutta: Indian Studies Past and Present.

Gillon, B. S. 1991. "Dharmakīrti and the Problem of Induction." Paper presented at the second International Dharmakīrti Conference. Vienna: Österreichischen Akademie der Wissenschaften: Philosophisch-Historischen Klasse, Denkschriften, 222. Band: Verlag der Österreichischen Akademie der Wissenschaften, Vienna.

Gnoli, R. 1960. *The* Pramāṇavārttika *of Dharmakīrti; the First Chapter with the Autocommentary*. Rome: Instituto italiano per il medio ed estremo oriente.

Gokhale, P. P. 1992. *Inference and Fallacies Discussed in Ancient Indian Logic*. Delhi: Sri Satguru Publications.

Gokhale, P. P. 1993. *Vādanyāya of Dharmakīrti: The Logic of Debate*. Delhi: Sri Satguru Publications.

Gosvāmi, M., ed. 1972. *Nyāyakusumāñjali of Udayanācārya with the Commentaries Āoda of Śankara Miśra, Viveka of Guṇ ānanda, Bodhanī of Varadarāja, Parimala of Mm. Shri Harihara Kṛ pālu Dvivedī*. S. Bagchi: Dharbhanga.

Gosvāmi, M. 1984. *Mīmāṃsādarśanam*. Vols. 1–4. Varanasi: Tara Book Agency.

Griffiths, P. J. 1999. *Religious Reading: The Place of Reading in the Practice of Religion*. New York: Oxford University Press.

Hahn, M. 1971. *Jñānaśrīmitra's* Vrttamâlâstuti. *Ein Beispielsammlung zur altindischen Metrik. Nach dem tibetischen Tanjur zusammen mit der mongolischen Version herausgegeben, übersetzt und erläutert*. Wiesbaden: Harrassowitz.

Hahn, M. 1989. "Sanskrit Metrics—As Studied at Buddhist Universities in the Eleventh and Twelfth Century A.D." *Adyar Library Bulletin*, 30–60.

Hattori, M. 1968. *Dignāga, on Perception; Being the Pratyakṣapariccheda of Dignāga's* Pramāṇasamuccaya *from the Sanskrit Fragments and the Tibetan Versions*. Cambridge, Mass.: Harvard University Press.

Hattori, M. 1977. "The Sautrāntrika Background of the Apoha Theory." *Buddhist Thought and Asian Civilization: Essays in Honor of Herbert V. Guenther on His Sixtieth Birthday*, ed. H. V. Guenther, L. S. Kawamura, and K. Scott, 47–58. Emeryville, Calif.: Dharma Publications.

Hattori, M. 1980. "Apoha and Pratibhā." *Sanskrit and Indian Studies: Essays in Honour of Daniel H. H. Ingalls*, ed. M. Nagatomi, 61–73. Dordrecht: D. Reidel.

Hattori, M. 2000. "Dignāga's Theory of Meaning: An Annotated Translation of the *Pramāṇasamuccayavṛtti*: Chapter V: Anyāpoha-parīkṣa I." In *Wisdom, Compassion, and the Search for Understanding: The Buddhist Studies Legacy of Gadjin M. Nagao*, ed. J. A. Silk, lx, 420. Honolulu: University of Hawai'i Press.

Hattori, M. 2006. "The Apoha Theory in the Nyāyamañjari." In *Word and Meaning in Indian Philosophy*. Acta Asiatica no. 90, 55–70: Tokyo: Tōhō gakkai.

Hayes, R. P. 1980. "Dignāga's Views on Reasoning." *Journal of Indian Philosophy* 8:219–77.

Hayes, R. P. 1986. "An Interpretation of *Anyāpoha* in Dignāga's General Theory of Inference." *Buddhist Logic and Epistemology: Studies in the Buddhist Analysis of Inference and Language*, ed. B. K. Matilal, 31–58. Dordrecht: D. Reidel.

Hayes, R. P. 1987. "On the Reinterpretation of Dharmakīrti's *Svabhāvahetu*." *Journal of Indian Philosophy* 15:317–32.

Hayes, R. P. 1988. *Dignāga on the Interpretation of Signs*. Dordrecht: Kluwer Academic.

Hayes, R. P. 1997. "Whose Experience Validates What for Dharmakīrti." In *Relativism, Suffering and Beyond: Essays in Memory of Bimal K. Matilal*, ed. P. Bilimoria, J. Mohanty, and B. K. Matilal, 105–18. Delhi: Oxford University Press.

Hoornaert, P. 2001. "Bhāviveka's Critique of *Parikalpitasvabhāva* and of Dignāga's *Anyāpoha* Theory." *Religion and Culture* no. 13:12–47. Hokuriku Society for Religious and Cultural Studies.

Isaacson, H. 2001. "The Opening Verses of Ratnākaraśānti's *Muktāvalī* (Studies in Ratnākaraśānti's Tantric Works II)." In Harānandalaharī: Volume in Honour of Professor Minoru Hara on His Seventieth Birthday, ed. R. Tsuchida and A. Wezler, 121–34. Reinbeck: Verlag für Orientalistische Fachpublikationen.

Isaacson, H. 2002a. "Ratnākaraśānti's *Bhramaharanāma Hevajrasādhana*: Critical Edition (Studies in Ratnākaraśānti's Tantric Works III)." *Journal of the International College for Advanced Buddhist Studies* 5:151(80)–176(55).

Isaacson, H. 2002b. "Ratnākaraśānti's *Hevajrasahajasadyoga* (Studies in Ratnākaraśānti's Tantric Works I)." In *Le parole e i marmi: Studi in onore di*

Raniero Gnoli nel suo 70° compleanno, ed. R. Torella, 457– 87. Serie orientale roma no. 92, vol.1. Rome: Istituto italiano per l'Africa e l'Oriente (IsIAO).

Isaacson, H. 2007. "First Yoga: A Commentary on the *Ādiyoga* Section of Ratnākaraśānti's Bhramahara (Studies in Ratnākaraśānti's Tantric Works IV)." In *Pramāṇakīrtiḥ. Papers Dedicated to Ernst Steinkellner on the Occasion of His 70th Birthday*. Part 1, ed. B. Kellner, H. Krasser, H. Lasic, M. T. Much, and H. Tauscher. Vienna: Arbeitskreis für Tibetische und Buddhistische Studien, Universität Wien; and *Wiener Studien zur Tibetologie und Buddhismuskunde* 70, no. 1:285–314.

Ishida, H. Forthcoming. "On the Classification of *Anyāpoha*." Unpublished manuscript.

Iwata, T. 2003. "An Introduction of Dharmakīrti's Svabhāva-hetu." *Journal of Indian Philosophy* 311–13, 61–87.

Iyengar, R. H. H., ed. 1952. Tarkabhāṣā *and* Vādasthāna *of Mokṣākaragupta and Jitāripāda with a Foreword by Mahopadhyāya Vidhuśekhara Bhattāchārya.* Mysore: Coronation Press.

Jha, G. 1973/74. *Śābara-bhāṣya*. Baroda: Oriental Institute.

Jha, G. 1985. *The Nyāya-Sūtras of Gautama*. Delhi: Motilal Banarsidass.

Jha, G. 1986. *The* Tattvasaṃgraha *of Śāntarakṣita with the commentary of Kamalaśīla*. Delhi: Motilal Banarsidass.

Kajiyama, Y. 1965. "Controversy Between the *Sākāra*- and *Nirākāra-vādins* of the *Yogācāra* School—Some Materials." *Journal of Indian Buddhist Studies* 14, no. 1:418–29.

Kajiyama, Y. 1966. *An Introduction to Buddhist Philosophy: An Annotated Translation of the Tarkabhāṣā of Mokṣākaragupta*. Kyoto: Rinsen.

Kajiyama, Y. 1989. *Studies in Buddhist Philosophy*. Kyoto, Rinsen.

Kajiyama, Y. 1998. *An Introduction to Buddhist Philosophy: An Annotated Translation of the Tarkabhāṣā of Mokṣākaragupta: Reprint with Corrections in the Author's Hand*. Vienna: Arbeitskreis für Tibetische und Buddhistische Studien, Universität Wien.

Kajiyama, Y. 1999. *The Antarvyāptisamarthana of Ratnākaraśānti*. Tokyo: International Research Institute for Advanced Buddhology, Soka University.

Kang, S. Y. 1998 *Zur altindischen Tradition der Debatte gemäss der medizinischen Überliefrung. Übersetzung und ideengeschichtliche Untersuchung von Caraka-saṃhitā Vi.8.15–28*. Hamburg: Wissenschaftliche Hausarbeit zur Erlangung des akademischen Grades eines Magister Artium der Universität Hamburg.

Katsura, S. 1979. "The *Apoha* Theory of Dignāga." *Indogaku bukkyōgaku kenkyū* 28:16–20.

Katsura, S. 1984. "Dharmakīrti's Theory of Truth." *Journal of Indian Philosophy* 12:215–35.

Katsura, S. 1986a. Jñānaśrīmitra on *Apoha*. *Buddhist Logic and Epistemology: Studies in the Buddhist Analysis of Inference and Language*, ed. B. K. Matilal and R. D. Evans, 171–84. Dordrecht: D. Reidel.

Katsura, S. 1986b. "On the Origin and Development of the Concept of *Vyāpti* in Indian Logic." *Tetsugaku: Journal of the Hiroshima Philosophical Society* 37:1–16.

Katsura, S. 1991. Dignāga and Dharmakīrti on *Apoha*. In *Studies in the Buddhist Epistemological Tradition*, ed. E. Steinkellner, 129–44. Vienna: Österreichischen Akademie der Wissenschaften: philosophisch-historischen Klasse, Denkschriften, 222. Band; Verlag der Österreichischen Akademie der Wissenschaften, Wien.

Katsura, S. 1992. "Dignāga and Dharmakīrti on *Adarśanamātra* and *Anupalabdhi*." *Asiatische studien / Études asiatiques* 47:222–31.

Katsura, S. 1993. "On Perceptual Judgment." *Studies on Buddhism in Honour of Professor A. K. Warder*, ed. N. K. Wagle, F. Watanabe, and University of Toronto, 205. Toronto: Centre for South Asian Studies, University of Toronto.

Katsura, S. 2000. "Dignāga on *Trairūpya* Reconsidered." *Indo no bunka to ronri. Tosaki Hiromasa hakase koki kinen ronbunshū*, 241–66. Fukuoka: A. Akamatsu.

Katsura, S. 2004. "The Role of the *Dṛṣṭānta* in Dignāga's Logic." In *The Role of the Example Dṛṣṭānta in Classical Indian Logic*, ed. S. Katsura and E. Steinkellner, 135–74. Vienna: Arbeitskreis für tibetische und buddhistische Studien, Universität Wien.

Katsura, S., and E. Steinkellner. 2004. *The Role of the Example Dṛṣṭāna in Classical Indian Logic*. Vienna: Arbeitskreis für tibetische und buddhistische Studien, Universität Wien.

Kellner, B. 1997a. *Nichts bleibt nichts: Die buddhistische Zurückweisung von Kumārilas Abhāvapramāṇa: Übersetzung und Interpretation von Śāntarakṣitas Tattvasaṅgraha vv. 1647–1690, mit Kamalaśīlas Tattvasaṅgrahapañjikā, sowie Ansätze und Arbeitshypothesen zur Geschichte negativer Erkenntnis in der indischen Philosophie*. Vienna: Arbeitskreis für Tibetische und Buddhistische Studien Universität Wien.

Kellner, B. 1997b. "Non-cognition *Anupalabdhi*—Perception or Inference? The View of Dharmottara and Jñānaśrīmitra." *Tetsugaku* 49:121–34.

Kellner, B. 1999. "Levels of Imperceptibility. Dharmottara on the *Dṛśya* in *Dṛśyānupalabdhi*." In *Dharmakīrti's Thought and Its Impact on Indian and Tibetan Philosophy: Proceedings of the Third International Dharmakīrti Conference*, ed. S. Katsura, 193–208. Vienna: Verlag der Österreichischen Akademie der Wissenschaften: Beiträge zur Kultur—und Geistesgeschichte Asiens.

Kellner, B. 2001. "Negation—Failure or Success? Remarks on an Allegedly Characteristic Trait of Dharmakīrti's *Anupalabdhi*-Theory." *Journal of Indian Philosophy* 295, no. 6:495–517.

Kellner, B. 2003. "Integrating Negative Knowledge into Pramāṇa Theory: The Development of the *Drśyānupalabdhi* in Dharmakīrti's Earlier Works." *Journal of Indian Philosophy* 311, no. 3:121.

Kellner, B. 2004. "Why Infer and Not Just Look." *The Role of the Example Dṛṣṭānta in Classical Indian Logic*, ed. S. Katsura, 1–51. Vienna: Arbeitskreis für tibetische und buddhistische Studien, Universität Wien.

Kellner, B. 2007. *Jñānaśrīmitra's* Anupalabdhirahasya *and* Sarvaśabdābhāvacarcā*: A Critical Edition with a Survey of His Anupalabdhi-Theory*. Wiener Studien zur Tibetologie und Buddhismuskunde no. 67. Vienna: Arbeitskreis für Tibetische und Buddhistische Studien, Universität Wien.

Kellner, B. Forthcoming. "Dharmakīrti's Exposition of *Pramāṇa* and *Pramāṇaphala* and the Sliding Scale of Analysis." Unpublished manuscript.

Kevalānandasarasvatī. 1992. *Mīmāṃsākośa*. New Delhi: Śri Satguru Publications.

Keyt, C. M. 1980. "Dharmakīrti's Concept of the *Svalakṣaṇa*." PhD diss., University of Washington.

Kosambi, D. D., and V. V. Gokhale, eds. 1957. *Subhāṣitaratnakośa*. Harvard Oriental Series no. 42. Cambridge, Mass.: Harvard University Press.

Krasser, H. 1991. *Dharmottara's kurze untersuchung der Gültigkeit einer Erkenntnis Laghuprāmāṇyaparīkṣā: Materialen zur Definition gültiger Erkenntnis in der Tradition Dharmakīrtis 2*. Vienna: Österreichische Akademie der Wissenschaften.

Krasser, H. 1995. "Dharmottara's Theory of Knowledge in his *Laghuprāmāṇyaparīkṣā*." *Journal of Indian Philosophy* 23:247–71.

Krasser, H. 1997. "Zur Buddhistischen Definition von gültiger Erkenntnis *Pramāṇa* in Jayantabhaṭṭas Nyāyamañjari." *Studien zur Indologie und Iranistik* 21:105–32.

Krasser, H. 2002. *Śaṅkaranandanas Īśvarāpākaraṇasaṅkṣepa: Mit einem anonymen Kommentar und weiteren Materialien zur buddhistischen Gottespolemik, Beiträge zur Kultur- und Geistesgeschichte Asiens* no. 39. Vienna: Verlag der Österreichischen Akademie der Wissenschaften.

Kyuma, T. 2009. "Superiority of Vajrayāna—Part I: Some Remarks on the **Vajrayānāntadvayanirākaraṇa* (*rDo rje theg pa'i mtha' gñis sel ba*) Ascribed to Jñānaśrī." In *Genesis and Development of Tantrism*, ed. Shingo Einō, 469–86. Institute of Oriental Culture Special Series no. 23. Tokyo: University of Tokyo, Institute of Oriental Culture.

Kyuma, T. Forthcoming. "On the Perceptibility of External Objects in Dharmakīrti's Epistemology." Unpublished manuscript.

Laine, J. 1993. "Some Remarks on the *Guṇaguṇibhedabhaṅga* Chapter on Udayana's *Ātmatattvaviveka*—Defense of Nyāya Epistemo-Logical Realism Against Buddhist Idealism." *Journal of Indian Philosophy* 21:261–94.

Laine, J. 1998. "Udayana's Refutation of the Buddhist Thesis of Momentariness in the *Ātmatattvaviveka*." *Journal of Indian Philosophy* 261:51–97.

Larson, G. 2001. *Classical Sāṃkhya*. Delhi: Motilal Banarsidass.

Lasic, H. 1999. "Dharmakīrti and His Successors on the Determination of Causality." In *Dharmakīrti's Thought and Its Impact on Indian and Tibetan Philosophy: Proceedings of the Third International Dharmakīrti Conference*, ed. S. Katsura, 233–42. Vienna: Verlag der Österreichische Akademie der Wissenschaften. Beiträge zur Kultur—und Geistesgeschichte Asien.

Lasic, H. 2000a. *Jñānaśrīmitras Vyāpticarcā: Sanskrittext, Übersetzung, Analyse*. Vienna: Arbeitskreis für Tibetische und Buddhistische Studien.

Lasic, H. 2000b. *Ratnakīrti's Vyāptinirṇaya: Sanskrit Text, Übersetzung, Analyse*. Wiener Studien zur Tibetologie und Buddhismuskunde, Heft 49. Vienna: Arbeitskreis für Tibetische und Buddhistische Studien.

Lasic, H. 2003. "On the Utilisation of Causality as a Basis of Inference: Dharmakīrti's Statements and Their Interpretation." *Journal of Indian Philosophy* 31:185–97.

Malvania, P. D. 1971. *Paṇḍita Durveka Miśra's* Dharmottara-pradīpa [*Being a Sub-Commentary on Dharmottara's* Nyāya-bindu-ṭīkā]. Patna: Kashi Prasad Jayaswal.

Matilal, B. K. 1968. *The Navya-Nyāya Doctrine of Negation*. Cambridge, Mass.: Harvard University Press.

Matilal, B. K. 1986. *Perception: An Essay on Classical Indian Theories of Knowledge*. Oxford: Clarendon Press.

Matilal, B. K. 1987. "Debate and Dialectic in Ancient India." In *Philosophical Essays: Professor Anantalal Thakur Felicitation Volume*, ed. R. R. Mukhopadyaya et al., 53–66. Calcutta: Sanskrit Pustak Bhandar.

Matilal, B. K., et al. 1998. *The Character of Logic in India*. Albany: State University of New York Press.

Matsumoto, S. 1981. "On the Philosophical Positions of Dharmottara and Jitāri." *Indogaku bukkyōgaku kenkyū* 58:969–66.

McClintock, S. L. 2002. "Omniscience and the Rhetoric of Reason in the *Tattvasaṃgraha* and the *Tattvasaṃgrahapañjikā*." PhD diss., Harvard University.

McCrea, L. J., and P. G. Patil. 2006. "Traditionalism and Innovation: Philosophy, Exegesis, and Intellectual History in Jñānaśrīmitra's *Apohaprakaraṇa*." *Journal of Indian Philosophy* 34:303–66.

Meuthrath, A. 1996. *Untersuchungen zur kompositionsgechichte der Nyāyasūtras*. Wurzburg: Altenberge.

Mikogami, E. 1979. "Some Remarks on the Concept of *Arthakriyā*." *Journal of Indian Philosophy* 7:79–94.

Mimaki, K. 1976. *La refutation bouddhique de la permanence des choses [Sthirasiddhidūṣaṇa] et la prevue de la momenraneite des Choses [Kṣaṇabhaṅgasiddhi]*. Paris: Insititut de civilization indienne.

Mishra, A. 2002. *Antarvyāpti*. New Delhi: Indian Council of Philosophical Research.

Miyasaka, Y. 1971/72. "*Pramāṇa-vārttika-kārikā*" Sanskrit and Tibetan, Chapters 2, 3, 4." *Acta indologica* 2:1–206.

Mookherjee, S. 1935. *The Buddhist Philosophy of Universal Flux: An Exposition of the Philosophy of Critical Realism as Expounded by the School of Dignāga*. Reprint, Delhi: Motilal Banarsidass, 1993.

Motilal, L. 1926–30. *Śrimad-Vādidevasūri-viracitaḥ Pramāṇanayatattvālokālaṅkāraḥ Sa-syādvādaratnākaraḥ*. Poona.

Much, M. T. 1991. *Dharmakīrti's Vādanyāyaḥ. Teil 1—Sanskrit Text. Teil 2—Übersetzung und Anmerkungen*. Vienna: Verlag der Österreichische Akademie der Wissenschaften.

Much, M. T. 1994. "Uddyotakara's Kritik der *Apoha*-Lehre *Nyāyavārttika* ad NS II.2.66." *Wiener Zeitschrift für die Kunde Südasiens* 38:351–66.

Mullens, J. G. 1994. "Principles and Practices of Buddhist Education in Asaṅga's *Boddhisattvabhūmi*." PhD diss., McMaster University.

Nagatomi, M. 1967. "A Study of Dharmakīrti's *Prāmāṇavārttika*: An English Translation and Annotation of the *Pramāṇavārttika*, Book 1." PhD diss., Harvard University.

Newland, G. 1999. *Appearance and Reality: The Two Truths in Four Buddhist Systems*. Ithaca, N.Y.: Snow Lion Publications.

Oetke, C. 1991. "*Svabhāvapratibandha* and the Types of Reasons in Dharmakīrti's Theory of Inference." *Studies in the Buddhist Epistemological Tradition: Second International Dharmakīrti Conference*, ed. E. Steinkellner, 243–68. Vienna: Österreichischen Akademie der Wissenschaften: philosophisch-historischen Klasse, Denkschriften, 222. Band: Verlag der Österreeichischen Akademie der Wissenschaften, Wien.

Oetke, C. 1993. "Bemerkungen zur Buddhitischen Doktrin der Momentanheit des Seienden: Dharmakīrtis *Sattvānumāna*." *Wiener Studien zur Tibetologie und Buddhismuskunde*, vol. 29. Vienna: Arbeitskreis für Tibetische und Buddhistische Studien Universität Wien, Wiener Studien zur Tibetologie und Buddhimuskunde.

Oetke, C. 1994. *Studies on the Doctrine of Trairūpya*, vol. 33. Vienna: Arbeitskreis für Tibetische und Buddhistische Studien Universität Wien. *Wiener Studien zur Tibetologie und Buddhismuskunde*.

Oetke, C. 1996. "Ancient Indian Logic as a Theory of Non-monotonic Reasoning." *Journal of Indian Philosophy* 24:447–539.

Oetke, C. 2003a. "Indian Logic and Indian Syllogism." *Indo-Iranian Journal* 461:53–69.

Oetke, C. 2003b. "A Review of 'Philosophy in Classical India: The Proper Work of Reason.'" *Indo-Iranian Journal* 462:135–55.

Ogawa, H. 1999. "Bhartṛhari on Representations *Buddhyākāra*." *Dharmakīrti's Thought and Its Impact on Indian and Tibetan Philosophy: Proceedings of the Third International Dharmakīrti Conference*, ed. S. Katsura, 267–86. Vienna: Verlag der Österreichischen Akademie der Wissenschaften: Beiträge zur Kultur—und Geistesgeschichte Asiens.

Pandeya, R. C. 1989. *Ācāryadharmakīrteḥ pramāṇavārttikam: Granthakartṛviracitayā Svopajñavṛttyā Ācāryamanorathanandikrtayā Pramāṇavārttikavṛttyā ca samupetam*. Dillī: Motīlāla Banārasīdāsa.

Patil, P. G. 2003. "On What It Is That Buddhists Think About—*Apoha* in the *Ratnakīrti-nibandhāvali*." *Journal of Indian Philosophy* 31:229–56.

Patil, P. G. 2006. "Consuming Scripture: Philosophical Hermeneutics in Classical India." *SITES* 7:47–60.

Patil, P. G. 2007. "Dharmakīrti's White-Lie." In *Pramāṇakīrtiḥ: Papers Dedicated to Ernst Steinkellner on the Occasion of His Seventieth Birthday*, Part 2, ed. B. Kellner, H. Krasser, M. T. Much, and H. Tauscher, 597–619. Vienna: Wiener Studien zur Tibetologie und Buddhismuskunde, no. 70.

Patil, P. G. 2009. *Against a Hindu God: Buddhist Philosophy of Religion in India.* New York: Columbia University Press.

Patil, P. G. Forthcoming. "History, Philology, and the Philosophical Study of Sanskrit Texts." *Journal of Indian Philosophy.*

Phillips, S. H. 1997. *Classical Indian Metaphysics.* Delhi: Motilal Banarsidass.

Pind, O. 1991. "Dignāga on *Śabdasāmānya* and *Śabdaviśeṣa.*" *Studies in the Buddhist Epistemological Tradition,* ed. E. Steinkellner, 269–80. Vienna: Österreeichischen Akademie der Wissenschaften: philosophisch-historischen Klasse, Denkschriften, 222. Band: Verlag der Österreichischen Akademie der Wissenschaften, Wien.

Pind, O. 1999. "Dharmakīrti's Interpretation of *Pramāṇasamuccayavṛtti,* vol. 36: *Śabdo 'rthāntaranivṛttiviśiṣṭān eva bhāvān āha.*" In *Dharmakīrti's Thought and Its Impact on Indian and Tibetan Philosophy: Proceedings of the Third International Dharmakīrti Conference,* ed. S. Katsura, 317–24. Vienna: Verlag der Österreichischen Akademie der Wissenschaften: Beiträge zur Kultur—und Geistesgeschichte Asiens.

Potter, K. H. 1991. *Presuppositions of India's Philosophies.* Delhi: Motilal Banarsidass.

Preisendanz, K. 2008. "Text, Commentary, Annotation: Some Reflections on the Philosophical Genre," *Journal of Indian Philosophy* 36, nos. 5–6:599–618.

Prets, E. 2000. "Theories of Debate, Proof, and Counter-Proof in Early Indian Dialectical Traditions." In *On Understanding Other Cultures,* ed. P. Balcerowicz and M. Major, 369–82. Warsaw: Studia indologiczne.

Prets, E. 2001. "Futile and False Rejoinders, Sophistical Arguments and Early Indian Logic." *Journal of Indian Philosophy* 29:545–58.

Raja, K. K. 1986. "*Apoha* Theory and Pre-Dignāga Views on Sentence Meaning." In *Buddhist Logic and Epistemology: Studies in the Buddhist Analysis of Inference and Language,* ed. B. K. Matilal and R. D. Evans, 185–92. Dordrecht: D. Reidel.

Randle, H. N. 1930. *Indian Logic in the Early Schools. A Study of the* Nyāyadarśana *in Its Relation to the Early Logic of Other Schools.* Oxford: Oxford University Press.

Ray, G. 1993. *Slokavārttikam.* Varanasi: Ratna Publications.

Ruben, W. 1928. *Die Nyāyasūtras: Text, Übersetzung. Erläuterung und Glossar.* Leipzig.

Saito, A. 2004. "Bhāviveka's Theory of Meaning." *Journal of Indian and Buddhist Studies* 52, no. 2:24–31.

Sāṃkṛtyāyana, R., ed. 1938–40. "Dharmakīrti's *Pramāṇavārttika* with Commentary by Manorathanandin." Appendix to *Journal of the Bhandarkar Oriental Research Institute*, 24–26.

Sāṃkṛtyāyana, R., ed. 1943. *Ācārya-Dharmakīrteḥ Pramāṇavārttikam (Svārthānumānaparicchedaḥ) Svopajñavṛttyā Karṇakagomiviracitayā Ṭaṭṭīkayā ca sahitam*. Allahabad.

Sāṃkṛtyāyana, R., ed. 1953. *Prajñākaragupta's* Pramāṇavārttikālaṅkārabhāṣyam *or* Vārtikālaṅkāraḥ *of Prajñākaragupta [Being a Commentary on Dharmakīrti's* Pramāṇavārtikam]. Tibetan Sanskrit Work Series no. 1. Patna: Kashi Prasad Jayaswal Research Institute.

Sanghavi, S. 1949. *Hetubinduṭīkā of Bhaṭṭa Arcaṭa: With the Sub-commentary Entitled Āloka of Durveka Miśra*. Baroda: Oriental Institute.

Sanghavi, S., and M. Jinavijayaji. 1949. *Hetubinduṭīkā of Bhaṭṭa Arcaṭa: With the Sub-commentary Entitled Āloka of Durveka Miśra*. Baroda: Oriental Institute.

Sāstri, M. K. 1987. *Īśvarapratyabhijñāvivṛtivimarśinī*. New Delhi: Akhil Book.

Scharf, P. M. 1996. *The Denotation of Generic Terms in Ancient Indian Philosophy: Grammar, Nyāya and Mīmāṃsā*. Philadelphia: American Philosophical Society.

Schmithausen, L. 1965. *Maṇḍanamiśra's* Vibhramavivekaḥ. Vienna: Hermann Böhlauss Nachf.

Sharma, D. 1969. *The Differentiation Theory of Meaning in Indian Logic*. The Hague: Mouton.

Shastri, D. 1984. Nyāyabindu *of Ācārya Dharmakīrti with the Commentaries by Ārya Vinītadeva and Dharmottara and Dharmottara-Ṭīkā-Ṭippaṇa*. Varanasi: Bauddha Bharati.

Shastri, H. P. 1910. *Six Buddhist Nyāya Tracts in Sanskrit*. Calcutta: Asiatic Society.

Siderits, M. 1986. "Word Meaning, Sentence Meaning, and Apoha." *Journal of Indian Philosophy* 13:133–51.

Siderits, M. 1991. *Indian Philosophy of Language: Studies in Selected Issues*. Dordrecht: Kluwer Academic.

Siderits, M. 1999. "*Apohavāda*, Nominalism, and Resemblance Theories." In *Dharmakīrti's Thought and Its Impact on Indian and Tibetan Philosophy: Proceedings of the Third International Dharmakīrti Conference*, ed. S. Katsura, 341–48. Vienna: Verlag der Österreichischen Akademie der Wissenschaften: Beiträge zur Kultur—und Geistesgeschichte Asiens.

Siderits, M. 2005. "Buddhist Nominalism and Desert Ornithology." In *Universals, Concepts, and Qualities: New Essays on the Meaning of Predicates*, ed. A. Chakrabarti and P. Strawson, 91–104. Abingdon: Ashgate.

Siderits, M. 2007. *Buddhism as Philosophy: An Introduction*. Indianapolis: Hackett.

Solomon, E. A. 1976. *Indian Dialectics: Methods of Philosophical Discussion*. Ahmedabad: B. J. Institute of Learning and Research.

Stcherbatsky, T. 1984. *Buddhist Logic*. New Delhi: Munshiram Manoharlal.

Steinkellner, E. 1967. *Dharmakīrtiś Hetubinduh*. Graz: Böhlau in Kommission.

Steinkellner, E. 1969. "Die Entwicklung des Kṣaṇikatvānumānam bei Dharmakīrti." *Wiener Zeitschrift für die Kunde Süd- und Ostasiens* 13:361–77.

Steinkellner, E. 1973. *Dharmakīrti's Pramāṇaviniścaya 2, Kapitel: Svārthānumāna*. Vienna: Verlag der Österreichischen Akademie der Wissenschaften.

Steinkellner, E. 1974. "On Interpretation of the *Svabhāvahetu*." *Wiener Zeitschrift für die Kunde Südasiens* 18:117–29.

Steinkellner, E. 1976. "Der Einleitungsvers von Dharmottara's Apohaprakaranam." *Wiener Zeitschrift für die Kunde Südasiens und Archiv für indische Philosophie* 20:123–24.

Steinkellner, E. 1979. "Miszellen zur Erkenntnistheoretisch-logischen Schule des Buddhismus." *Wiener Zeitschrift für die Kunde Südasiens und Archiv für indische Philosophie* 23:141–54.

Steinkellner, E. 1991. "On the Logic of *Svabhāvahetu* in Dharmakīrti's *Vādanyāya*." *Studies in the Buddhist Epistemological Tradition: Second International Dharmakīrti Conference*, ed. E. Steinkellner, 311–24. Vienna: Österreichischen Akademie der Wissenschaften: philosophisch-historischen Klasse, Denkschriften, 222. Band: Verlag der Österreichischen Akademie der Wissenschaften, Wien.

Steinkellner, E. 1996. "An Explanation of Dharmakīrti's *Svabhāvahetu* Definitions." In *Festschrift Dieter Schlingloff*, ed. F. Wilhelm, 257–68. Reinbek: Dr. Inge Wezler Verlag fur Orientalistische Fachpublikationen.

Steinkellner, E. 1998."Dharmakīrti." In *Routledge Encyclopedia of Philosophy*, ed. E. Craig, 51–53. New York: Routledge.

Steinkellner, E. 2005. "Dignāga's *Pramāṇasamuccaya*, Chapter 1." Available at www.oeaw.ac.at/ias/Mat/dignaga_PS_1.pdf.

Steinkellner, E., and H. Krasser. 1989. *Dharmottaras Exkurs zur Definition gültiger Erkenntnis im Pramāṇaviniścaya: Materialien zur Definition gültiger Erkenntnis in der Tradition Dharmakīrtis 1: Tibetischer Text, Sanskritma-*

terialien und Übersetzung. Vienna: Verlag der Österreichischen Akademie der Wissenschaften.

Steinkellner, E., H. Krasser, and H. Lasic. 2007. *Jinendrabuddhi's* Viśālāmalavatī Pramāṇasamuccayaṭīkā. Beijing: China Tibetology / Austrian Academy of Sciences.

Steinkellner, E., and M. T. Much. 1995. *Texte der erkenntnistheoretischen Schule des Buddhismus*. Göttingen: Vandenhoeck & Ruprecht.

Stern, E. 1988. "*Vidhiviveka* of Maṇḍaṇamiśra, with Commentary *Nyāyakaṇikā* of Vācaspatimiśra, and Supercommentaries, *Juṣadhvaṇikaraṇī*, and *Svaditaṅkaraṇī* of Parameśvara, Critical and Annotated Edition." PhD diss., University of Pennsylvania.

Taber, J. 1996."Is Verbal Testimony a Form of Inference?" *Studies in Humanities and Social Sciences* 3, no. 2:19–31.

Taber, J. 2002. "Mohanty on Śabdapramāṇa." *Journal of Indian Philosophy* 30, no. 2:161–90.

Taber, J. 2004. "Is Indian Logic Nonmonotonic?" *Philosophy East and West* 54:143–70.

Taber, J. 2005. *A Hindu Critique of Buddhist Epistemology: Kumārila on Perception*. New York: Routledge/Curzon.

Tanemura, R. 2009. "Superiority of Vajrayāna—Part II: Some Remarks on the **Vajrayānāntadvayanirākaraṇa* (*rDo rje theg pa'i mtha' gñis sel ba*) Ascribed to Jñānaśrī." In *Genesis and Development of Tantrism*, ed. Shingo Einō, 487–514. Institute of Oriental Culture Special Series no. 23. Tokyo: University of Tokyo, Institute of Oriental Culture.

Tani, T. 1984. "A Conflict Between Logical Indicators in the Negative Inference Svabhāvānupalabdhivādin Versus Vyāpakānupalabdhivādin." *Indogaku bukkyōgaku kenkyū* 322:1100–1106.

Tani, T. 1997. "Problems of Interpretation on Dharmottara's *Kṣaṇabhaṅgasiddhi* 1, 2 and 3." *Bulletin of Kochi National College of Technology* 41:19–77.

Tani, T. 1999. "Reinstatement of the Theory of External Determination of Pervasion *Bahirvyāptivāda* Jñānaśrīmitra's Proof of Momentary Existence." In *Dharmakīrti's Thought and Its Impact on Indian and Tibetan Philosophy: Proceedings of the Third International Dharmakīrti Conference*, ed. S. Katsura, 363–86. Vienna: Verlag der Österreeichischen Akademie der Wissenschaften: Beiträge zur Kultur—und Geistesgeschichte Asiens.

Thakur, A. 1957. *Ratnakīrtinibandhāvali*. Patna: Kashiprasad Jayaswal Research Institute.

Thakur, A. 1959. *Jñānaśrīmitranibandhāvali*. Patna: Kashi Prasad Jayaswal Research Institute.

Thakur, A. 1975. *Ratnakīrtinibandhāvali*. 2nd ed. Patna: Kashi Prasad Jayaswal Research Institute.

Thakur, A. 1987. *Jñānaśrīmitranibandhāvali*. 2nd ed. Patna: Kashi Prasad Jayaswal Research Institute.

Thakur, A. 1996. *Nyāyavārttikatātparya-ṭīkā*. New Delhi: Munshiram Manoharlal Publishers.

Thakur, A. 1997a. *Nyāya-sūtra. Gautamīyanyāyadarśana with Bhāṣya of Vātsyāyama*. Delhi: Indian Council of Philosophical Research.

Thakur, A. 1997b. *Nyāyavārttika*. Delhi: Indian Council of Philosophical Research.

Tillemans, T. J. F. 1999. *Scripture, Logic, Language: Essays on Dharmakīrti and His Tibetan Successors*. Boston: Wisdom Publications.

Tillemans, T. J. F. 2004. *Dharmakīrti's Pramāṇavārttika: An Annotated Translation of the Fourth Chapter Parārthānumāna Vol. 1 k. 1–148*. Vienna: Österreichischen Akademie Der Wissenschaften.

Tucci, G. 1929. *Pre-Dignāga Buddhist Texts on Logic from Chinese Sources*. Baroda: Oriental Institute.

van Bijlert, V. A. 1989. *Epistemology and Spiritual Authority: The Development of Epistemology and Logic in the Old Nyāya and the Buddhist School of Epistemology, with an Annotated Translation of Dharmakirti's Pramāṇavārttika II Pramāṇasiddhi, vv. 1–7*. Wiener Studien zur Tibetologie und Buddhismuskunde, vol. 20. Vienna: Arbeitskreis für Tibetische und Buddhistische Studien Universität Wien.

Vetter, T. 1964. *Erkenntnisprobleme bei Dharmakīrti*. Vienna: H. Böhlaus Nachf., Kommissionsverlag der Öseterreichischen Akademie der Wissenschaften.

Vetter, T. 1966. *Dharmakīrti's Pramāṇaviniścaya, 1. Kapitel: Pratyakṣam. Einleitung, Text der Tibetishcen Übersetzung, Sanskritfragmente, deutsche Übersetzung*. Vienna: H. Böhlaus Nachf., Kommissionsverlag der Öseterreichischen Akademie der Wissenschaften.

Vidyabhusana, S. C. 1921. *A History of Indian Logic Ancient, Medieval and Modern Schools*. Calcutta: Calcutta University Press.

von Rospatt, A. 1995. *The Buddhist Doctrine of Momentariness. A Survey of the Origins and Early Phase of This Doctrine Up to Vasubandhu*. Alt- und Neu-Indische Studien no. 47. Stuttgart: Steiner.

Watson, A. 2006. *The Self's Awareness of Itself: Bhaṭṭa Rāmakaṇṭha's Arguments Against the Buddhist Doctrine of No-Self.* Vienna: De Nobili Research Library.

Williams, P. 2000. *Buddhist Thought: A Complete Introduction to the Indian Tradition*. London: Routledge.

Woo, J. 1999. "The *Kṣaṇabhaṅgasiddhi-Anvayātmika*: An Eleventh-Century Buddhist Work on Existence and Causal Theory." PhD diss., University of Pennsylvania.

Woo, J. 2001. "Incompatibility and the Proof of the Buddhist Theory of Momentariness." *Journal of Indian Philosophy* 294:423–34.

Yaita, H. 1985a. "On *Anupalabdhi*, Annotated Translation of Dharmakīrti's *Pramāṇavārttikasvavṛtti* I." *Taishō daigaku daigakuin kenkyū ronshū* [*Journal of the Graduate School of Taisho University*] 9:199–216.

Yaita, H. 1985b. "On *Anupalabdhi*, Annotated Translation of Dharmakīrti's *Pramāṇavārttikasvavṛtti* II." *Chizan gakuhō* [*Journal of Chizan Studies*] 34:1–14.

Yogindrananda, S., ed. 1968. *Śrīmadācāra-Bhāsarvajña-praṇītasya Nyāyasārasya svopajñaṃ vyākhyānaṃ Nyāyabhūṣaṇam* (Saḍdarśanaprakāśanagranthāmālā 1). Vārāṇasī: Saḍdarśanaprakāśanapratiṣṭhānam.

Yoshimizu, C. 1999. "The Development of *Sattvānumāna* from the Refutation of a Permanent Existent in the *Sautrāntika* Tradition." *Wiener Zeitschrift für die Kunde Südasiens* 43:231–54.

INDEX

Abhayākaragupta, 3
Abhinavagupta, 143n71
Abhinavaraṅganāthabrahmatantrapa rakālayati, Srimad, 134n8
absence, 56, 136n28, 158n110; appearance of, 76; awareness of distinction and, 59; exclusion as referent of words expressing, 60; four types of, 152n37
affirmation, 65, 68–69, 151n32
analogy *(upamāna),* 136n28
Analysis of Pervasion [Vyāpticarcā] (Jñānaśrīmitra), 21
appearance, 47, 48; absence and, 76, 96; methods of awareness and, 61–64; object of awareness and, 94
Asaṅga, 135n14
Atīśa, 3
Ātmatattvaviveka (Udayana), 134nn8–9
awareness, 4, 23, 138n40, 163n154; awareness events, 8, 10, 12, 13, 133n4, 138n40; blocking, 79–80, 164–65n164; determinate, 53, 54; different methods of, 61, 63–64, 75–76; errors in, 79, 80–81, 89, 156–57n89, 165n167; exclusion of other and, 57–58; four objects of, 33; internal and external objects in relation to, 26; nonappearance of external object in, 48; objects of, 1, 48, 67, 69, 70, 94, 160n129; positive entities and, 43; pseudoperceptual, 10; recurrence produced by universals, 83–85, 167n183; reflective, 54, 56, 82, 90, 151nn28–29; sources of knowledge and, 7, 8. *See also* conceptual awareness; inferential/verbal awareness; perceptual awareness; valid awareness

Bhāsarvajña, 85, 159n118, 168n200
Bhāṣya (Prajñākaragupta), 90
Bhūṣaṇa, 71, 72
Buddhist epistemological tradition, 9–16, 22, 24, 31; Dignāga as founder of, 133n3, 135n18; English translations, 34–41; on negation, 150n20; on perception, 33; Sanskrit philosophy and, 16–17
Buddhist philosophy, 1, 4, 137–38n39; debates on exclusion, 2; on sources of knowledge, 7–9; text traditions and, 3–6; on ultimate and momentary reality, 18; Vikramaśīla as learning center, 3

cause-effect relations *(kārya-kāraṇa-bhāva),* 26, 75, 81, 85
Commentary (Dharmottara), 56
Compendium on Sources of Knowledge [Pramāṇasamuccaya] (Dignāga), 5, 14–15
conceptual awareness, 1, 28, 53, 72, 78; of absence, 56; appearance in, 62; class property and, 58; defined, 133n4; desire and, 74; determination and, 47; differentiation and, 96; exclusion and, 49–50, 55, 94; external objects and, 46, 67, 169nn210–11; false, 77; intermediate properties and, 64; memory and, 81, 82, 146n101; object of, 69, 93; object of experience and, 61, 84; particulars absent from, 63, 87–88, 170n218; positive entities and, 52, 153n42; sense faculties and, 81; unreality of images in, 47–48; validity and, 12, 13. *See also* awareness; perceptual awareness
conceptualization, 51, 164n160; appearance of properties and, 69; determination as synonym for, 22, 31–32, 46–47, 87–88, 90, 92; mental images and, 26; perceptual awareness and, 9, 63; as property possessor, 90; universals and, 23; verbalization and, 34
conditionally adopted positions *(vyavasthā),* 26–34, 44, 49, 51, 52, 95; arising of nonexistent thing, 55; expression of positive entities and, 60; external objects and, 94; "natural" connections and, 73; restriction of, 67; truth and, 92–93
consciousness *(vijñaptimātra),* 21

Debating God (Jñānaśrīmitra), 134n10
determination *(adhyavasāya),* 13–14, 25–26; absence of, 96; activity and, 89–90, 90–91; appearance of unreal object and, 92; conceptualization as synonym for, 22, 31–32, 46–47, 87–88, 90, 92; conditionally adopted positions and, 92; exclusion and, 96; external object and, 46, 60; inference and, 18–19; object of awareness and, 94–95; semantic values and, 28; superimposition and, 94, 172n250; universals and, 24
Dharmakīrti, 1, 2, 8, 133n5; on awareness, 50, 91, 139n52; on categories of inference, 26, 43–44; on conceptualizing and determining, 32–33; on determination, 13, 19, 87; on enabling, 159n117; epistemological tradition and, 9–15; on exclusion and universals, 60; on inference and perception, 18, 19; on language and awareness, 61; on negation, 56; on nonapprehension of cause, 75; on perception, 17, 33, 34, 140n65; on pragmatic efficacy, 138n49; on property possessors and properties, 72; on sources of knowledge, 14; text tradition of, 3–4, 135n18; on universals, 164n157
Dharmapāla, King, 3